The Reminiscences

of

Admiral Charles K. Duncan

U. S. Navy (Retired)

Volume IV

U. S. Naval Institute

Annapolis, Maryland

1983

Preface to Volumes III and IV

In these final two volumes of his superbly detailed oral memoir, Admiral Duncan describes the culmination of his naval career--a tour of duty as Chief of the Bureau of Naval Personnel from 1968 to 1970 and one as Commander in Chief Atlantic Fleet/Commander in Chief Atlantic/Supreme Allied Commander Atlantic from 1970 to 1972. These two volumes are beneficial for a historian because the admiral goes beyond just describing the events which occurred during his tenure in each billet; he provides detailed explanations of the duties involved in each and illustrates these with examples from his own service.

One of the duties of the Chief of Naval Personnel is to control the flow of manpower in the Navy in order to live within the personnel strengths mandated by Congress. This was a strenuous challenge in 1969-1970, the admiral explains, because Congress didn't get around to establishing the Navy's desired end strength until the fiscal year was well under way. In that job, he was required to testify frequently before Congress. Admiral Duncan provides an insider's view of the preparations that go into such testimony and the resulting demands on his time. Especially fascinating is his discussion of the interaction between the Chief of Naval Operations and the Chief of Naval Personnel in making up slates of flag officers to fill various duty assignments.

During the final two years of his 39 years of commissioned

service, Admiral Duncan wore three hats--one that was strictly U. S. Navy; one that was a joint-service U. S. command; and the third that was a multinational NATO command. He carefully delineates the demarcation lines between the three jobs and makes the case for separating the fleet command from the joint-service command, as is done in the Pacific. Despite having capable staff officers, the admiral considered himself unable to devote to each of the three jobs the time it deserved. The historian will find here discussion of both the political and military usefulness of NATO and the ways in which the Supreme Allied Commander Atlantic can foster that usefulness through periodic naval exercises and through ties with high-ranking officials in other countries. As a joint-service commander, the admiral must take a purple-suiter approach to ensure that the requirements of various component commands are satisfied. And as a fleet commander in chief, he is concerned with the readiness of ships, planes, and personnel. In all three jobs, considerable emphasis is given to planning and doing what is necessary to see that available forces are suitable for the plans.

Admiral Duncan rounds out his oral history with an account of his relationship with Admiral Elmo R. Zumwalt, Jr., who was Chief of Naval Operations from 1970 to 1974. He tells first of being senior to Commander Zumwalt in the Bureau of Personnel at a time when Zumwalt was demonstrating great potential for higher rank. Then came his years in the Pentagon with Secretary of the Navy Paul Nitze when Zumwalt's star continued to rise.

Finally, Admiral Duncan concludes by talking about Admiral Zumwalt's controversial CNO years. He considers Zumwalt to have had the potential to be one of the greatest CNOs ever but feels that the potential was not realized because Admiral Zumwalt came to the job without suitable four-star experience and because the CNO would not take the advice of those who did have the experience.

As with the earlier volumes in Admiral Duncan's oral biography, these have benefited from the interviewing skill of my predecessor, Dr. John T. Mason, and from the very thorough preparation done by the admiral to ensure completeness. Following transcription of the interview tapes, Admiral Duncan made extensive revisions to the text in the interests of accuracy and clarity. The index was prepared by Ms. Susan Sweeney of the Naval Institute.

Paul Stillwell
Director of Oral History
U. S. Naval Institute
July 1983

Admiral Charles K. Duncan, U.S. Navy (Ret.)

Former: Supreme Allied Commander Atlantic (NATO)
Commander in Chief Atlantic (Unified Command)
Commander in Chief Atlantic Fleet

Admiral Charles Kenney Duncan, U.S. Navy, became NATO's seventh Supreme Allied Commander Atlantic in September 30, 1970. On the same day he became Commander in Chief Atlantic (the U.S. Unified Command) and Commander in Chief Atlantic Fleet. He retired from active duty on November 1, 1972 in the grade of Admiral.

Admiral Duncan's assignments during his thirty-nine and one-half years of active duty as an officer in reverse chronological order, were as follows:

April 1, 1968 to August 1970 — Chief of Naval Personnel and Deputy Chief of Naval operations (Manpower and Naval Reserve). The Distinguished Service Medal was awarded to him for "exceptionally meritorious service" during that period. The citation accompanying the medal praised his "dynamic leadership and outstanding foresight," his deep concern for the morale and welfare of Navy personnel," and "his dedicated service and brilliant record for achievement."

1967 - 1968 Commander Second Fleet, Commander of NATO's Striking Fleet Atlantic, and Commander Joint Task Force 122.

1965 - 1967 Commander Amphibious Force, Atlantic Fleet. Promoted to Vice Admiral in June 1965. For his service as Commander Amphibious Force, Vice Admiral Duncan was awarded the Legion of Merit with a citation which commended "his outstanding operational and planning ability, leadership, and sound judgement."

1964 - 1965 Commander Cruiser — Destroyer Force Atlantic Fleet.

1962 - 1964 Assistant Chief of Naval Personnel for Plans and Programs.

1961 - 1962 Commander U.S. Naval Base Subic Bay, Philippines. While there Rear Admiral Duncan became President of a Philippine charitable association and also Vice President of the Philippine Tubercular Association. He was made an "adopted son" of the Provinces of Bataan and Zambales.

<u>1959 - 1961</u>   Commander Amphibious Training Command, Pacific Fleet

<u>1958 - 1959</u>   Selected for promotion to Rear Admiral in the summer of 1958, Rear Admiral Duncan was immediately assigned as Commander Amphibious Group One.

<u>1956 - 1958</u>   Assistant Chief of Staff for Operations for the Commander in Chief Pacific Fleet.

<u>1955 - 1956</u>   Commanding Officer of the Amphibious Attack Transport Chilton operating in the Atlantic, Caribbean, and Mediterranean. Chilton won the Amphibious Force "Battle Readiness Plaque" during the period of Captain Duncan's command.

<u>1953 - 1955</u>   Executive Assistant to the Chief of Naval Personnel.

<u>1952 - 1955</u>   Member of the Plans and Policy Section of the Supreme Allied Commander Atlantic Staff. This was the first year of that Command's activation. Captain Duncan was the only U.S. Naval officer in that section.

<u>1951 - 1952</u>   Commander Destroyer Division 62 in the Atlantic Fleet. Promoted to Captain.

<u>1948 - 1951</u>   Plans Division of the Commander in Chief Atlantic Fleet. Selected for promotion to Captain during this tour.

<u>1948</u>   Student at the Armed Forces Staff College in Norfolk, Virginia (six months

<u>1946 - 1948</u>   Executive officer of the fast battleship Wisconsin.

<u>1944 - 1946</u>   Director of Naval Officer Procurement, Bureau of Naval Personnel. More than 100,000 Naval officers were commissioned while Lieutenant Commander, later Commander, Duncan was Director. During the latter part of this period Commander Duncan served as a member of the Navy's "Holloway Board" to study the Form, System, and Method of Education of Naval Officers". The conclusions and recommendations of this Board established the modern NROTC and also provided for direct commissioning of college graduates at the Officer Candidate School in peacetime, among other matters. This was Commander Duncan's first shore duty since graduation in 1933.

<u>1943 - 1944</u>   Commanding Officer USS Wilson (DD408). Wilson took part in combat actions in the South and Central Pacific. For his service as Commanding Officer

Lieutenant Commander Duncan was awarded the Navy Commendation Medal with Combat "V", and a gold star with Combat "V" in lieu of a second award.

<u>1942 - 1943</u> Executive Officer USS Hutchins (DD 476), Lieutenant Commander Duncan commissioned Hutchins, built in the Boston Navy Yard. After a short period as anti-submarine escort in the Atlantic, Hutchins went to the Pacific, taking part in action in the Aleutians and the South Pacific.

<u>1941 - 1942</u> (December 20, 1941 to August 1, 1942) Aide and Flag Lieutenant to the Commander Service Force Atlantic Fleet.

<u>1940 - 1941</u> Aide, Flag Lieutenant and Personnel officer to Rear Admiral Reichmuth, Commander of Destroyers of the Atlantic Fleet. Lt(jg), later Lieutenant, Duncan was assigned to the Staff of Commander Destroyers the first year of that command's existence, starting June 1940. It was during this period, while the Destroyer Command was turning over 50 destroyers to the British, that he met his wife, Sheila Taylor of Halifax, Nova Scotia. They were married the following summer, in July 1941, in Bermuda.

The Destroyers Atlantic command went through the interesting period of operating convoy escorts in the North Atlantic in the summer - fall of 1941 before the U. S. was at war.

<u>1938 - 1940</u> Engineer Officer of the destroyer Schenck (159) in the Atlantic, as Lt. (jg).

<u>1933 - 1938</u> Ensign Duncan was assigned to duty in the cruiser USS Salt Lake City on graduation from the Naval Academy in June 1933. He served five years in Salt Lake City in various departments - engineering, navigation, fire control, and as a turret officer. As a turret officer he received his first commendation, one for having the highest score in cruiser turrets in target practice.

<u>1929 - 1933</u> Midshipman, Naval Academy. Entered at age 17.
Entered the Navy June 1929, retired November 1, 1972.

Upon retirement in November of 1972 from his assignment as Supreme Allied Commander Atlantic, Commander in Chief Atlantic, and Commander in Chief Atlantic Fleet, Admiral Duncan and his wife lived in the country near Leesburg, Virginia.

While there he became identified with local Loudoun County volunteer work and on the Board of Managers of the Navy Relief Society.

He and his wife now live in Coronado, California, where they moved in the fall of 1976. He is a member of the Board of Trustees of the San Diego Museum of Art.

Admiral Duncan is a member of the Secretary of the Navy's Advisory Board on Education and Training. He was also a member of the Board of Advisors to the President, U.S. Naval War College in Newport, R.I.

In the Spring of 1974 Admiral Duncan was installed in Athens as Honorary President of the "Greek National Oragnization Encouraging NATO's Aims."

As Supreme Allied Commander, Atlantic, in which Command he conducted the largest NATO naval exercises held up to that time, he received the Award of the Grand Cross of the Order of Oranje Nassau with Swords from Her Majesty the Queen of the Netherlands, and the Grand Cross of the Order of AVIS (the oldest military order) from Portugal. Admiral Duncan, as Supreme Allied Commander Atlantic, was given an audience with His Majesty the King of Belgium, Her Majesty Queen Elizabeth II, Queen of Great Britain, His Majesty the King of Denmark, and His Majesty the King of Norway.

Admiral Duncan still retains close links with NATO Organizations, attending the ceremonies at the NATO Summit Meeting in Washington in late May 1978, and a NATO Sea Symposium held in Annapolis, Maryland, in June 1978.

Admiral Duncan was born in Nicholasville, Kentucky, on December 7, 1911. He moved to Lexington, Kentucky, at age 9 and subsequently attended Lexington High School, Kavanaugh Preparatory School, and the University of Kentucky. His mother was a full Professor and a Head of Department at the University, one of the first women to hold such position. Admiral Duncan is a Kentucky "Colonel." Member of the Chevy Chase Club. He is an Episcopalian.

Admiral and Mrs. Duncan have a son, Bruce Duncan, of St. Michaels, Maryland, and one granddaughter. Admiral and Mrs. Duncan's current address is 813 First Street, Coronado, California 92118. Telephone: (714) 435-4244.

Updated: March 1981

DECLARATION OF TRUST

The undersigned does hereby appoint and designate as his (her) Trustee herein, the Secretary-Treasurer and Publisher of the United States Naval Institute to perform and discharge the following duties, powers, and privileges in connection with the possession and use of a certain taped interview between the undersigned and the Oral History Department of the United States Naval Institute.

1. Classification of Transcript.

   (✓)a. If classified UNDERLINE OPEN, the transcript(s) may be read or the recording(s) audited by the qualified personnel upon presentation of proper credentials, as determined by the Secretary-Treasurer of the U.S. Naval Institute.

   ( )b. If classified PERMISSION REQUIRED TO CITE OR QUOTE, the user will be required to obtain permission in writing from the interviewee prior to quoting or citing from either the transcript(s) or the recording(s).

   ( )c. If classified PERMISSION REQUIRED, permission must be obtained in writing from the interviewee before the transcribed interview(s) can be examined or the tape recording(s) audited.

   ( )d. If classified CLOSED, the transcribed interview(s) and the tape recording(s) will be sealed until a time specified by the interviewee. This may be until the death of the interviewee or for any specified number of years.

2. It is expressly understood that in giving this authorization, I am in no way precluded from placing such restrictions as I may desire upon use of the interview at any time during my lifetime, nor does this authorization in any way affect my rights to the copyright of my literary expressions that may be contained in the interview.

Witness my hand and seal this 4 day of March 1978

Charles K. Duncan
(Admiral USN (Ret.))

I hereby accept and consent to the foregoing Declaration of Trust and the powers therein conferred upon me as Trustee:

R/E Bowker Jr

Interview No. 18 with Admiral Charles K. Duncan, U.S. Navy
(Retired)

Place: His residence in St. Michael's, Maryland

Date: Wednesday, 3 November 1976, the day after the elections

Subject: Biography

By: John T. Mason, Jr.

Q: Today we're going to talk about another hat you wore. You've been talking about your experiences as SACLant, but you also became CinCLant on the same date, 30 September 1970, and so we'll have that story today.

Adm. D.: I wanted to talk about the Commander in Chief, Atlantic, which is a Unified Command, separately, because if I talked about it in connection with the other titles and other commands it would become blurred and that is one of the main things I wish to bring out in my talk. The Unified Command title in the Atlantic has, indeed, been blurred and this has had some bad effects.

Now, when I am speaking of the command, I noticed in my notes that I appeared to have a high percentage of negative comment about various things, rather than positive, and I am not negative at all about the Unified Command or Commander in Chief, Atlantic, not at all. But there is no use spending time taping all the various good points and good things that happened, although some are worth noting, but I believe the value of the recollection is to record areas where, with my experience, I would recommend change. Also events and situations which took place under the circumstances under which I served would indicate that, perhaps, other arrangements were better.

The Unified Command title, Commander in Chief, Atlantic, is in accordance with the Unified Command Plan, which is prepared by the Joint Chiefs of Staff, approved by the Secretary of Defense, and probably the President, I do not recall. It represents authoritative direction, in any event, and is based upon the law, which is a very important point. It is based upon law passed by Congress.

Q: 1958.

Adm. D.: Earlier actually, and modified by various executive orders. The early laws pertaining to the Department of Defense Unified Command system were passed back in 1947, 1948 back in there.

Q: Yes, then the modification of the National Defense Act in 1950.

Adm. D.: Right. Many naval officers from the outset did not

believe in the Unified Command plan, or the Unified Command system, for various reasons, and many today don't believe in it. Even more officers and especially in the junior ranks, don't understand it, have never studied it. Their operating levels are not necessarily conscious of the exact command lines and they tend to think it is not important.

Whether one agrees or disagrees, it is the law of the land and it is going to be.

I personally believe that it is absolutely necessary in modern warfare, absolutely necessary if operations are to be run at all efficiently. If you're going to do things well in war, you should run them that way in peacetime. I believe that most knowledgeable people in the upper echelons agree with this.

The importance of Unified Command is much more accepted in the areas where the Unified Commander is separate from the Service components such as the Fleet. That is such as the Commander in Chief, Europe; the Commander in Chief, Pacific; the Commander in Chief, South; and others. Each has three service components, as they are usually called - it will usually be such as: Air Force, Pacific; Army, Pacific; and the Pacific Fleet. Those components are separated. I will go a little more into the organization later, but the mere melding or combination of the Atlantic Fleet Command with the Unified Atlantic Command, and the absence of a continuing Air Force and Army component under CinCLant has pretty well blurred exactly what CinCLant is and what CinCLant does in the minds of most junior people.

Q: Except in time of war or threat of war when it becomes apparent?

Adm. D.: Or if they get in exercises and they don't perform properly, maybe they find that they should have known about it. Or when they get more senior and more experienced, not older necessarily, and they come up against the power that is given to a Unified Commander. For example, areas of responsibility, as far as the United States is concerned, are only assigned to a Unified Commander. The only areas in the Atlantic that are authoritatively assigned are those assigned the Commander in Chief, Atlantic. The Atlantic Fleet has no area responsibility, except as derived from an operation order from the Commander in Chief, Atlantic.

The Fleet can, and we will discuss this separately, divide up an area then assigned. There is no document from the Secretary of Defense or the Joint Chiefs of Staff, who are responsible for operations worldwide, assigning areas to the U.S. Atlantic Fleet or the U.S. Pacific Fleet. You would find, I would make a guess that about 60 per cent of the officers did not know that. The area of the Atlantic Command encompassed all the waters from the north pole to the south pole, from Pakistan in the Indian Ocean, surrounding all of Africa, westward into the Atlantic, surrounding all of South America, westward into the Pacific Ocean and running vertically up the west of South America, running up to the central American coast, I forget the exact point. In other words, the Atlantic Command is an absolutely tremendous area command. The Atlantic and Pacific Commands are the largest area commands. The Atlantic Command, as I often told War Colleges where I spoke, had operations going on at both poles at the same time. We had submarines cruising under the north pole. Fleet submarines, but under the authority delegated by the Commander in Chief, Atlantic. At the same time we had operated by the Atlantic Fleet operations the year round in Antarctica, and flying over the South pole.

This is not realized by everyone, this tremendous authority and responsibility, the seriousness of the responsibility of an area such as that. Let us say something happens to a ship in the Atlantic Command area and the press or maybe others say "with the whole Atlantic Fleet they didn't do anything about it." Well, computation of the area involved versus available forces would make it highly unlikely that we would have a unit in every place in that area where something might happen of interest to the United States.

Much power is given to the Unified Commander within this area. He can arrange to make agreements with foreign military and civil authorities with regard to operations. He can arrange directly an exercise with a foreign country at whatever level they wish it addressed and they may delegate or they may not.

Q: When he does something like that there is no infringement upon his other hat as SACLant?

Adm. D.: No, because SACLant is entirely NATO. I am going to give some examples of the great value of the CinCLant-SACLant combination, which I will be coming to. I mentioned some in our SACLant discussion.

No, this is a U.S. authority to deal with a foreign nation. I believe we discussed in our last session the fact that SACLant, if he holds exercises, has to have the exercise approved in Brussels by NATO at whatever level they decide, usually the permanent Ambassadors of fifteen nations. So this authority of CinCLant is really a very serious authority. I think it shows confidence and trust, which I think they should have, in the maturity and experience of the Unified Commander. Quite obviously, going into these matters you can very easily get into sensitive political areas, such as where you hold an exercise and what you are interpreted to be practicing. It can be very delicate politically and we have had very delicate political situations. There were certain caveats, such as in sensitive areas major exercises would have to be approved by the Joint Chiefs. Some of our exercises had to be approved by the President. Then, within certain prescribed limits, we could go ahead and make the arrangements and we would merely advise the Joint Chiefs that this exercise was going on. After all, the staffs and the Unified Commander are experienced, they know their opposite numbers in the other country, and the politically delicate points. Believe me, in every exercise and country there are tremendously delicate points. We lived with them and knew them, and we avoided things that would upset either country.

The knowledge that this authority exists doesn't seem to permeate in the U.S. Navy. I am going to talk more about the advantages and give you some examples of those exercises a little later. The authority goes further. It authorizes the Commander in Chief to make operating agreements, as we did, with Iceland, with Norway, Mauritius, with Portugal - I could name many countries where we had agreements. We, of course, sent these to Washington. I don't mean we kept them just to ourselves at all. In certain cases the agreement would cross a threshold where they would have to get approval. But, in effect, the Unified Commander was acting for the United States and everybody involved well knew this.

Usually, I would start with the Chief of Defense of the country concerned. If I wanted an exercise with Norwegian forces I would send a message to the Chief of Defense of Norway. Incidentally, he usually had to clear it with his own parliament, but I didn't deal with the parliament, quite obviously. I might start with the political Minister of Defense, according to the nature of the exercise, and what you might call staff-level advice from Norway on what approach would best sell this exercise in Norway, and how delicate it was politically to do this and that.

I want to come back to that particular subject because it is very important, but I am bringing out here that the Atlantic Fleet has no such authority. No U.S. Navy fleet has any such authority unless specifically delegated to act as agent. The CNO has certain authority, for example, for making training arrangements with foreign fleets. Except as a member of the Joint Chiefs CNO technically does not have the authority to make arrangements with foreign countries to have operational exercises. This is a Unified Command prerogative.

As to the chain of operational command, many do not understand it and feel it is sort of blurred because all these three commands I am discussing were together with one Commander. The chain of operational command goes from the President, to the Secretary of Defense, to the Joint Chiefs of Staff, to the Unified Commander, that is, the Commander in Chief, Atlantic, and thence to the Atlantic Fleet. It is extremely important that the command chain in nuclear weapons matters comes down the route.

Traditionally, when we were young officers and there wasn't any Unified Command, we believed that the Chief of Naval Operations was what his name said, the Chief of Operations, and that he operated the Fleets. He does not any more. He is a member of the Joint Chiefs and, as a member of the Joint Chiefs, he operates. The part that the CNO plays - this is getting a little bit off the subject, of course - in the materiel, training, standards, standards of operations, and the total hours of operations, and that type of thing. But in emergencies and particularly in these foreign areas, he technically is not the chief of "operations". This adds to the blurring of the title of the Commander in Chief, Atlantic, and his responsibilities and authority because he is one man with two other commands. In practice, naturally, matters don't follow such technicalities all the time! If the CNO wants something done he frequently told the Fleet, and it got sorted out satisfactorily.

Naval officers all feel pretty comfortable operating in a completely Navy environment. It is nice, it is easy to operate just in the Navy, with Navy people directing Navy operations. You feel comfortable with that. But today, in peacetime and, of course, absolutely in war, the Navy cannot in this country possibly operate, for example in the ocean areas disregarding the U.S. Air Force with its weapons capabilities and electronic emissions. The Navy cannot operate without a unified approach to the problems. Nor can you, as a matter of fact, take combat action without a unified command with the Army, the Navy, and the Air Force in the area in which they are operating adjacent to one another and interfering or cooperating, as the case may be, with one another. Now, this is not as comfortable nor as easy as working with the traditional Navy chain of command where you know what to expect. That is a very comfortable situation. I had noticed this in exercises. Officers and commands, get rather uncomfortable with unified operations and are happiest when they slip back right into the normal Navy chain of command, which is quite natural. I understand it completely. I feel the same myself, except that they had better learn to operate under unified directions and make the other way more comfortable, because that is the way things are going, and if there is a war that is the way it will be fought.

I mentioned, for example, that the chain of nuclear command goes through the Unified Commander. The Unified Commander doesn't control the detailed operations of the Polaris-Poseidon submarines, but under the Joint Chiefs controls policy, and from the President controls any nuclear weapon release. So this is a very important chain, indeed. I am not, incidentally, trying to describe all of the methods of release of the nuclear weapons because, in the first place, it is highly classified, and it should be, and, secondly, it gets technical and complicated. The basic approach is that the chain of command is as I have described to you.

Now, as I have mentioned, certainly the notional or the book solution of Unified Command as taught in joint schools is with the Commander commanding three components, Air Force, Army and Navy components. He commands joint task forces which he may set up himself or which he can be directed to set up. He commands directly, in most cases, island commands such as Iceland. I will come to those later in the Atlantic.

Now contributing to the blurring of the command picture in the Atlantic is the fact that the "school" solution or whatever one wishes to call it, the classic organization, which is present in Europe, is not present in the Atlantic. In the

European theater you have a Commander in Chief, CinCEur, under him are three component commands, Army, Navy and Air Force Europe. He sets up certain subordinate joint commands or task forces.

But in the Atlantic only the Navy component, the Atlantic Fleet, is active all the time. So I think you can see why the Commander in Chief, Atlantic, to many people in the Navy, has been sort of a myth. They haven't had to pay too much attention to it because it is always the same boss, Admiral X. There was a habit in years past, which was changed, of sending out messages from the Headquarters combining both titles in the message originator's call. A message would be sent out as from Commander in Chief, Atlantic/Commander in Chief, Atlantic Fleet. This practice did away with, some people would say, the artificialities of writing a message to yourself. Technically, you had to write a message from the Commander in Chief, Atlantic, to the Commander in Chief, Atlantic Fleet, who would in turn put out a clear-cut Commander in Chief, Atlantic Fleet, message. The short cut practice saved time and I won't say that it is not used at all but we discouraged it to try to clarify this matter of whose responsibilities were being exercised.

When CinCLant held operational exercises he did not have large Army forces and Air Forces under his command. He had a four-star General, Air Force, and a four star General, Army, report to CinCLant. He established joint task forces.

Just to flash back to an example of an actual operation: In the Dominican Republic operation, when, first Admiral Page Smith and then Admiral Moorer was the Commander in Chief, Atlantic, the commander of all U.S. forces in the Dominican Republic, after the amphibious phase, was an Army General. He reported directly to Admiral Moorer as CinCLant.

So, both in exercises and in actual emergency operations, the system functions and those who participate begin to see, how it is supposed to operate.

I don't mean to be either condescending or to disparage our young naval officers and some not so young, incidentally, who had avoided all contact with joint matters. As a matter of fact, maybe it is the Navy's fault for not educating the officers by correspondence course or by more attendance at junior staff colleges. Many have never been exposed to the Unified Command Plan. Many have never heard of it. They get to be commanders of destroyers or submarines. The junior submariners have probably the least concept because submarine operations are so individual. You send out one submarine on one mission. He knows who his commander is, it is a Navy commander, and it is very clear-cut as far as that submarine commander is concerned. A submarine officer can go up sixteen years in the submarine service and never realize that he really is under a joint command structure. I am not blaming the individual officer. In fact, I think it is the Navy's fault.

I have mentioned that in the Atlantic we had only the Navy component, the Atlantic Fleet, permanently. CinCLant had, during exercises, the Army and the Air Force. CinCLant had continuously permanent island commands, of which I will speak in more detail. Iceland was an island command reporting directly to the Commander in Chief, Atlantic, and the Azores, the base at Lajes, was directly under CinCLant. As a matter of fact, in the Azores I had an Air Force General, Tom Aldrich, an exceptionally able man, commanding. It worked perfectly and set a good example. As far as operating forces are concerned, we only had substantial Army and Air Forces during the relatively infrequent exercise periods, about once a year. We did have a permanent Air Force fighter squadron in Iceland. We had very small Army detachments, usually very specialized. I will mention later certain operations that were ongoing every day.

There are some advantages to the commands having only one commander. But I believe the disadvantages of the combination of the three titles, Supreme Allied Commander, Atlantic, Commander in Chief, Atlantic, and Commander in Chief, Atlantic Fleet, outweighed the advantages.

To cite some of the advantages having these three titles combined in one man really made for very easy, really beautiful working situations in certain cases. Especially for any Commander in Chief who had the extensive background to take advantage of the situation of having three hats.

For example, as Supreme Allied Commander, Atlantic, or as the Unified Commander, Atlantic, CinCLant, I wanted to push a certain type of exercise. I might want the U.S. submarine force to exercise certain of their functions. Or, on the other hand, suppose NATO specially wanted to exercise either in a certain area or at a certain level, and especially with new equipment such as nuclear submarines. The only way NATO could get nuclear submarines was for the Supreme Allied Commander, Atlantic, to turn his hat around and tell the Commander of Submarine Force of the Atlantic Fleet to assign two or three nuclear submarines. Otherwise, they would not have, because nuclear submarines were overworked all the time. I will discuss this later, but I think the nuclear submarines were consistently overworked and it came down to a matter of priorities. So, wearing three "hats", I, as Supreme Allied Commander made the judgment. So, if I had convinced myself that there should be three nuclear submarines in the exercise, I arranged it. I could turn my hat around and order it, knowing what the tradeoffs were, what I deprived my Atlantic fleet of, what sort of end results would be seen down the road by my imposing additional loads on these submarines. I think it is quite easy to see, if you go into a NATO conference and some high official wants a particular type of exercise or a particular thing to take place, how authoritatively SACLant can speak, because he controls whatever it is, carriers, aircraft, submarines, etc. He could say, yes, we will do it, or no, we cannot do it, or I will look into it, as the case may be. It gave him complete confidence that if he committed himself he could carry out what he had committed.

So, there is that advantage of operating on three levels and having the resources with which to carry out the wishes of your collective command responsibilities.

Another advantage is that it prevented misunderstandings between staffs. I had an entirely separate staff for Supreme Allied Commander, Atlantic, the NATO command. I had a small separate staff for the Unified Command, and I would say fully half and maybe more of my Fleet staff officers double-hatted or performed a dual role as CinCLant staff officers. They worked for the Commander in Chief, Atlantic, and the Commander in Chief, Atlantic Fleet. Further, I might add, adding to blurring the command situation for people who came to see the staff. Nevertheless "wearing" these three hats and knowing them pretty well, listening to the staffs briefings, I could foresee, not every one perhaps, but certainly any major cause for friction that might come up. I would not let something happen that would cause great friction between the staffs or between the commands. The NATO and the U.S. command staffs were separate entities. They wrote letters to one another and they sent messages, even though the NATO staff was in another wing of the same building with the U.S. staffs. They dealt with them as though they were in Europe as far as formality when they got into this sort of thing. So there was the opportunity for the Commander to pretty much see that there was certainly a minimum of friction between staffs.

Now, frictions grow up between staffs and I am not going to go into that now. For example, with no fault attaching to any command or individual it was sometimes difficult to work with the U.S. CinCEur staff in Germany. They had a tremendous staff and frequently I had to send my Deputy, Admiral Jimmy Holloway who is now CNO, over to iron out a couple of things. I instituted something at headquarters in Norfolk which I believe and hope contributed further to understanding and to lack of friction. Every officer, and it was usually done in small groups, reporting to any of these staffs for duty was briefed within two to three weeks of his arrival by the other staff. A U.S. officer reporting to the Atlantic fleet staff got briefed by the SACLant staff, and vice versa. Very important on all sides. You can picture an officer coming into the NATO staff in Norfolk from a very small nation with a very small military service and a very small Navy. It was difficult for him immediately to translate himself to the level of operations planned for war, and which were in being all the time on the U.S. side and were in being only in exercises on the NATO side. I think it helped a great deal to have these officers briefed on Atlantic fleet operations. We could brief them, not in the most sensitive areas, but certainly in a few confidential and reasonably classified areas.

I have said that the disadvantages of combining the three into one commander outweighed the advantages in my opinion and I made recommendations on how best to resolve the situation.

Q: You're going to deal with these disadvantages?

Adm. D.: One of the disadvantages was that the Supreme Allied Commander, Atlantic, the NATO commander, and the Commander in Chief of the two U.S. commands just did not have the hours in a day to do justice to all of these three commands. For example, to be available to a U.S. Admiral or the Danish Admiral, to be available to all these commanders and all the ramifications of the Command.

The ramifications of all commands were great. I mentioned earlier the Supreme Allied Commander, Atlantic, for example, having bases in foreign countries, supporting the NATO budget and the infrastructure. And the U.S. Atlantic Fleet having bases all over the area that I have described to you earlier, I use "bases" very loosely here, stations or posts, several islands in the Caribbean, and also having permission to use facilities in Europe. There are just tremendous ramifications to the possibilities of these three commands. The immediate subordinates should have access to you because they feel, many times, that they must get to the Admiral himself. The Commander should be seen in all these places. That is part of military knowledge, that a good commander is seen by as much of his command as possible. You just run out of hours in the day. It isn't a matter of intellectual scope because really it is an Atlantic area military operation. It wasn't the scope especially. It was simply not enough time.

The members of my NATO staff from other nations, I know, felt that I did not give enough time to NATO affairs. I know that the Atlantic fleet - I know this from my own experience in the Fleet - thought that the Fleet should have the full time of a four-star officer. I think it should have the full time of a four-star officer. This is going way back now to when I commanded a ship, I would feel that you can't get to the Admiral, you can't see him, he is in Europe all the time. And indeed the schedule was full as long as you wanted to schedule it, from eight in the morning until midnight.

So it was just a matter of time. I was very fortunate in that I had had three successive commands in the Atlantic Fleet in very recent times preceding my going to be Commander in Chief. I had been on board every destroyer of the Atlantic Fleet, every amphibious ship of the Atlantic Fleet, on board every carrier of the Atlantic Fleet and on many submarines. I had conducted as Commander Second Fleet and Com-Strike Fleet Lant; Fleet exercises, NATO striking fleet exercises, and had been joint task force commander for joint exercises for CinCLant. I came to the position with a lot of relevant experience behind me. I didn't have to go look at the Naval Air Station, Roosevelt Roads, or the Naval Station, Guantanamo, Cuba. I had been there many, many times.

As far as I know, except for the Atlantic and Diego Garcia, which the Atlantic Fleet was building during my tenure in the Indian Ocean, I really can't think of a base of the Atlantic Fleet or a station of the Atlantic Fleet I did not visit. I came with this experience, so I would think that it would be very difficult for an officer to come to this three-hatted position where his primary operational experience as a flag officer had been in the Pacific, to even acquaint himself with every facet of the three Commands in two years. That doesn't mean he wouldn't be a good Commander because his staff prepares the problems and offers solutions and he can be a good Commander.

I just say that I felt fortunate in that I didn't have to do a tremendous amount of reading or visiting before I was effective. And I do think it points to leaving the Commander in Chief, especially if he is going to "wear" three hats, in command for a long period. Every CNO I have talked to about this has agreed, but it never turns out that way.

Q: He still remains two years?

Adm. D.: Well, the appointment for the Unified Command is two years and that gets into certain political ramifications of the unified command again. It can be renewed. All officials say commanders should remain at one place a long time. In fact no one is stronger than new civilian Secretaries. They say "we must leave people in their jobs four and five years". And they are the first to say, "I want Admiral Moorer". Or they want to put so and so in such and such a place, right away.

I did have an advantage, which helped me, by going there with considerable background. I feel that I could have given full time to the Atlantic Fleet and I could have given full time to the Commander in Chief, Atlantic, job and the Supreme Allied Commander, Atlantic job. Certainly the Fleet deserves the full time of a four-star officer. It is one of two components, the Pacific Fleet and the Atlantic Fleet, which really constitute the strength of the U.S. Navy and the Atlantic should have a separate Commander in Chief as it does in the Pacific.

I think the example of Europe is a pretty good one. While there may have been some inter-echelon friction, it was not so great that it ever came to my attention in Europe, where the Commander in Chief, Europe, had under him Air Force, Europe, Army, Europe, and Naval Forces, Europe. I do not recall hearing of any friction that surfaced. There may have been slight frictions between staffs, but I never heard of any knock-down arguments between the three component commanders and the boss in Europe, the Commander in Chief, Europe.

I have discussed this matter of commanding with you previously under SACLant. One intangible aspect which enters in is the regard in which the Navy holds the position of Fleet Commander in Chief. Becoming a Fleet Commander in Chief is a naval officer's dream. Practically no one I knew thought they would ever be Commander in Chief of a Fleet. Every naval officer who gets near four star rank thinks, I believe, that that is really the prize job. You are really in charge of the operating forces that you have grown up with. It is something a line naval officer knows pretty much from top to bottom. It is a rewarding command; it is a lot of fun, you have no doubt that it is vital to the U.S. Navy and vital to the United States. It has all those elements that go to make up satisfaction in your assignment. So it is a pretty hard thing for an officer who is SACLant, CinCLantFlt, CinCLant to have to recommend that he be divorced from the Fleet. Had they been split when I was there and someone said, "Which do you want, command of the Fleet or the Unified Command?" It would have been a most difficult decision. I am not sure to this day I could tell you which I would opt for. Had I spent two years as Commander in Chief of the Fleet and then been offered the higher job, that would have been fine. This has just occurred in the Pacific. Admiral Weisner was Commander in Chief of the Fleet and fleeted up to be Commander in Chief, Pacific. But if someone said to me or to many naval officers, "Now, you are going to get one of these commands, either the Fleet or the Unified and the NATO Command," it would be a most difficult choice for most people. It would depend somewhat on the individual. There are certain people so oriented to staff or military-political affairs that they would quickly opt for the higher position. I believe you could

say that an Army General would automatically opt for the
higher position, both because it is higher and because in the
Army, staff work and military-political international affairs
takes precedence over troop command. In the Navy there is a
strong feeling of the desirability and pleasure of commanding
ships, units and aircraft operations directly.

Incidentally, a "fleet-up" proposition such as in the
Pacific is obviously the right way to do it. However, much
one talks about this fleet-up it doesn't work out because
there is always someone in high office demanding an officer's
service or perhaps someone has a heart attack. It just
doesn't usually work out in the Navy. It works out better,
I believe, in the Air Force where, I have been told, they
can tell you who will be the Chief of Staff of the Air Force
three changes from now, at least within one or two people.

Now I would like to shift slightly and give you
an example of the "short shrift" that was given to the Atlantic
command because of this blurring of the three commands. The
command was blurred in the eyes of Washington and blurred
in the eyes of commands on the same level. Some of this
blurring might have been for their advantage. It is difficult
to tell why certain people do certain things.

I will give you a quick example of blurring at the
high levels, and I can say this because I know the people
very well. Mr. Laird, Secretary of Defense, of whom I will
speak later, fully understands the command structure of the U.S.

military and the command structure of NATO. It was rather remarkable the way he got around, with all of the things going on in Washington. When I was Commander in Chief, I would see him at a Unified Commanders' conference and at a NATO conference and at SecDef meetings. When I was relieved, I naturally wanted him at the change of command and he came. We sent him the schedule. The Fleet command was to change hands I believe at one or one-thirty. Then at about 3:30 there was a separate relieving ceremony for the NATO command. I should have said the Fleet command and the Unified Command changed hands at the same ceremony on board a carrier. The NATO command, Supreme Allied Commander, Atlantic, changed hands in front of the Supreme Allied Commander, Atlantic headquarters. Different people participated. NATO ambassadors came down. NATO officials came over from Europe such as General Steinhoff, the Chairman of the Military Committee. It was taken for granted in NATO circles that there would be a separate ceremony. The SACLant people would have been terribly hurt had they tried to wrap it all up in one. When we invited Mr. Laird, the answer came back from his staff- staffs always overprotect their bosses "You will have to have all these ceremonies at one time," which showed a complete lack of understanding and knowledge by some very important staff people.

I sent a message back and said, no, that could not be, the ceremonies would be separate, it could not be combined. We continued to be queried and it was strongly suggested that we combine these two changes of command because "the Secretary of Defense doesn't have that sort of time." To make a long story short, he did come down and he did stay for both ceremonies. It was a long day for him and I appreciated it, but it was very good for both commands, I would say even essential, that the Secretary of Defense came down. By way of contrast, when I went to see the relieving of Admiral Cousins by Admiral Kidd, there was not one single civilian from the Defense Department of the United States at the change of command. So maybe the Secretary of Defense staffs protected them too much.

I was going to give you another example of the disadvantage factor of the blurring of the commands in the Atlantic. For some years the Commander in Chief Pacific and the Commander in Chief Europe had jet aircraft airborne command posts. They were primarily for use in nuclear warfare. They were for the use of senior commands which had nuclear weapons in their forces under their command. They - I believe - were converted jet tankers from the U. S. Air Force. One was always ready to take the C in C at any time in case of emergency. In times of alert there were four or five of these aircraft so that the C in C and his staff could be kept in the air almost continuously. They were valuable to the C in C when he was required to go great distances from the Headquarters, as the C in C could embark with necessary staff and be ready to operate from any where in the world.

The Commander in Chief Atlantic did not have any of these aircraft assigned to him when I was C in C. This was really inexplicable, as the Atlantic Command controlled more strategic nuclear weapons than the Pacific Command and the European Command together.

I cannot tell you when the first effort was made by CinCLant to get airborne command posts. I suspect that Admiral Moorer made the first real efforts in 1965-1967. I know Admiral Holmes made efforts. These matters take a long time. These aircraft were jealously guarded, scarce resources.

When I became Commander in Chief I pushed as hard as I could and made personal representations in Washington to get some airborne command aircraft. I did not get much support from Navy - either CNO Zumwalt or his staff. They weren't very conscious of the Unified Commands during their first years in Washington. The Joint Chiefs of Staff controlled the allocation of these aircraft, with the concurrence of Secretary Defense.

The situation was almost inexplicable. I have tried to think back as to why they let this situation grow up, and I put it to two things. Primarily, the blurring of the image of the Commander in Chief, Atlantic. Secondarily, the fact that during the sixties the Polaris submarines were coming into the active Fleet steadily. The Navy, of course, had had nuclear weapons for years in the carriers and certain weapons that we had in storage and in submarines and surface ships. Sea based intercontinental weapons really came in during the Polaris introduction, and this came in gradually. I think the highest building rate was six per year, increased by President Kennedy in 1962-63. So the intercontinental weapon build-up took place gradually in the sixties. As I recall, the Atlantic had thirty of the Polaris-Poseidon submarines, the Pacific only ten.

So perhaps the Commander in Chief, Atlantic, didn't himself dwell on this increasing power relative to what others were doing, and maybe he wasn't too conscious of what the other commands had.

I pursued this matter as vigorously as I could. That was only one of a multitude of projects. The Pacific and European Commands used the rule that "possession is nine points" and were reluctant to give up any of their aircraft, and their aircraft was the only source. We couldn't get the money to build or convert new ones. The only source was to take some away from the European command and the Pacific command, and that was the ultimate solution. At that, they only shared equally and they turned over the oldest aircraft that they had -

Q: That's human nature, isn't it!

Adm. D.: All this is human nature. One of the reasons that it took so long was just a lot of good foot-dragging on their part. They just couldn't get around to it. You could write letters back and forth for years and just argue. In the meantime, they don't turn over any aircraft. They still had their four or five aircraft, and the Atlantic Commander had none, and had none when I left. The first one, I believe, came into position within about three months after I left. We did have the location and operating organization all set up. It was an Air Force unit based across Hampton Roads actually at a Tactical Air Force field. We were all ready for the aircraft in every respect, both the Air Force and we. It was very trying to get the actual physical airplanes out of the other two commands. It took a direct order from the Joint Chiefs with a time schedule to get things moving.

I come back to the fact, why did this occur? Partly because of the blurring of the image, the lack of clear-cut focus of the image of the Unified Command in the Atlantic. Of course, a lot of their reasons I probably don't know. You don't always know, as I said earlier, just exactly what reasons people do have for doing or not doing things.

Q: And will you eventually get to some of the interesting events that happened in your period there?

Adm. D.: Yes, I will get to some, and there are others that you could remind me of or other areas, types of things -

Q: I do have some in mind.

Adm. D.: We had daily and delicate reconnaissance going on under the aegis of the Unified Commander because we were using U.S. Air Force assets and Navy assets. The operational commander of these assets was always on some other echelon, but it was CinCLant who was the agent who said where, when, and who coordinated. That was one of the ongoing operations. Some of the reconnaissance operations involved more than one Air Force Command - such as SAC.

I've mentioned already that we had in Iceland an Air Force fighter squadron. In Iceland we had a force called the Iceland Defense Force. Part of it was the Air Force fighter squadron which made more intercepts of Russian Aircraft than any squadron, Navy or Air Force, in the world. They got a unit commendation for it recommended by CinCLant. They were flying single-engine jets. I brought this matter out in War College speeches and most didn't really believe it. They started asking me questions, but we had the facts.

Q: Why the large Russian traffic? North of Norway, in that area?

Adm. D.: Well, the Russians made reconnaissance, which is no secret today. The exact things they did were classified, and one always questions why was it secret. It was secret because of how much we knew about it and how we knew about it. That is why some things are secret. The Soviets made frequent flights to Cuba passing within the Iceland radar range. They made frequent reconnaissance over the Atlantic. Unless they are going over to Labrador or the North Pole, they had to come within the Iceland fighter range. So the Iceland squadron got a tremendous amount of intercept practice and, incidentally, with no accidents, which is absolutely amazing. We also had an Iceland marine detachment. We had certain classified sensors there in the way of radar and that type of thing. The marines really constituted a security detachment. It wasn't a tremendous marine detachment but it was the only ground force we had. They would have been beefed up, of course, had an emergency situation indicated.

Q: What sort of rotation system was employed for this marine detachment in Iceland?

Adm. D.: This was a changing thing. As I recall, without dependents, it was a one year tour and, with dependents, two. This, as I say, was a very fluid thing because Iceland imposed some pretty severe conditions on our people and, especially for an unmarried man, it was a very difficult post. Another subject but a very interesting one, they didn't like the Iceland girls going with our boys. It was their country and it was their policy, so it wasn't up to us to try to dictate to them, although many in the U.S. wanted to. I discussed in the SACLant segment of our talks in some detail the delicate nature of having U.S. forces in Iceland. I also mentioned the great advantages of having both my NATO command and my U.S.

Unified Command authority in working with Iceland. I described my visit to Iceland in one of the recurrent crises where the Icelanders threatened to throw U.S. forces out. It would be difficult to say whether I had more at stake as SACLant or as CinCLant in making my visit there in the summer of '71 (as I recall). The forces there were, of course, CinCLant forces. CinCLant was responsible for the day to day operations of the forces, the air anti-submarine squadron, the radar detection system, the Air Force fighter squadron, the air field, the security, etc. These actual operations were delegated to the Atlantic Fleet or to the Iceland Island Commander, but the responsibility was on CinCLant. And in some aspects, the ability to operate out of Iceland was of more direct concern to CinCLant and the U.S. than to NATO.

I may have discussed the invaluable agreements that SACLant had with Iceland which authorized the Commander to introduce aircraft of other countries into Iceland for operations or for familiarity. Sometimes we would do this in a NATO exercise, at other times in a bilateral or trilateral CinCLant exercise. We tried usually to bring in aircraft from foreign units which would expect to operate from there in time of war. But not always. The Icelanders had their favorites and we naturally paid attention to the intangible aspects.

The Azores were somewhat similar to Iceland but not as active in all types operations and while I was there, not as delicate politically. The Azores were vital to NATO, CinCLant and CinCLantFlt from the anti-submarine standpoint.

I would be staggered to think that Portugal would ever not allow the U.S. in there under the current capabilities of our weapon systems. The Azores are vital to the submarine effort in the Atlantic and South Atlantic. I have already mentioned that CinCLant had a fine Air Force General there. It was an important stopping place for air transports going to Europe and the Middle East. The fact is aircraft couldn't make it to the Middle East without it. There were alternatives for getting fighters to Europe. We had a VP antisubmarine air squadron stationed in the Azores and certain upkeep facilities. We had a very good air station.

Q: I suppose this is an unfair question to ask you, but I will ask it, anyway. In the light of the importance of the Azores to our military future, is there any connection between this incipient movement in the Azores for its independence from Portugal itself.

Adm. D.: It would be difficult for me to analyze. I am sure that you are aware that we, the U.S., really kept at arm's length any "tilt" toward any internal politics of the Portuguese. It certainly would be hoped if they became independent that the Azores would want the U.S. there, and I would predict they would. Incidentally, I don't think they will become independent, that would be my prediction. As many small places, they may find that independence really is not the pot of gold at the end of the rainbow they think. I heard nothing really serious on this matter.

Q: Unless they could make some kind of a treaty arrangement with us which would include monetary considerations?

Adm. D.: Our presence there is a big monetary consideration, there is no question. I was not in any position of authority, I was retired when the coup occurred in Portugal, when everyone in NATO was really very worried about the strength of the communist movement there. Had there been communist rule in Portugal, we would have been out of the Azores or, as you said, there might have been an independence movement. I am sure a communist government would never allow the United States there. If anything was underplayed in the press it was that possibility, maybe because military people didn't want to talk about it and surface it. There is no secret about these things. It is according to what is played up. But it would have been a major blow to NATO, not only a nation going communist within NATO, but the possibility of losing the contribution the Portguese made and the contribution made in the Azores. Think of the strategic position of Portugal and its airfields at the entrance to the Strait of Gibraltar.

Q: It's all very interesting.

Adm. D.: Yes. It would have been a major calamity. Fortunately, now it appears that there is a stable democratic government there. All I know now, of course, is from reading the papers. It would appear that there is no move in Portugal to get the United States armed forces out of the Azores.

Q: Terceira?

Adm. D.: The U.S. airfield is at Lajes. This is different compared with Iceland, where we were there under the aegis of NATO. Lajes was the result of a U.S.-Portuguese bilateral arrangement before NATO ever came along. I suspect that the Portuguese like the current arrangement about the airfield at Lajes because the U.S. bears all the costs. At a NATO sponsored airfield there are shared costs.

Q: Springing out of World War II?

Adm. D.: That is right. I know that I did mention in my talk about SACLant the fact that we were building a new NATO airfield down in the Madeiras on Porto Santo.

The Portuguese were extremely cooperative with me. Perhaps I have mentioned too much the advantages of the CinCLant/SACLant double hatting. Here was a clear example. I had certain problems or matters as CinCLant that I wished to discuss on the political level with the Minister of Defense and the Minister of Foreign Affairs. As CinCLant I could not go freely, personally, to them direct. But as SACLant I could. They gave me as much time as I wished. The affairs were so commingled that I went from U.S. CinCLant subjects to SACLant subjects, back and forth. This was very helpful.

Now, I am not inferring for a minute that I used this mode to bypass our U.S. Ambassador in Portugal. I was very conscious, as far as the United States is concerned, that the senior representative of the President is the Ambassador. That never escaped me, and on U.S. matters I touched base with him and kept him informed. Nevertheless, I did have this entree as an international officer and, if nothing else, it let me know the Cabinet officers personally and I could talk to them freely. I did not try to bypass the Ambassador. I did not consult with the Ambassador on purely NATO matters because it would have been in very poor form to do that. But I informed him in due course on NATO matters. I consulted with him on U.S. matters.

Now, we have spoken about CinCLant day-to-day operations, reconnaissance, the Island Commands, and now we might turn and talk a bit about the exercises that were held for the Unified Command. We are talking CinCLant now.

It was absolutely essential that we hold joint U.S. exercises, with the Army, Navy and Air Force, of the Atlantic. It is quite simple, you either exercise in peace or you won't be effective in war. New weapons were coming on, new electronics, new communications procedures and new communications equipment. This had to be an ongoing thing. You couldn't just write on paper that you would do this and that in time of war. You had to practice it.

It was difficult to get as many exercises as the Commander wished, but I think you can say this of any Commander any time. I didn't have enough NATO exercises, I didn't have enough joint exercises, I didn't have enough Fleet exercises. There are always constraints of money, and especially in that period with our forces in Vietnam, the lack of resources, or else we ran our few resources to death. So there is always a compromise. Looking at it from a Unified Commander's standpoint, I didn't feel that I had enough exercises per year to attain the degree of readiness which, as a Commander, I wanted and which I think I had in the Fleet. But I was not in charge of the Army and the Air Force. They had their own priorities and their own money problems. It was a little difficult very frankly to get complete cooperation from the Service components, and not because they were uncooperative people. It is because they have their own problems with money, resources, and time. The best we could do, then, was one large joint exercise a year.

I will make an aside here and say that sometimes in Atlantic Fleet exercises we could get some Air Force participation and help on sort of a "mission basis". They were pretty good about that. But as far as putting on or mounting out a big exercise, it was very difficult to do, very difficult to get them to allocate as many forces as were needed for the length of time wanted.

Q: For an exercise of this combined nature, roughly how many personnel would be involved?

Adm. D.: I would have to take a little time to compute exact numbers. We are talking on the level now of a task fleet, in other words, an amphibious force - this is mostly Navy at the start - logistic support, a carrier striking force, submarines and antisubmarine carrier group. We are talking about an airborne lift of an Army regiment. I don't know the exact name of the components as well as I used to, but we got a sizeable air-dropped Army component. We had to get the necessary Air Force to carry the Army troops, for which the Army had to pay. We had probably a couple of squadrons of Air Force transports, probably three, four or five squadrons of fighters or fighter-bombers. In other words, to use the Army term, we were at the division level. We tried to make it as large as we could. Once it was laid on, the other Services would want to respond within their limitations to match the level the others had, otherwise they became a sort of little auxiliary part. They are all very conscious of the attention of the press, and the attention of certain analytic organizations run by the Secretary of Defense who came down and looked at these joint operations.

In any event, I never got one quite as large as I wanted or as long as I wanted. Nor could I get the kind of joint exercise I wanted. In the two years I was there we had two fine big joint exercises. In both I tried to get them held in the Vieques area or, alternatively, Puerto Rico, in both of which we had exercise areas where we could exercise pretty much at will. In both cases the Air Force reneged on the basis of money. Both times we operated in Army and Marine areas along the east coast of the continental U.S. - LeJeune and certain Army and Marine areas that they have had for years.

What CinCLant wanted was to force them to relocate units, to displace from home bases and established communications and logistics, to go through what you have to go through in war. In war you pack up everything, you put it in an airplane or in a ship and go and set it up somewhere else. This is when you really test your readiness, and I did not succeed in getting the Air Force to do it. The reason was lack of money and it is pretty hard to argue with. Still there was some speculation that they wanted to operate from established bases in order to look good because of Secretary Defense observers and the press.

The Army, incidentally, also was not too keen about it because they budget on an exercise basis. The Navy doesn't. The Navy budgets for so much oil, so many steaming hours, and so forth. Navy doesn't budget on each exercise. Army only has so much for exercises and so much for each exercise. If you tell them they have to embark in Florida, instead of Fort Bragg, that costs an awful lot of money for railroad trains or trucks or aircraft. I must say it opened my eyes to the minute extent to which the Army analyzed the cost of their exercises.

Q: Did a political factor raise its ugly head, too, when you wanted Vieques? I recall that in '71 and '72 the question of Culebra came up and Chafee finally made a determination that we would pull out in a few years.

Adm. D.: That question did not arise. I do want to address that briefly later. The question did not arise because the environmentalists and others had not solved the Culebra issue yet, and so I predict they will be starting on Vieques, which is our only remaining place. So I had no pressures there not to go to Vieques. The main pressures, I would say, were two, money and time. I have said earlier, when people give you a reason for not doing something, you don't know what their real reason is. I don't know. I couldn't possibly tell you their thinking. Their decision was attributed to money problems and time for the units to exercise, how much effort do you direct to this, to that. Armed forces have to be given time for many other things, for other exercises, for upkeep for training, for many things. However, based on those two reasons, they refused to relocate to either Puerto Rico or Vieques.

I had, incidentally, participated as a lower echelon commander when they did go down there. It is a terribly important thing, to make units disassemble their equipment, pack it for moving, unpack it, set it up, and get it going. I would say the more junior the person you are dealing with, the less they want to displace from home bases. They want their radar or communications or command post, of which they have mobile ones and very good ones, to work perfectly. Shore based electronic equipment doesn't like to be moved very much. So I must say that I felt there was considerable merit to the thought my staff had that the Air Force simply did not want to move out of established bases. They could use their regular communications circuits, they had communication land lines that were dependable, they did not have to disassemble any of their air-warning radar stations. Their location of those stations forced the maneuver area, which then brought it into the standard command and control area, so they were literally working from home bases.

Q: But, as you imply, that lessens the value of an exercise, doesn't it?

Adm. D.: Yes, and I pounded on this as hard as I could. Yes, it does, but they wouldn't go anywhere.

Q: They're not going to be able to choose their locale!

Adm. D.: That is right, and the fact is in wartime maybe they would be going to Norway in a snowstorm, instead of to Vieques. I think maybe the higher the Command the more inclined they would be to push the readiness aspect, and the lower the echelon the more they would resist it. I guess the high command bowed to the many arguments about money and the trouble and effort, et cetera, and made a very firm stand. I think the Air Force might very well have dropped out had CinCLant insisted. I don't know. I went as far as I thought I could go, and did not succeed.

All the services have these mobile command posts, communications facilities and radar facilities that can be packed up and moved anywhere in the world. In the Navy, of course, we are very proud of the fact that we have everything in a ship and it is mobile. Mobility is extremely important. They all recognize this.

The junior people like units all set up and running and it disturbs them if they set up and they don't run, and usually they don't for a little while after moving. It is a lot of trouble to displace and there is always a risk.

Another practice that militates against experiments and sophisticated exercises is the one in all the services of giving flag/general officers short tours. As one gets more senior and as Washington has loomed so important, the career patterns have been that an officer may spend three years and maybe in the Army four straight years in Washington, in the Pentagon. I know one BG who had spent 13 straight years. Maybe an officer gets one year of Army field command or one year with a carrier task force, or one year with a Marine division. The result is in that year he wants to be good, he is a hot shot, he wants everything to work perfectly. He only has one year, he probably only gets two big exercises, and what he wants is a well-planned exercise that works absolutely perfectly. I have already discussed this point.

That feeling in all Services leads to the reluctance to displace the equipment. I remember back when I was Commander, Amphibious Force. I was aware of this feeling among some Marines. With the full help and acquiescence of the senior marines we forced the subordinate units to displace. If it was any location they could get to, they would go and set the unit up six weeks in advance and have it all tested out and tell you, "Well, we had to do that or it would waste exercise time."

This is a natural, human thing. I expect if I were running it, I might do the same thing. It is up to the higher Commanders to force them out. I have said in this interview that I really think that instead of striving for perfection we should strive for maximum confusion in an operation.

Q: Why not, innovation being an important part of it?

Adm. D.: It brings about innovation. There is the well-known fog of war. In war there is confusion on the battlefield. Equipment is not going to work in war, things won't go so smoothly. Not only that, but the enemy will be shooting at you, and you will be farther from your source of supply. It is trite to say so, but the only way to get ready for war is to practice as nearly as you can with the conditions you will face. You have these competitive factors coming in. The officer and, indeed, his subordinate units want to look as good as possible. Units like to report, "Everything has worked perfectly, communications worked 98 per cent of the time." We know in war they don't.

Q: Is this because of one eye being fastened on the fitness report?

Adm. D.: Not specifically - but in a very broad sense. These officers are good - I'm talking about the flag officers and general officers now - they know they only have limited time with an operational unit. At best they get two major exercises during their year. They are hot shots. They feel they are going some place, and they sure don't want to stumble publicly, as it were, in their two chances. So this is a big factor, and not necessarily a selfish thing. They are accustomed to doing things right and they want to do it right, and their idea of right is to have it work perfectly. My idea of right would be to have mass confusion in the fog of war, if you could impose it on them. In a joint operation participating units are even more determined to look good. There is no denying that there is strong competition between the Services. Competition is good. There is a certain amount of jealousy and a certain amount of suspicion, not on the part of all but on the part of some. Increasingly, and especially in this period of the late sixties and early seventies with the antiwar sentiment, there was real scrutiny by the press and real scrutiny, as I have said, by certain analytical organizations in the Department of Defense, some of whom were quite antimilitary. They would like nothing better than to analyze an operation and say, "They are absolutely no good, they are just wasting money or the weapon system is no good." There are people dedicated to being anti-military. You have seen some of them in the public eye, without naming names, people who were in Defense. There is nothing they would like better than to see the military fall on its face.

Now, I don't ascribe that attitude to all of the organizations who observed exercises. I am for being scrutinized and having outside analytic organizations measure specifics, such as what per cent of our communications got through. I don't want the participating unit to tell me. I would like to have WESEG or the Defense Communication Agency come down and tell me, and, incidentally, they did. They also tapped our phones. It is quite legal if it is an operational matter. We had expert observers and analytic teams telling us how good our communications were, how secure they were, whether we were good at security, if we were security-conscious, the number of circuit outages, and the reliability of communications. This is very valuable. I am for it, but it puts the operational Commander in each Service on his mettle, and each Service wants to come out looking good. Some are afraid somebody will come out with a report that the Air Force communications are better than the Navy's or the Navy had more aircraft up every day than the Air Force, or they performed more missions per aircraft than the Air Force did, The Services don't like this sort of thing, especially in public print. I would say that if it were a perfect world from the military commander's viewpoint, I would like to have the most stringent, caustic criticism or analysis possible, but kept within the Services. I admit that when it is displayed in the papers and The New York Times writes that the Air Force communications fell down, you have introduced an element where human nature takes over and it is hard to be objective.

Remember, in 1970 the Vietnam War was still going on. In this antimilitary period, with the military under critical scrutiny and under attack from some real strong sectors in the United States, some of whom had previously been our friends and who had supported the military, it was almost dangerous to look bad. The Services did not want a public, honest laying out on the board of every defect.

I still say that on the highest level the decision should be taken to see that mass confusion develops in exercises, make it as hard for units and Commanders as possible, impose casualties they have never had before and especially in the field, the kind of casualty that results when an enemy bomb lands in the command post.

We did try some of that. We tried to initiate taking command posts out of action, but they would raise the specter of safety and you just cannot overrule anyone when they tell you that this may cause a collision of aircraft. You are just not going to disable their communications or their command post, although we thought, on my level, it possible to hand off the control of aircraft to others. But this brings back that whole cycle I have been talking to you about. Who gets put out of action and who gets control? If X service is out of action and Y service takes control and does a splendid job - well, these are the things that make it difficult.

Q: This is the Unified Command?

Adm. D.: Yes. But applicable to all exercises. Joint ones are the most delicate.

Q: They're all working for the same thing.

Adm. D.: Which means that we don't have enough joint exercises. In some ways it was somewhat easier in NATO, even though foreign sensibilities are very delicate. Nevertheless, there seemed to be a little bit more resilience in taking imposed, artificial casualties and that sort of thing.

I think I could ascribe a lot of the apparent difficulty to the quality and the ambition of the young flag officers and general officers, the anti-military sentiment in the Department of Defense and in the press and the desire to look good and not have your Service in any way not look as good as the next.

An example of how far the competitive spirit goes. We had to be very careful about, for example, letting Marine air attack with the Air Force defending, or the Air Force attack with the Navy defending in fighters. On one exercise, we just finally cancelled it out. We had some Air Force national guard units on active duty and they were determined they were going to be the most aggressive aviators there were, and we had some near misses of collisions. It got so that we had to have some ridiculous rules about how close they could come to each other, because they were so aggressive and determined to come out on top. That shows you the competitive spirit, which has good aspects, but when carried to extremes is self-defeating.

To sum up that part of the exercise, I didn't get out of the exercises what a Commander would like to get because I was subject to too many constraints. There were good parts to it. There are good parts to any exercise where there is comparatively large-scale three-service operations. I had the four-star Army General from CONARC and the four-star Air Force General from TAC report to me as commanders of their components. They sent to us absolutely splendid staff officers who beefed up our joint staff and made it a real joint staff, which it was not normally, as I described earlier. We couldn't possibly operate in war with the normal staff that we had. The other Services sent us very fine staff officers and, with a little workup period, it was a splendid operating staff in the headquarters. We also beefed up certain staffs in the field where we had to make a joint staff out of what was a one Service staff.

So there were a lot of pluses. There were minuses. We didn't realize the full benefits of having spent the money and devoted the effort to an exercise. We could have realized more if there could be a really "no-holds-barred" exercise. In the U.S. military I don't think there was a really no-holds-barred exercise that I can think of. I can't speak of current practices.

Q: Are there any examples of no-holds-barred exercises in foreign military - ?

Adm. D.: I don't know of them, so I won't say there aren't. For U.S. exercises remember the factor of safety. When you talk about "no holds barred" with submarines, you just have to have operating rules, what you can and cannot do. The same for aircraft.

Q: I wonder if the Russians are quite as much concerned about safety in exercises?

Adm. D.: I do not know. It is said that they are not as concerned about the safety of men, but that is a generality. I think history has shown that they are not concerned about the individual man very much from the way they used armies. But I think they are very concerned about attaining the maximum degree of perfection and that their Commanders, just like ours, are going to work just as hard to attain it.

I hope I have pictured the fairly large-scale joint exercise as absolutely essential if there is to be a reasonable approach to the readiness for combat that the United States should expect of the armed forces.

I do want to mention briefly one other good aspect of the joint exercise versus the single-service type of exercise, and that is the opportunity to bring the State Department into the exercise. It is quite obvious, I think, to everyone that, especially in the initial stages of any confrontation or actual combat situation today, it is a military-political situation. The planning should go forward coordinated, and the State Department and the Services must work together. The Unified Commander, CinCLant, is the agent to work with the U.S. Ambassadors of the countries in the area for which CinCLant is responsible. We had fairly close touch with all the Ambassadors in the Caribbean. As a hypothetical example, if there should be a revolution that endangered our Ambassador and his mission, it would be CinCLant, the Unified Commander, who would get into communication with the Ambassador and would do whatever was directed by Washington or what was required to do in the situation. If there were a gigantic storm that caused great casualties in a country and the U.S. gave assistance, as we did in Haiti when I was there, the Ambassador gets involved. The chain of communication is between the Unified Commander and the Ambassador to the country. They know this and the Unified Commander knows it. Therefore they are more willing on both sides than perhaps in many years past, to exercise together. In our CinCLant joint exercises, I do not know if it was the first time but it was the first time in a long time, that we had gotten the State Department to send an Ambassadorial-level official to play the role of the Ambassador of the hypothetical country that we were involved in. Also, there was set up in the field a State Department communication post, with the State Department official there, who acted as the State Department. We played a military-political game, ending up in an eventual combat situation. All through the exercise there was an interchange between the Ambassador, State Department, CinCLant, and Defense. We played all these roles. That is, we set all these roles up. We didn't actually use Washington, but we would set up Washington representatives, and the State Department did participate with us, and very well. They sent good people who were interested, and it added a great deal to impose their thinking on our subordinate Commanders. "You shouldn't do that or you shouldn't do this, or take this into consideration." These are thoughts that are well imposed while the Commanders are young.

I was very pleased with the State Department's participation. I believe I mentioned earlier, in my SACLant talk, that the Europeans are ahead of us in this sort of thing, I think because they have been invaded so many times. Their civilian arm plays their "war game". They have suffered more, they have seen more civil disorder resulting from the impact of military operations and that sort of thing, than we have.

So I was very pleased with this aspect of the exercises. This was one of the prerogatives or responsibilities of the Unified Commander, to establish contact and maintain relationship with the State Department's representatives in the area.

I am going to continue to go over various facets of the Commander in Chief, Atlantic, responsibilities and day-to-day functions.

One of the biggest jobs, both quantity or volumewise and also from a standpoint of importance, was war planning, joint war planning, for the vast area of responsibility. This included the maintenance of the lines of communication and the supply of U.S. CinCEur in Europe. It also included contingency planning on four continents. In the military, the word "contingency" is used all the time to denote a plan short of all-out war. It usually deals with a specific country, in many cases a specific island, or perhaps a specific area. Just to take a hypothetical example, of someone decided to block a key strait in the sea routes, there might be a contingency plan for what one would do in such circumstances.

Q: There are dozens of such plans, are there not?

Adm. D.: There are dozens, and that is one of the things that create volume. For example, we had in the Atlantic command, I am sure, over seventy such contingency plans. As a matter of fact, we were just in the process in my latter time there of really getting this effort organized properly into two or three basic plans with about seventy different annexes.

Q: And how often are these plans updated?

Adm. D.: The frequency of updating is another very difficult problem. It takes a tremendous amount of work to keep these plans updated and so we had a routine. It did not have set dates on it, but it really amounted to a contingency review.

We had a plan for every conceivable country and every circumstance we could conceive or which we were directed to consider within our area. In fact, if we had not had such plans we would not have been doing our job.

Q: How are these tied in with JCS plans?

Adm. S.: All of our contingency plans are submitted to the Joint Chiefs of Staff and almost all of them are made under either a specific or general JCS directive. However, we could initiate our own situations. Some situations are so obvious that you could discuss them openly, not classified. For example, you wouldn't need the Joint Chiefs of Staff to tell the Commander in Chief, Atlantic, to make a contingency plan for Guantanamo Bay, Cuba. It is a rather natural requirement with what has occurred in the last twenty years with the exposed and vulnerable situation of Guantanamo Bay, full of U.S. military people and civilians and their dependendents. You need a contingency plan whether the JCS directed it, or the Command initiated it.

Frequently, however, the Joint Chiefs would direct that a contingency plan be made for, let us say, a certain island country under given circumstances. We tried to foresee all reasonable possibilities. One can easily think of many hypothetical situations, such as infiltration from other countries resulting in perhaps a communist takeover and danger to American lives, that type of thing. You can envision many scenarios for different contingencies. It was a big work load. They were under almost continuous review in a way. By the time you went through the whole catalogue of plans you were employing some of your best talent continuously updating them as to forces, because the plans got into detail as to specific companies of marines, specific ships, aircraft, and went right down to the most minute planning.

This work load was shared right on down the line by the U.S. Atlantic Fleet and by the U.S. Army and U.S. Air Force units concerned. That is where the JCS came in. There were very few contingency plans that were single-service plans. There were a few, because the Atlantic Fleet was always present and we always had Marines and we had aircraft and we had ships, so there were some relatively simple situations that could be handled within our Service. Even there, you were usually supported by the U.S. Air Force in reconnaissance, or something of that sort, or perhaps the U.S. Army in certain civil aspects of the action.

Only the Joint Chiefs of Staff could direct the Army and the Air Force to make units available for this contingency or that. We would then turn to the appropriate Army or Air Force command and ask them to designate a Commander and give us the troop list or the equipment list, whichever it may be. Then we went to the designated Commander and he and his staff planned with us. When the plan was all ready it was usually presented, according to the importance of the plan and the level of the plan, to the actual Commanders who were designated or, in many cases, it was presented to the four-star General of the Air Force and/or the Army who would be the component commanders.

Some of the plans were so small that it wasn't foreseen as necessary to activate the component commanders. They would merely provide units to CinCLant, who was a Joint Commander

and who could form a subordinate Joint Task Force. That
Joint Task Force was, of course, commanded by the Commander,
Second Fleet, who switched his title and became Commander, Joint
Task Force 122. He had a joint staff and it was an augmented
one for planning or operations. The point I was making here was
that this work load involves very detailed planning because
when you get into the more serious contingency planning you
plan right down to airplanes and targets and weapons. The
communications planning, as you can imagine, is extremely
meticulous in detail. Perhaps they are especially delicate
from a political standpoint - maybe that isn't the best
word - not from a strictly military standpoint. It brings
in a different sort of planning, say, than war. If you are
already at war, the big decision has been taken and you are
joined with the enemy in a clear-cut situation. Your
planning then is really, especially at sea, truly military.
When you get into land areas, of course, you undoubtedly get
into some political aspects of the matter. Contingencies
really run a development pattern. Certain events took place,
negotiations and minor action coupled with State Department
action at the same time. In other words, these situations
built up from what one might call a show of military
presence and negotiations on the government level on to
the actual application of military force, and that in graduated
degrees.

From Washington the President could order a part of this plan executed and he could, through the Secretary of Defense and the regular command chain, stop it at any time. When we had growing evidence of emergencies arising in some of the countries for which we had emergency plans or contingency plans, these plans, of course, would be broken out of the file and everybody would study them. We would start posting the details of the forces in the command center. We have done that many times for real because we didn't know, we had to be ready to go. I am sure the same thing took place in the White House. They broke out the plans and posted the forces and Commanders. This was done all up and down the chain, in the JCS and in the Service headquarters, and according to the situation the actual forces were alerted.

These plans were extremely detailed. They were a little different from plans, let us say, during World War II for the taking of Kwajalein where the action had already been joined. An even clearer-cut case would be the taking of an unpopulated place, where there was no civilian population. Or war at sea where there aren't the delicate political aspects, a battle just between opposing forces afloat. In attaining readiness to execute we had to stay completely in tune with the State Department, with any governmental action in Washington, not get ahead and not get behind, and be ready to deliver what we were supposed to deliver in the way of force and in the exact degree at the exact time.

Q: Now, let me ask, was there any effort made and, if so, how was it made, to test the effectiveness of these potential plans? I mean, after all, they were plans on paper, but come to the actual reality, how would you test them in advance of putting such a plan into operation?

Adm. D.: We tested them in our exercises, and that was one of the reasons I said we needed more exercises. We wanted to test the most complicated and the most serious ones, and we did that. We also tested not just the most serious ones but the most likely ones, which might not be awfully hard to do from a purely military standpoint, but might be quite delicate. You can think of places where complete chaos and breakdown could occur in certain small countries.

What I thought you were going to ask, and I was going to mention was about the fact that the press frequently, if we were holding an exercise even on the coast of North Carolina, would say "Oh, they are testing the emergency plan against Cuba." Or, the press would report that the military has a contingency plan for the Middle East. Well, I hope somebody has a contingency plan for every place. We probably have contingency plans for places that would surprise a lot of people. If we don't have -

Q: Didn't the press put some inference on this, that this was a threat?

Adm. D.: They, of course, interpret that the "Pentagon" is planning to intervene. They chose to interpret the existence of a plan or an exercise as proof of intent by the U.S. to intervene. The Pentagon is planning for a myriad things which we hope are not ever going to be carried out. This is a very hypothetical situation - the Pentagon should be planning for some unknown X country, let us say, to occupy Iceland, or for someone to take over Bermuda. We could not, of course, stand for anyone taking over Bermuda. Now this is really hypothetical because in the furthest stretch of my imagination I cannot conceive of a foreign power taking over Bermuda. If they do, everything is about over.

We would plan for any possible contingency and when we held an exercise a really keen observer could detect similarities. Sometimes we combined the aspects of a couple of plans in one exercise. We always gave fictitious names and drew fictitious terrain, but we put enough into it to make it a fair test of the problem. That is where these Ambassadors came in that I was talking to you about. We went through the whole play from the time it was still on the diplomatic level. Then through the time when military force was readied and used. Initially it might be only a naval presence, then military force used in small degrees. And then maybe clear on through to the civil control stage such as took place in the Dominican Republic. That case wasn't U.S. civil control, but our forces on the spot tied in with the Dominicans. We would play through all of these phases. The reporters frequently would, and it could be fishing, of course, accuse us of planning for invading this or that country or taking over Bermuda, if I can use that example.

Or, as you have said, we can think of places in Africa, for example. I can conceive that there is a plan for some African country. I am not addressing that particular thing, but I can conceive of possible circumstances. Almost any place you can think of in the world which affects our interests at all, I hope the Pentagon has planned for. If we did not plan we would not generate proper requirements for forces and special equipment. Planning is the basis for realistic force requirements.

So when the press tries to make it as a provocation that the Pentagon is using this plan as a threat, that they are planning to do this, the press is merely distorting to a certain extent because the plan probably has existed for years.

I can't imagine us getting caught without one. I can't give you actual examples, except to say that we would have to have a plan for any embassy in the Atlantic area, in case of natural disaster where people are in danger, to relieve the U.S. civilians and other personnel or an Ambassador. You can see the number of plans that that would produce.

Q: What steps did you take to protect yourself from unofficial, silent observers like stray trawlers from interpreting an exercise in its true nature?

Adm. D.: They would have some difficulty. We did have Soviet AGIs in almost every exercise we ran in the Caribbean, and that was one of our principal exercise areas, and we did practice contingency plans down there. It would have been very difficult for them, however, by observing the exercise to tell what plans we were simulating, even if they read the communications. They did read our communications, but whether they broke our codes I honestly do not know. A lot of our communications were in plain language. Most voice communication was in plain language. They undoubtedly copied all of our communications. That was easy to do with all the electronic array that they had on their ships. They also analyzed every radar frequency that we had and they saw what took place physically. The marines flew off in helicopters from the helicopter carriers and the Air Force came over and dropped an Army brigade. They could see this visually. They stayed right with us. I mentioned earlier that one of them anchored actually within the U.S. three-mile limit in one of my exercises at an earlier time. But I do not believe that they could tell exactly what scenario we were practicing. For one reason, some of our plans called for rather large forces, which we could not begin to duplicate.

Let us say some plan called for three Army divisions, it would probably be simulated with three battalions, so we would actually take one division of the three, or a piece of the exercise.

So it would be very difficult for them. I expect that the press did theirs mostly by deduction and intuition. For example, the Dominican Republic.

Let us say that there had been news stories out of there that things were breaking up. It wouldn't be too hard to deduce that we were holding an exercise that might well test the Dominican Republic plan. The United States did go in and assist the Dominicans.

I don't believe the Soviets could match it up, which was your question. A lot of these exercises went by pattern. We would put certain units ashore by boat - we tested every mode - we would put them ashore by helicopter, we would air drop troops. This was a part of almost any plan we had. We always had the elements of oilers and supply ships and amphibious ships, and carriers standing off ready to make air strikes. You could take this package of forces and write different plans. You had a flexible force package really, and it did different things in different places.

The way we wrote the exercise up in the operation order helped to conceal actual plans while still simulating the terrain and circumstances. We had outsiders take a look at our plan to see if they could match it. We wouldn't use cute names for places or operations, as was in vogue for a while, which really gave away what you were doing. The fact is we had a book to pick names for operations and plans out at random which did not relate to anything factual. Years ago it was the custom to use names that any high-school boy could relate to a specific situation. That was done away with. Even our own troops, I would say, outside of the people who had to read the entire plan, such as the people in the combat information centers and communicators, didn't know what we were really simulating, what island or plan. Let us say we were operating near and on Vieques. We had overlays with fictitious depth of water, for example, or we put in a fictitious land mass. It would take someone who had read the plan thoroughly and knew of the existence of other plans to relate them, and really it didn't matter all that much. The crews and the junior officers didn't really care. They all knew that we had plans. It wasn't an object of great curiosity.

Some people deride contingency planning, they say you are just wasting your time, it is a papermill, and you will file them away and that is the end of that. The fact is that it is through developing contingency plans and war plans, more especially contingency plans, that you come up with logistic requirements. How much oil you need for this operation, how fast does the ammunition have to come in, is it going to be brought in by air, do you have enough airlift, how much effort are you going to have to request from the Air Force, are there enough merchant ships for this operation, and where are you going to get them? The Commander may conclude that he needs a request to Washington to commandeer some of our merchant ships. When you work up to the war plan situation, you again query, "Do you have enough merchant ships?", and the answer is no before you really get started. We don't have enough for any war plan, I can say that without fear of exposing anything. Everybody knows that.

Preparing a plan is one of the important sources of developing requirements. You may find that you need two more communications circuits to talk to this agency or that. You need a portable communications equipment to airdrop in a certain place. You may have estimated you need four communications units. Then, when you test it in an exercise, you may find you need five, and you may need some special communications equipment you had not foreseen.

So you do develop requirements. Some people are fond of saying it is never going to happen as you have planned and exercised. Quite true. Everyone knows that who is knowledgeable. A contingency situation or a war is never fought according to plan. That doesn't denigrate the importance of the plan for trying to foresee all possible circumstances and developing these requirements. If you waited until a contingency happened, and then went in and found you need two vital mobile communications equipments and no one has procured them, it could be very serious. The way to get procurement, especially of unique equipment, is to do this contingency planning and to hold realistic exercises.

Q: How do you work with the service fleet then, for the supplies that would be necessary? They have to be cognizant of your plan, too, do they not?

Adm. D.: Are you talking about navy service ships?

Q: Yes.

Adm. D.: That would be a part of the fleet planning. As I have mentioned, on the Unified Command level, each supporting echelon has to make its own supporting plan. That goes right on down. An individual ship won't make a plan, but the next echelon up will. They will make a plan to dispatch a specific ship with such and such a load. In the case of the logistic portion, a supply depot will know that if a certain plan is executed they must get on the dock ready within two days a specific list of supplies. So many days' of C-rations, so many spare parts, and that sort of thing.

For example, in the case of carriers in a great many of the contingency plans, the planning went right down to the aviation squadron. They had specific target folders and practiced simulated approaches on important targets. The planning was this detailed. That was, of course, only on the most serious and most likely contingencies. We didn't have it for every single contingency plan. In some plans, specific pilots knew what they were going to do.

You can see again this detailed planning originates a lot of requirements. If it were an amphibious landing in the Antarctic - that is a good hypothetical example, that brings up a requirement for skis and heating units, et cetera, et cetera. An operation in the tropics brings up the need for certain equipment for your troops going ashore.

The planning process is under rated by a fair number of people. It is an extremely important process. It develops a certain mental discipline, which is needed. If you have not approached these problems, you find it very difficult to get into them in an emergency. Developing these plans and having them refined is almost like an academic discipline. It is both a training ground and a product of a planner's mind.

Now, to shift to a slightly different subject, which we have already mentioned, I would like to mention the Unified Commander's authority to arrange and to conduct bilateral or multilateral exercises with foreign countries. I mentioned that, according to agreements made, the approach might be at the Ministerial level, it might be the Chief of Defense level, or it may be that the foreign country has authorized working at a Navy-to-Navy level. In that case we would delegate the exercise to the Fleet and the Fleet would work with their opposite number in the foreign country.

An example. We conducted quite a few extremely valuable bilateral exercises with Norway. This gets back to the advantages of the combined Unified Commander, SACLant hats. Many of the airfields in Norway were SACLant-sponsored, NATO-funded airfields. In NATO exercises the U.S. aircraft worked out of these airfields, the U.S. was familiar with them. To put on a bilateral exercise with Norway was a comparatively simple thing. Both sides knew what they wanted to test and they may want to test different things. Maybe they would want to test their little submarines against us, and maybe we wanted to test various operations working in that very rugged terrain and climate in north Norway.

In that particular case, I knew the Norwegian Chief of Defense very well. He was a close friend. The fact that the Minister of Defense had been in my house and had dinner didn't hurt any. He trusted the Chief of Defense of Norway and myself to work out something that would be in the best interests of both countries and not embarrass anyone.

It was generally easier for me to arrange a bilateral or trilateral exercise in my U.S. Commander in Chief, Atlantic, hat than as SACLant. The difference in actual war plans between the U.S. and NATO as far as basic goals were concerned hardly existed. Even a school solution run by somebody in Argentina would come out generally the same sort of operation.

So, in a sense, we were always testing the war plans without any specific danger or revealing plans or having it take on any particular political connotation. Any exercise contributed to readiness.

We had quite a few exercises testing operations that were of value to NATO, to Norway, and to us through these bilateral arrangements. The same in other countries, each with its own concerns and problems.

I wish to discuss in some detail the matter of relationships between my commands-SACLant, CinCLant, CinCLantFlt and the Commander U.S. Naval Forces Europe. If they continue as they were my resume may be of interest, if the relationships have changed, my description of those existing in 1970-72 illustrate certain basic mistakes not to make.

CinCUSNavEur - the abbreviation, had a peculiar status which confused the staff there, especially those officers who had had no experience with the NATO structure or the Unified Command in the Atlantic. CinCUSNavEur was the Navy component commander for the Unified Commander in Europe - CinCEur. CinCusNavEur was the opposite - companion command to CinCLantFlt. Fleets had no area boundaries, except as they derived from the Unified Commander's boundaries.

CinCLant's area of responsibility went up to the shores of Europe - as did SACLant's. CinCEur and thus CinCUSNavEur had responsibility for the Baltic and the Mediterranean.

CinCUSNavEur had no combat role in the command structure of NATO, in case of a NATO war. Obviously if the U.S. got into a confrontation in the European area without NATO, CinCus-NavEur had a role. In a NATO war they would be primarily a logistic agent.

This situation CinCUSNavEur controlling no waters in the Atlantic, even four miles off the coast of Norway or France, confused staff officers.

Possibly further confusing them, by mutual agreement between the two C in Cs, CinCUSNavEur had a "hat", or a title as Commander of part of the Eastern Atlantic under CinCLantFlt. But this command was only activated by specific mutual agreement when it fitted a need, or if directed to do so by the CNO.

So, in the examples of bilateral exercises with Norway, which we have discussed, CinCUSNavEur's staff frequently got confused. CinCLant-CinCLantFlt would hold a bilateral exercise with Atlantic Fleet ships going into Norwegian and British ports and fleet aircraft flying in and out of Norwegian airfields with no reference to CinCUSNavEur.

In one exercise I decided to exercise the command of U.S. ComEastLant - who was also CinCUSNavEur as I have described. This was good to do to be ready for any eventuality. I had worked these kind of exercises out with Admiral Wendt, who then retired. In this specific exercise there were apparently several new staff officers in NavEur's operations staff. I, as CinCLant, had made all detailed arrangements with Norway, including restrictions on press participation and press releases.

Operational control of the exercise - primarily an anti-submarine one - was delegated to the U.S. ComEastLant. CinCUSNavEur's staff really took charge, ordering the ships to comply with CinCUSNavEur operation orders, which the ships did not ever have. The NavEur staff initiated press releases and even some press flights to the carriers, which was embarassing to me and the Norwegians. They even lost their perspective to the point that as CinCUSNavEur, not even in the exercise, they reported on the operation directly to CNO.

I have gone into some detail here, because obviously if good staff officers got so confused, the organization should have been clarified. Further, it is to me an example of lack of emphasis on command relations and command structure at the Naval War College. The Army and the Air Force stressed it. This incident I have described was also partially my fault for not discussing all the details personally with the Commander in Chief of U.S. Naval Forces Europe. We got along well. I have mentioned previously that U.S. naval officers tend to fight or avoid any command arrangement except straight U.S. Navy.

I have previously discussed the advantage of my CinCLant "hat" in arranging trilateral exercises with Spain and Portugal, which I could only do as CinCLant. We had one of our bases in Rota, Spain. Most of the Spanish ships had been sold or transferred to them.

Q: They were of U.S. origin?

Adm. D.: Former U.S. destroyers, submarines and small carriers. The Portuguese and the Spanish are very close together both geographically and culturally. After all, they occupy the same Iberian Peninsula, and what is more natural than that they should work together. The U.S. stand is well known, that Spain should be in NATO.

Q: It's hard for a non-Scandinavian to understand that attitude of theirs toward the Iberian Peninsula.

Adm. S.: I think I remarked on this in my discussion on SACLant. As told to me, the Dutch even hark back to the days of the Spanish occupation of the Netherlands, unbelievable as that may seem. The whole upper continent never forgave the Spanish for aiding the Germans. It is amazing, they can forgive the Germans and the Japanese, but not the Spanish.

I could also arrange exercises with South American countries. We had a standing one, but I don't want to go into that now because that was completely delegated to the Atlantic Fleet. If we wanted to hold an exercise with the Brazilians I could initiate it, or the Brazilians could with me, as Commander in Chief, Atlantic. This was a very valuable power and it is a power that the Fleet doesn't have. The CNO technically doesn't. Obviously, he can move into his JCS seat and if he can get through the JCS he can arrange anything he wants. Quite obviously, with the same naval officer holding the three Atlantic commands, the CNO could certainly push any sort of exercise he would like. During my tour there was not much interest in operations by Admiral Zumwalt, the CNO.

Incidentally, we could also, in arranging these exercises, arrange for the introduction of one country's forces into another, where perhaps they wouldn't tolerate it under a two country arrangement. I will use a hypothetical example. The Greeks could not arrange a bilateral with Norway and hold a practice amphibious landing in Norway. Politically it just wasn't on, this couldn't be done. But we could arrange a multilateral exercise and, especially in larger exercises where there are many components, they don't pay much attention to who is participating.

So that was one value of authority.

I mentioned very briefly, but I want to develop it a little more, the authority of the Unified Commander to make operating agreements with foreign governments. This, again, causes confusion and blurring among the more inexperienced staff officers. This authority actually stemmed from the Unified Command plan. I don't have the exact authority right at hand now. We made operating agreements in the Indian Ocean, we had bilateral operating agreements with many of the countries which were also NATO members.

I have already mentioned the Iceland situation. The agreements went right down to how late the personnel could stay in town. With several countries we had agreements as to how many ships could be in at one time and what other country's ships we could bring in. The agreements weren't of a nature that normally required governmental attention. That was a matter of judgment and we, of course, were very careful. If we got into sensitive areas, off it went to the Pentagon and the State Department before we did anything. Most were relatively straightforward operating matters.

Q: How often were they vetoed by the State Department?

Adm. D.: I don't recall a specific veto. I recall arguments about how far north we could operate, which, I must say, frustrated me considerably. To be sure, sea areas are a gray area now, because different nations are claiming different limits. The old limit of territorial waters and the only one ever really recognized by the majority of countries was three miles. Sort of generally agreed now, more a gentlemen's agreement than anything else, is twelve miles, merely because nations claimed it and why be provocative. Nations now, including the U.S. are claiming 200 miles for specific purposes. None claim 200 miles as far as passage of warships is concerned. I saw no reason why we shouldn't operate anywhere outside the three mile limit. The Soviets did.

I remember once the State Department balked at some planned North Atlantic operations and used some loose language about "Russian waters", which would make the Norwegians absolutely furious because it was off the coast of Norway. It wasn't anybody's waters, it was the high seas.

That is about the only time I remember them getting into the act very much. I have said earlier that we checked proposals and problems out with them.

As I mentioned earlier we were told we could not run exercises in certain sensitive areas of the world, so we didn't try, naturally.

I am of the opinion and all naval people are, that the U.S. simply musn't consent to any restrictions about warships operating on the high seas. The waters are subject to international law and they do not belong to any country. The press and TV often talk about operating in Vietnam waters, or operating in Japanese waters or Korean waters, even though it is sixty miles off the coast. This is unfortunate. What they mean is the nearest identifiable piece of land the reporter knows about. They should say "operating in international waters, sixty miles off the coast of Korea". Reporters are not particularly conscious of those fine points and it sounds more stimulating or provocative the way they do it. They aren't knowledgeable about the places they write about.

Q: I don't know why not. If they write for the knowledge of the public, why shouldn't they?

Adm. D.: Well, they should but the fact is they don't.

In this discussion, I don't mean to be negative. These points that I bring up where we had confusion or a little difficulty illustrate the importance of the Unified Command structure and a failure by the Navy to indoctrinate its officers in all the ramifications of the many different command structures existing with which they have to live and work and have knowledge.

I will give you one example of the kind of difficulty relating to making these agreements with foreign countries, which only the Unified Commander could make, unless he specifically delegated authority. These agreements were only for operations or perhaps details of use of airfields or bases. They did not infringe on the prerogatives of the State Department, who was kept informed. The Indian Ocean was split between the Commander in Chief, Pacific, and the Commander in Chief Atlantic. Command responsibilitites went roughly to a line dropping down vertically from east of Karachi, Pakistan. It used to be farther over and included Diego Garcia, but that shifted while I was the Commander in Chief. It has since been changed again.

Commander in Chief, Europe, had no responsibility in the Indian Ocean at all at that time. He was given operational control of the Middle East Force. There is no use going into the many pros and cons of why this was done. It was that way when I got to CinCLant and I didn't object to it because it really was a practical matter. CinCEUR (C in C US NavEur) was dealing with the oil states so much and the flagship homeported in Kuwait.

Q: One ship, didn't he have?

Adm. D.: He had two destroyers, a flagship, and occasionally we sent him a submarine from the Atlantic Fleet. All his ships were from the Atlantic Fleet. One was homeported and the others rotated. Naval Forces, Europe, had no ships there.

In any event the Middle East Force, headed by a Rear Admiral, belonged under the operational control of U.S. CinCEur, who, of course, put it under the C in C Naval Forces, Europe. Quite naturally, the units very frequently came into the waters which were the responsibility of CinCLant and into waters which were the responsibility of CinCPac. We had a mutual agreement that, under normal circumstances, we would not change the operational control as the units crossed command boundaries. It was sort of a general rule that if you go into someone else's area you change operational control to the area commander who has responsibility. That is not a hard and fast rule. By agreement, you can operate in another commander's area in great depth, but this must be with the consent of the one responsible for the area. Suppose there is a submarine incident there, it is the area commander who is responsible.

There was a standing agreement that when the Middle East Force visited African ports, it would remain under CinCUSNavEur operational control. When the Portuguese were still in Mozambique, Mid East Force visited ports there, some of which were very important fueling ports to us. Lourenco Marques was one of our fueling ports. The Middle East Force went around and kept the U.S. flag showing and kept in touch with authorities which is a valuable thing. No one on my staff felt that CinCLant should take operational control merely because they were operating in Atlantic waters.

About 1971, somewhere down in the staff of Naval Forces, Europe, they decided they wanted an agreement, just a minor operating and refueling agreement, at Diego Suarez. U.S. CinCEur told the U.S. Naval Forces, Europe, staff to make this agreement. The U.S. Naval Forces, Europe, staff sent back to the Chief of Naval Operations and asked permission to do so and it was granted. I happened to check on this particular one, and permission was granted at the lieutenant commander level. He didn't know it, but the CNO or OpNav had no authority to interfere to get into the making of agreements by Unified Commanders. The JCS of course could. This particular area was under a CinCLant's authority, and yet a staff officer got a message back from the CNO, never seen personally by the CNO giving them authority to make an agreement outside his area. This only came to our attention by sheer accident. We protested and it was called off.

I cite this to show both the responsibility and authority of a Unified Commander and the lack of knowledge at the working levels of these responsibilities and their importance. You can't have several agencies or commands making agreements with foreign countries on operational matters. It just cannot work that way. They must know with whom they are dealing. A single authority must know the constraints or parameters of the agreement having made and what the purpose of it is.

I will give you another example. This concerns the day-to-day working of the Atlantic Command in emergency operations. This incident brings in command lines and command directives, which, as I pointed out, everyone doesn't read.

In the winter of 1971, you may remember, the Cubans suddenly and without warning seized a ship commanded by a U.S. civilian citizen. It was of Panamanian registry. They charged, and I suspect it was quite true, that this ship had delivered people and material on the Cuban coast illegally. I don't know, but I wouldn't be surprised if it were true. The Cubans seized this ship and immediately we started getting all sorts of directives. The press said, in effect, they did not see how such a seizure could occur with the whole Atlantic Fleet out there and wondered how we could permit such a thing. The Cubans took the captain off, as I recall. They took the ship into port. The Atlantic Command was given various instructions.

Actually, it was an act of piracy under international law. There is no question about that. Whether the United States can protect every ship in the world and in every part of

the seas from piracy is a different matter. The U.S. can't.
Indeed would the U.S. want to in certain cases? There was
tremendous interest about this aspect. I would also make
a guess that there were ships and boats of U.S. registry
which possibly had engaged in similar activities. I don't
know, but it is certainly quite possible because we read in
the papers where there was a Cuban group in Florida who were
supplying arms to dissidents in Cuba by various means. I did
not know the details nor did I have to. The point is my
command was told not to let anything like this happen to any
ship under U.S. registry. I cannot remember all the rules of
engagement because there were about five pages of what we
could and could not do. When there is crisis management
from Washington, they really give you the most minute directions,
as we have found in many crises, including the big Cuban missile
crisis.

In this incident we immediately established sea and air
patrols, if nothing else to find out what was going on. We had
very detailed "rules of engagement", as they are called. It
doesn't mean you are going to engage. It means rules of contact,
rules for handling a particular situation such as how close
units can come to units of other nations and what your action
should be if somebody shoots at you.

We mounted air and sea patrols and set up certain barriers
and patrols merely to identify traffic going around Cuba. No
one knew whether or not they might come out and take a U.S.
ship. Of course, if they did, it was our job to prevent that.

Q: What is the penalty in our eyes for piracy?

Adm. D.: That is a matter for the international court. We as a nation could take drastic action by force. Of course, that goes back to the old actions of the Barbary pirates.

Q: Well, someone told me not too long ago about acts of piracy off the Chinese coast after World War II in which we did apprehend pirates, Chinese pirates in sampans, and turned them over to the British, who summarily executed them. That was their interpretation.

Adm. D.: I cannot say about that. If there were piracy against a U.S. ship, it would be incumbent on any military officer in whose area they were to protect the ship and take physical charge of the people and await instructions from Washington. This would be getting into international law where the general rules don't fit. You are not at war, you don't sink the ship or anything. Instructions would be given from Washington on exactly what to do. I have never encountered this in my career, so that is why I stumble in telling you exactly what we would do. Any military commander can and should take action in an emergency situation, according to his best judgment.

In a sense, we were facing that situation, but it was a little different because we weren't dealing with just some individual pirate. This was a Cuban governmental action, which puts an entirely different face on it. These were Cuban combat ships which went out and took this action. It was a

Cuban combat ship that went out to the first one that I was describing to you. I don't remember whether it was a Komar-class torpedo boat or what it was. It doesn't matter. The Unified Commander's job, which was delegated to the Fleet, was to institute patrols and find out where the Cubans were and what and where the U.S. ships were. The Unified Commander had to ensure that ships of U.S. registry were not seized or harmed, which certainly isn't the easiest job in the world in an ocean area such as that, with the long coastline Cuba has. A lot of our U.S. coastal ships just hippity-hop right along the international boundaries as close as they can. It saves oil.

We didn't know what they were going to do next. We inferred from our newspapers that, indeed, perhaps some ships had been engaged in some sort of illegal activity, but that made no difference. They were on their legal mission at this time. Of course, we were going to protect those ships. We were instructed to do so.

Q: Since you mention this particular incident involving Cubans, perhaps I should ask you about the action of the fleet in the same period, in 1971, '72, when there was great speculation, and perhaps it was more than speculation, that the Russians were establishing a submarine base in Cuba.

Adm. D.: I will address the establishment of bases in Cuba secondly. I want to finish up with a point of command relationships illustrating some of the things I have talked about before in this particular situation.

There are a lot of these situations that are political dynamite. They naturally come to the attention of the White House and it is run from the highest level. Indeed, all of official Washington - I am talking about the Secretary of State, the President, the Secretary of Defense, the JCS Chairman, they are all into the details of these things. Admiral Moorer was running back and forth to the White House daily. He would come back from the White House, pick up the phone to me, as Commander in Chief, Atlantic, and say:

"We want you to get two more ships up there to the north, two more destroyers. How soon can you do it?"

We would take a look at it and I would tell him.

Now, the point I am bringing out here is that there is an executive order that gives the Chairman of the Joint Chiefs of Staff the authority to act in an emergency on his own, without asking the other members of the Joint Chiefs of Staff, but informing them later when there is time. Admiral Moorer, being pressed by the President, or told to do something by the President or the Secretary of Defense and being personally intimately familiar with the Atlantic having been CinCLant, CinCLantFlt, and CNO, might have picked up the phone knowing who was on the other end, knowing their responsibilitites and their authority, and took the action. Some of the middle level staff in OpNav were just horrified at this method of directing Atlantic Fleet units, but it illustrates what I have been talking about, that the CNO doesn't operate the Fleets, except as he is a member of the JCS. Perhaps the line is very fine.

Had there been time to call a meeting of the Joint Chiefs, they would have made the same decision, and the JCS would have sent a message directing me, not the CNO, to do this. The CNO, in this situation, could tell us, "Send fifteen destroyers down south for training and invite adjacent countries to join," or something like that. Or, "let's mount a big training effort," or "let's fire more torpedoes off Vieques." But when it came to a matter such as this Cuban incident, which was an emergency operation, the Chief of Naval Operations was not the action officer. OpNav was in a support role. I immediately advised Admiral Zumwalt. I would call him up as soon as we got action going and tell him exactly what had transpired and what directives I had received.

Q: This is referring to the submarine?

Adm. D.: No, I am back to this Cuban incident, where the Chairman told me, as CinCLant, to send two more destroyers from Guantanamo up north on the patrol line. I would as soon as possible call up the Chief of Naval Operations and say that I was doing this at the direction of the Chairman. The Chairman, I am sure, in turn when his staff got around to it, would send a note or call over and tell the Navy what was going on, but he technically was acting quite correctly, quite legally. I advised Admiral Zumwalt at that time, that in these fast-moving situations, if he wanted to be in on it he was either going to have to get an office down there or get one of his Deputies down there to keep up with the day-to-day operations.

We had Navy officers on the Joint Staff but they worked for the Chairman, they didn't work for the CNO. It was the duty of certain section of the JCS staff to keep the Services informed. You can be sure the Army had a close worship arrangement. But in emergencies things don't always go smoothly or efficiently.

Some middle-level OpNav officers were baffled that all these directives would go from the Chairman of the Joint Chiefs to a Unified Commander to get ships under way to go out on what really could be a combat mission without even consulting the CNO. I did what I could to smooth it over and kept the Navy cut in. This was an unusual situation, in normal day to day business all the Services had effective links with the JCS.

Q: Does that not point up a fallacy in the revised National Defense Act?

Adm. D.: I am not sure what you're referring to.

Q: The fallacy of taking it away from the CNO, the control of the Fleet.

Adm. D.: No, I don't think so because what we were discussing here happened to be a single-service action. I must say had that been an Army officer chairman he would have called the CNO or the Navy operational Deputy who would have written up the message, releasing it in the name of the JCS. It would have been a Navy action. But Admiral Moorer knew it so well. He knew all the ships by name. He was quite legally correct and he sure was efficient and it got done. Had that been General

Maxwell Taylor, I doubt that he would have called me on the phone and said, "Send two destroyers up there." He would have called up whoever the CNO was and said, "Have your boys get a message ready." The CNO would probably would have been in on the conference in the first place because they were dealing with a purely Naval action. But as it was, I am sure as far as the President and the Secretary of Defense were concerned, they were dealing with a naval officer and they didn't have to worry about anything like that. Anyway, that was the Chairman's responsibility. Back to your question, under the Unified Command system I believe it is correct and the only way the Unified Command system could work is for the JCS to give the orders to the Unifed Commander in emergency, confrontation, or national policy situations. Can you imagine the USAF Chief of Staff giving operational orders to European Air Force units, bypassing the U.S. Commander in Chief Europe? It won't work in a unified theater. The Service Chiefs ran training, shifting units around, all those things.

Some OpNav officers didn't understand the legality of the Chairman's action or why it was done. The several examples I have given you of this lack of understanding perhaps indicates more study of command matters by naval students.

I would like to reply briefly to your query about the establishment of submarine bases and the movements of Soviet ships in the Cuban periphery and Cuban ports.

As far as U.S. responsibility and authority went it was a CinCLant matter. In this case, because CinCLant had only the

Atlantic Fleet to work with on a day-by-day basis, except for some USAF reconnaissance aircraft, it was all delegated to the Fleet C in C. Some coordinated reconnaissance was shared with the Air Force.

I think it is sufficient to say, because it is a very simple thing to do that we merely kept track of Soviet ships. The Soviets had to approach through international air space or international waters. No ship or aircraft could go in or out without being in a position where they could be closely observed quite legally. The Atlantic Fleet kept track of where they went and how long they stayed. Through other intelligence sources we knew that, while there were some facilities for the Soviets, there wasn't a base in the technical sense, as we think of a base in this country. There were a considerable number of flights of Soviet aircraft nonstop around the North Cape and all the way to Cuba. They would stay there for various periods and then return home. Submarines and submarine tenders went into various ports, especially Cienfuegos in the south, but also other ports. We knew their movements and knew what they were doing.

I think the significance of this was not so much in what was bandied about in the press about a base or no base, the point was that the Soviets showed their ability to operate at that distance. They demonstrated the potential in case of a U.S. Soviet confrontation of using Cuba as a base, especially during what you might call a diplomatic phase of any confrontation, where they could use Cuban ports freely. Quite obviously, after an all-out war started they couldn't use Cuban ports. It is too much under our eye, under our guns, too close to the U.S. Short of open conflict, they could use Cuba indefinitely. They could leave the ships there a year if they wished. They sent down submarine tenders, as a preliminary or getting-ready measure, this could be a very valuable action. So it demonstrated more of Soviet capabilities and possibilities than in what little bit they put ashore.

Q: But it was, in a way, a minor missile crisis all over again.

Adm. D.: Minor. You could argue about whether it violated the Kennedy agreement that they were not to introduce missiles aboard these missile submarines into Cuba and this sort of thing. If the submarine carried even a short-range cruise missile, you could argue that it was a violation.

Q: It was in a relatively short period of time after the original missile crisis?

Adm. D.: Relatively, yes.

Q: Ten years?

Adm. D.: Slightly less. Of course, as far as bases were concerned which is where the attention was focussed in the press, with a submarine tender, you don't need a base, except for recreation. The tender is the base. They can go anywhere and did. They went to Africa and submarines operated from the tenders for long periods. The submarine tenders operated in the open seas and submarines came alongside the tender. This was an innovation.

Q: This went on for a matter of several months, didn't it?

Adm. D.: I can't tell you the exact period, but as I recall it was over a year or more that this sort of thing went on. In fact, these port visits by Russian ships had gone on, as I recall, over a period of several years. However, the frequency and numbers increased. The Soviets also introduced nuclear submarines. That got people stirred up, a nuclear submarine going in there. This was quite a different action from having a cruiser come in. Anyone knows a cruiser, if you were in a war, couldn't operate out of Cuba. A submarine in there especially a missile sub, is quite a different thing. It involves covert operations they can do in peacetime. It gave the Soviets readiness for confrontation, if they based submarines forward.

I would like to turn quickly and mention another specific of the type things that CinCLant got involved in. This follows on pretty much from what I have been talking about, that is, in the military-political role.

CinCLant had the mission of protecting the Panama Canal from attack by air and sea.

Following considerable study and with the desire to reduce big staffs and to take cognizance of South American sensibilitites, CinCLant was directed to make a study of CinCLant taking over all responsibilities in Panama. This study was made in cooperation with the Southern Command, a four star Army General was the C in C. CinCLant sent a staff group down who stayed there about a month or so. We were directed to go so far as to outline how the responsibilities would be carried out if the Secretary of Defense dissolved the Southern Command entirely. Some of the effects had political overtones, such as who controls the military attachés in South America, to whom do they report, who funnels the military aid, who generates final military aid requirements. Incidentally I think that responsibility shifted to Washington, in any event. There were some political overtones to our study effort.

I bring this example up to show you the sort of thing CinCLant was thrown into. I believe our collective judgment at CinCLant was that we did not want to have the close-in defense, or security is a better word, of the Panama Canal. We already had the responsibility for any real threat that would come from an enemy, from outside. Therefore, we did not want to get bogged down in the details of an Army regiment and the U.S.A.F. fighter squadron locally in Panama. These were for the close-in, physical security of the canal. This was largely security against Panamanians. Even though we were instinctively against getting involved locally, we made a very thorough study with back-up arguments for our conclusion.

I went down and spent two or three days with the Army General, conferred with our U.S. Ambassador, and the Panama Canal Governor, a retired four-star General.

Q: Was Bunker there at that time?

Adm. D.: No. The shift in responsibilities did not eventuate, and, as I said earlier, we were not sorry.

I bring it up to show the sort of thing CinCLant got into and to bring up another point.

CinCLant did have close relations with South American countries. We arranged exercises with South American countries. Several of their Chiefs of Defense or Chiefs of Naval Operations came to Norfolk to call on me. I felt that we had some feeling and knowledge of South American affairs. We had responsibility for all the waters around all of South America and Central America.

Q: Did you do this through the OAS?

Adm. D.: Oh no, not at all, nothing to do with the OAS. They are headquartered in Washington. We were conscious of them but we worked directly with individual countries and delegated actual naval operations, which were the main thing, to CinCLantFlt. I will talk about that when we get into Fleet matters.

As to the Panama Canal, knowing something about South America and being briefed by these experts, I came to the conclusion that it was not a suitable task for CinCLant. It would be like guarding a dam and we thought that was an army task, a close-in task. CinCLant had other vital missions to perform. I personally thought, and I told the General, who was a fine, capable and sensitive man, that I didn't think a four-star U.S. officer would be in Central America in ten years.

I didn't think that the Latin-American countries would stand for
that sort of thing. I also came to the conclusion at that time,
which I now translate to the present, that the current U.S.
administration's stand concerning Panama is correct. We,
the United States, will have to make some sort of a partnership agreement or arrangement with Panama that gives them some
dignity and recognize their sovereignty. Regardless of
whether we may not like the current leader, or don't like
his policies or his alleged communist leaning, on which I am
not an authority. This relates to the whole way of dealing with
South America and gaining their partnership, rather than trying
to tell them what to do. In the last part of the 1900's a
large, powerful country of 215 million with a large presence
in a Latin country, can't tell that country of a million and
a half people the U.S. is going to be sovereign inside their
country. If the Latin country had a 150 million people and
were themselves powerful, it is possible that they might permit
it and just shrug their shoulders. A country of only a
million and a half cannot permit imposition of foreign
sovereignty because it is destroying their dignity. They don't
rule their own country. They at times could not even come in
parts of their own country. The United States can and has closed
off the Panama Canal Zone to the Panamanians. This became
crystal clear to me when I went down to Panama and I was briefed.
The U.S. Governor of the Canal Zone had been the Army General
at the time of the student uprising about 1964, I forget
the exact date now. He was very knowledgeable, as one would expe

As a result of these briefings I concluded that the status quo could not possibly continue into the latter quarter of this century. I also became convinced that the Commander in Chief, Atlantic, with his responsibilities vis a vis the Soviet Union had no business being bogged down in the details of what was going to be a very messy military-political situation, which it is developing into.

This merely illustrates a couple of facets of CinCLant's work.

I would like to turn to an entirely new subject. While I was CinCLant, Admiral Moorer the Chairman of the JCS called, as far as I know, the first conference of Unified Commanders ever to be held. He held it in an underground command facility, an underground national command post near Washington. He got all the Unified Commanders and put us under ground for three days, leaving on the third day. We had a series of excellent briefings. We had an opportunity to express our opinions. All the Unified Commanders in Chief were there. It came to me forcefully that for the first time I was getting to know just slightly the Unified Commanders who were my peers and with whom I was bound both realistically and every other way to carry on a U.S. war effort, if required. I did not know them nearly as well as I knew the NATO Chiefs of Defense, because NATO Chiefs of Defense and Supreme Commanders met two or three times a year and traveled together by plane and bus. The Unifed Commanders never meet. I hadn't even seen some of them. I had a telephone in my office and we occasionally held telephone conference calls, and that is as close as I had been to most of them. I don't think I had ever seen but one of them before, Andy Goodpaster. I knew him very intimately because I sat by him at a NATO table about five times a year.

So I think the Chairman of the JCS had a very sensible idea. You always wonder why wasn't it done before, and I don't think there is any explanation of that sort of thing. It was a very fine thing. As far as I know they are continuing, but I do not know firsthand.

It really showed me that we didn't know each other as well as we knew our opposite numbers in other countries, because we had not been gotten together, ever.

To pursue this thought further, the first time I ever met the Commander in Chief of NORAD was on a NATO military committee tour, where they took us out and showed us the underground headquarters of NORAD. I went there with foreigners. The North Atlantic Air Defense Command is a vital "specified" command directly under the JCS.

To wind up this part of CinCLant's functions and activities, I as most Unified Commanders, went to all of the Service War Colleges and spoke. That has been discontinued pretty much now and I am not prepared to argue whether it is good or bad. Through these speaking opportunities I did have an opportunity to get across certain views that I wanted to get across.

Q: In the light of what you've said this afternoon about the lack of knowledge on the part of naval officers about unified commands, does it seem advisable to cancel out on those lectures?

Adm. D.: Well, they could compensate partially by substituting instruction in the command structure. At the Naval War College, after speaking as a Unified Commander, I told the officer students I was putting on my blue suit and speaking just to the U.S. Navy people. I told them that in every War College where I had spoken, I got many questions about the command structure but they were all from Army and Air Force officers and I never got any from Naval Officers.

Q: They knew.

Adm. D.: I took a couple of rather obscure points but very important ones, such as the one I just cited to you about the JCS Chairman's ability to take certain actions, and asked them if they had ever heard of it and apparently they had not. Other Services were much more conscious of the upper command responsibilities than was the Navy.

The Navy, on the other hand, has its strong points. We were the best day-to-day operators of any Service.

Another thing I did as CinCLant, I was able to and did go directly to the Secretaries of the other Services to ask for certain classified support for operations which I can't discuss. I was authorized to do this and it speeded up things. As Atlantic Fleet Commander I would have had to go through all sorts of echelons in the Navy. It would have taken forever.

I would now like to discuss an intangible situation which, while understandable, gave me a lot of concern and some frustration. I am going to discuss it in a lot more depth when I talk about the Atlantic Fleet, but I will introduce it now. What I am speaking of was the attitude toward the Atlantic, and, to some extent, toward NATO, which seemed to me not to address squarely the realistic vital U.S. security situation. I think that the Atlantic situation in this period I am talking about, when I was Commander in Chief, was downgraded and was overlooked. Maybe the most important result that came of this was not what occurred, because we didn't have a Soviet war, but that it established some ways of thinking and rather dangerous credos or standard views in the military in general and the Navy in particular.

We were in an actual war in Vietnam. People were dying, we were losing equipment, it was costing us a lot of money, our reputation was at stake, we might be embarrassed. The most important thing was that fighting was going on and men were dying. Quite naturally and correctly the major attention was turned toward Vietnam and it was quite clear that priorities were to be given to Vietnam. I agreed 100 per cent and there certainly was no doubt in anybody's mind, from Sec.Def. Laird up and down. "Vietnam is Number One Priority." I don't quarrel with that at all, but what I point out is that it crowded out of the mind necessary considerations of the most important area, should we be so unfortunate as to get into an all-out war with the Soviet Union. That didn't occur, but we didn't know then that it would not occur. In other words, if we were in an all-out war of survival with the Soviet Union, I'm talking about conventional war now, not nuclear war, that is an entirely different discussion - Vietnam, of course, would have been nothing. It was not vital to our national security. It was a victory for communism, but it was not vital to our security. It was relatively nothing compared with the Soviets controlling the seas and severing our lines of communication. The Soviets could win a war by preventing us from using the Atlantic. We couldn't win by using it, but we could lose by not being able to use it. The Soviets well know this and that is why they plan their forces and their Navy as they do.

I felt that this fact was being ignored. I want to put this clearly. Not that I expected them to give the Atlantic priority, but serious consideration was neglected. Officials didn't look to the Atlantic or to NATO and give proper consideration. Yet there was no air action at sea in the Vietnam War, there was no submarine action, there was no Soviet threat from submarines in the Vietnam situation, and no air threat from the Soviets. And yet the Soviets had a very real capability to cut our lines of communication to Europe, which, if continued, would have been the end of Europe very quickly. Most scholars think within a month or two.

So it seemed to me that they were letting military and civilian officials get distracted. This may have been natural. Nevertheless, they should have retained more of an overall view and better perspective. It had even greater effects, in my opinion, some long-lasting ones among naval officers.

The loss of Vietnam wouldn't have affected our survival. Efforts there were taxing the forces that we had at hand. The reserves weren't called up, they didn't really build up the Fleets. It was really taxing us in many ways and we certainly were paying a big price in blood. Every military man knew that in Vietnam we weren't doing what was necessary to win a war militarily. So we were concentrating everything on a war that was not being run correctly, and we all knew it was not being run correctly. I will say that most of us were too optimistic in thinking that we would get along anyway. But we knew it was not being fought to win. And at the same time, the Soviets were gaining, as they still are, in their position to control the Atlantic, which could be a fatal matter, as far as the United States as we know it. I am talking still about conventional war. Had the Soviets challenged us in the Atlantic during the Vietnam War the U.S. would have been in horrible shape.

I might say that any high officer or high official in Washington had to pay primary attention to Vietnam. I would have if I had been there. I paid a lot of attention to it in the Atlantic because we were directed to give it first priority and support. I will talk about that when I get into the Atlantic Fleet and the effects that it had.

I will also say that at the very highest levels in Defense the people there - Secretary Laird, for example - I think had a very balanced view. He put Vietnam first priority for personnel and resources and was very conscious of it. At the same time, he paid a lot of attention to NATO. He attended every meeting. He was into it up to his ears. He had a very balanced world view. I think Admiral Moorer had a very balanced world view, but, of course, he was the Chairman, he was the senior military officer, the President's principal military adviser, and he had a war on his hands. He couldn't spend time seeing that his subordinates were knowledgeable about other things. He had an immediate task to do for which he was responsible.

Q: And which he had inherited, as had Laird?

Adm. D.: Exactly. I will say that there is no question but that under normal circumstances the CNO in the person of Admiral Zumwalt would have taken a more balanced view. The fact is that he came to the CNO position from two years of being completely emotionally, physically and mentally involved in Vietnam. I don't think that anyone could come back to Washington as the head of the Navy and shed that experience overnight. The fact is that he had not served in the Atlantic in any high position. I don't know when he had served in the Atlantic. Zumwalt did not look toward the Atlantic, he had not ever been in NATO, and had no time to engross himself in NATO at all. As the head of Service, Zumwalt did not attend NATO meetings. The Chiefs of Service furnished forces, it is the Chairman of the Joint Chiefs who attends the NATO meetings. Moorer attended all the meetings, as did Laird.

It was not at the top level but at the middle grade

where they really went completely, to my mind, off balance. Let me cite a couple of evidences of what I'm talking about. I wish I could articulate better. These instances represent building up blind spots, not sitting back and getting the proper perspective of the whole worldwide position of the United States.

Here is the first example. There was a speech by the Director of the Defense Intelligence Agency to the Unified Commanders' conference I went to. In his speech - it was a worldwide brief of the threat and what was going on, he noted there was one Soviet ship in the Atlantic. That was the only mention he made of the Atlantic. He was illustrating the threat of the Soviet Union, and he stressed that there were fifteen ships in the Indian Ocean and forty to fifty in the Mediterranean. He didn't mention--and I wrote him a letter about it - there were 179 Soviet submarines in the Barents Sea and the Kola Inlet with immediate access to the Atlantic Ocean. All he mentioned was where the Soviet navy was operating that day, where the threat was, and he had one ship in the whole Atlantic. He was an Army Lieutenant General.

Incidentally, from a U.S. standpoint, especially from CinCLant's standpoint, if the Soviets had put all their submarines in the Indian Ocean that would be a big plus for the United States. It was a very good place for Soviet submarines.

Q: It would take the pressure off.

Adm. D.: Yes. They would have a hell of a time operating down there and they would be in some way quite vulnerable.

Q: They weren't about to, however?

Adm. D.: No, I don't think so. Soviet presence in the Indian Ocean is important because it shows their ability and their sense of worldwide operations. But he never mentioned that the bulk of the entire Soviet Navy was based in the Kola Inlet with most of their naval air and the majority of their entire Fleet was based where it had access to the Atlantic. This was the director of the DIA lecturing to the Unified Commanders on the worldwide situation.

Q: Was there not any chance to question - ?

Adm. D.: I wanted to but they went through it so fast and moved to the next subject so fast. I probably should have but it seemed to me at the time that I didn't feel I should open it up. I did talk to Admiral Moorer about it and I did write a letter. I told Admiral Moorer how disturbed I was about what I thought was a distorted view given to these high Commanders by supposedly the best source of intelligence we had in the Department of Defense.

Incidentally, the DIA General wrote back a nice letter, a polite letter, but he really didn't change his view. He said that the emergence of Soviet fleet operations in farflung ocean areas appeared to him to deserve emphasis. He said it was not his intent to minimize the Soviet maritime power in the Atlantic.

Another example which gets back to my theme that if the leaders don't educate the middle level or make them look into things, they can get way off the track.

I wrote a letter to Admiral Moorer about this one. The significance is rather intangible but I think it is quite significant. You may wonder why I seize on this one. It is because when a high official's attention is on one situation people who have an axe to grind and who would like to change the way things are run, get opinion or conclusions into high-level papers, and then later they can quote them. This is quite a game in Washington. You slip something in a long paper, Kissinger approves it, and you say, "Mr. Kissinger has approved this." The person who wanted to make the point just finished writing it in the memorandum in small print.

This concerns what is known as a NSDM, a National Security Decision Memorandum. The title of this paper was "A Review of Noncombat Missions in Europe," emphasis on "in Europe." This was commented on by the Joint Chiefs of Staff. Secretary Laird signed this paper to Mr. Kissinger. You see how these things go. This wasn't low-level officers talking to one another. They had gotten Mr. Laird's signature on a significant paper going to Mr. Kissinger. It could easily have gone to the President. When you get on that high level, you can then lift quotes for your own benefit. I am not seeing ghosts or anything, but I had concern about the motives of some of the people and the ignorance of others.

This example shows I think, the ignorance of the middle level officers who wrote the paper. Admiral Moorer was too busy, he may never have seen the paper. They were trying to reduce forces in Europe for a lot of reasons such as pressure from Congress and other elements, and to save money for Vietnam. They were looking for ways. Admiral Moorer would normally delegate this sort of thing. What they were doing was combing over Europe, how to save some people and money. We were spending money like water in Vietnam. These are the sort of important matters they slipped in the paper as just casual items. Unbelievably, in this review they had listed as a part of the non-combat missions in Europe, my headquarters in Norfolk, SACLant head-quarters. They also listed headquarters of another "hat" I "wore" that we haven't discussed and it is inconsequential to discuss called Commander in Chief, Western Atlantic, which is a subordinate NATO command. They had them both listed in Europe. They were in Norfolk, Virginia.

Well, that is not earth-shaking, but it is ignorant, I think, and shows that the JCS staff level didn't know much about the European theater or the Atlantic theater. Also that perhaps some one had an idea of combining SACLant under SACEur.

Illustrating the tradeoffs to improve the combat forces in Europe, they said the first priority is to augment combat forces for Europe. In the first place, that was outside the purview of the paper. In the second place, it ignored completely how they were to be augmented and ignored completely the role of the Fleet in augmenting the combat forces of Europe.

Apparently some Navy middle-level staff officers worked on the paper. Under the heading of improving the situation, they said "homeport a carrier task group in northern Europe." The paper said it was important because the forces would be under C in C Naval Forces, Europe. That was directly contrary to the Unified Command plan. If the carrier were homeported in the United Kingdom, which was never done, it would have been under the Atlantic Fleet and the Atlantic command.

So I felt, very frankly, that they were taking advantage of this attention to Vietnam to write in opinions, conclusions or directives which some people had wanted for years. For example to include the Eastern Atlantic clear up to about Bermuda, under the European command as a supporting force. Some people were clever and wrote items in to get a certain conclusion into the paper, and others were so ignorant they didn't even know what they were writing about. Also written in the paper, although CinCLant commanded the Azores and Iceland, and were plainly specified in the Unified Command plan, was a section which listed the Azores and Iceland as "in-theater forces for Europe". Maybe there was some ignorance, maybe some other motives.

These errors were all through this particular paper, which was a very high level paper. They then went on in a discussion about Naval Forces, Europe, headquarters in London. The paper said to be sure that the Headquarters were retained in London, so that the HQ controlled the combat forces in the eastern Atlantic. The CinC US Naval Forces Europe had no mission to do that, as I have pointed out previously. Whoever wrote this simply never read the Unified Command plan. He was just writing, I suppose, what he thought. He didn't want the command to move from London to Naples, so he wrote this conclusion in that CinCUSNavEur couldn't command the Atlantic from Naples. Of course, they didn't have a mission to command the Atlantic. It had nothing to do with whether they moved or didn't move.

This may all seem like the most minor nitpicking. I am illustrating that this was an indicator of the situation that, due to the natural attention to fighting the war in Vietnam, promoted a lack of attention to a really vital theater, the Atlantic.

Q: It was really a distortion, wasn't it?

Adm. D.: And sort of shocking, really, to see the great gaps in the knowledge and information. What ticked me off to write Moorer - I wouldn't care what they said to one another, I wouldn't care particularly - is that it was a paper signed by Laird to Kissinger. Mr. Laird could not nitpick a paper such as that.

That, I think, really is the end of the discussion of the Unified Command, the Atlantic Command. I have said that the CinCLant should be separated from the Fleet command. I still believe it very strongly. The situation has promoted confusion. I think that the Atlantic command is a tremendously important part of the U.S. command structure. Therefore, it should be separated. It would help the Fleet and it would help clarify in people's minds the command lines.

I believe that I recognize the value of the authority and responsibility I had as Commander in Chief, Atlantic. I was disappointed that I was unable to make it a clear-cut, focused thing in the minds of all the forces that I commanded and in Washington. In Washington in naval circles the Atlantic Command as a entity was pretty much ignored, because the Commander in Chief was this officer, whoever was down there, who was also the Atlantic Fleet C in C and that was about the end of it.

I believe some day the split probably will happen. It certainly would happen in case of conflict or in case of preparation for conflict, serious preparation for conflict. I think the Unified Command plan is bound to continue - I cannot conceive of its ever being discontinued. It must continue.

Q: In the operational sense?

Adm. D.: Yes. So I think we will leave CinCLant and the next time we will discuss the Commander in Chief, Atlantic Fleet.

Q: All right, Sir.

Interview No. 19 with Admiral Charles K. Duncan

Place: Nimitz Library, Annapolis, Maryland

Date: Tuesday morning, 24th January 1978

Subject: Biography

By: John T. Mason, Jr.

Q: There has been quite an hiatus since our last session but I am glad we are getting with this now, and today you plan to talk about your Commander in Chief Atlantic Fleet tour of duty, 1970 to 1972.

Adm. D.: Yes, and I must say that it was obviously no fault of yours and entirely my fault, but really the fault of uncontrollable events that such a long period has passed by without continuing the narrative. I hope that in the process nothing has been lost, and perhaps something has been gained.

Q: Time for reflection is always a helpful thing.

Adm. D.: In our previous interview I covered, in that period of '70 to '72, two of the commands, the NATO command as Supreme Allied Commander of the Atlantic and the Unified

Command, the Commander in Chief Atlantic, both of which were very important. I would like to cover in this final session, in roughly three sections, first the Atlantic Fleet itself, second the Commander in Chief of the Atlantic Fleet and his relations, which were my personal relationships, with Admiral Zumwalt. The reason I do this is because I believe Admiral Zumwalt will be one of the most written about Chiefs of Naval Operations in current history, and I was one of the two Commanders in Chief of the major Fleets. I could have remarked on several of the Chiefs of Naval Operations and one could pick one another apart on small things. I don't spend this time in a sense of picking anyone apart, I do it because I believe that, according to one's judgment, for good or bad Bud Zumwalt made a terrific impression on the U.S. Navy and therefore there will be studious research on his tour as CNO and some writing. And finally, a short summary or an assessment of some good and not so good points as I see it, of a naval career.

First, talking a little about the Fleet. To state the obvious, having the position of CinCLantFlt which is the largest fleet in the entire world, was the absolute epitome of a naval officer's career or a naval officer's dream. I am saying this truly, it was far beyond any early dreams that I had. I admit that as I rose in rank and found myself somewhat accelerated over my peers, I then began to think where I could best fit--where could I go? As I became a senior Vice Admiral and then an Admiral I realized my niche was as a Commander in Chief of the Atlantic Fleet. I never asked anyone for the position. I probably mentioned in discussing the CNP position that I submitted a list of nominees to Bud Zumwalt in the summer of 1970 for the SACLant/CinCLant job. None of these lists contained my name, nor did I ask orally to be considered. Tom Moorer had apparently not nominated me before he was relieved as CNO. I assume that Bud Zumwalt and John Chafee (Sec.Nav.) initiated my nomination themselves. I do not think I would have made a good CNO, I did not particularly want to--that is not sour grapes--no one asked me to be CNO. I can honestly say that in the latter part of my career I just thought that I was well suited to be Commander in Chief Atlantic Fleet and I knew that I would love it. I think personally that it is a more satisfying position than being CNO, but there is no question that Chief of Naval Operations is the most important assignment in our Navy.

At the time I had the Atlantic Fleet, 1970 until late 1972, just to give you a rough idea of the size of the fleet: there were about two hundred thirty-three thousand men, including the marines; there were something over four hundred ships; (I am not being scientifically exact about these numbers) and there were several thousand aircraft, both Marine and Navy. This is a command of which to be very proud in any country at any time, and I am personally extremely grateful to the Navy for assigning it to my charge. It represents a great amount of trust when they do that.

Q: The largest component of all that was the Second Fleet?

Adm. D.: Well, the Second Fleet - if you remember our earlier discussions, was an operating command that drew from the "Type Commands", they did not "own" ships permanently. Commander Second Fleet was assigned ships from different Type Commanders, Air, Submarine, Service, Cruiser-Destroyer Forces etc., and of course, in their international role, from other countries, and in their joint role from the U.S. Army and the U.S. Air Force. The Commander of the Second Fleet is the principal sea operator of the Atlantic Fleet, that is quite correct and I believe it is that to which you are referring.

You will remember that I described my earlier positions as the Commander of the Cruiser Destroyer Force Atlantic Fleet, Commander of the Amphibious Force Atlantic Fleet, and Commander of the Second Fleet which was all excellent preparation. By the time I arrived at this point I had a good realization of the strengths and of the weaknesses of the Fleet. In the Fleet I continued to press, with some success, for my favorite programs, which we have discussed. Such as, the necessity to go to sea, the necessity to fly and to shoot if we were to become battle-ready. I pressed very hard and with considerable success to get ships to be assigned their very lengthy overhauls, that is from three to eight to ten months, in their home port. This has been a favorite project of mine, I was in a position where I could exercise considerable authority, I will note that I did this with very little support from Washington or from the CNO. I do not mean CNO was against it, he was for it but he had had to be for a great many things, he has only so many assets that he can apply to his struggles. I will say I did this overhaul in a homeport project with very little support from Washington or the CNO.

Q: Actually it was your problem, your command?

Adm. D.: It was my problem, except that Washington set rules that hamstrung me and which I could not fight. For example: for many of the Atlantic Fleet ships--in the Amphibious Force, the Service Force and the older destroyers--there is not room in navy yards for their overhaul--example the Norfolk shipyard. Therefore many had to be sent to civilian contractors. This I didn't like, especially as some of them were what we call "bicycle shops"--they were only marginally qualified. The Fleet was required by Washington (and I use Washington a little loosely here because you can't pin it on any one group; it was the unions, it was the Congress, the GAO, the Pentagon giving in to the GAO, you will recognize the many pressures brought to bear on this sort of thing) to take the lowest bidder for a civilian contract. They did not make the decision as to where the ship would go until maybe a month or so, sometimes even less, before the ship was to depart for the yard. Under this formula, there was absolutely zero attention given to the men, to the crew and to the officers or their families. If the yard happened to be in Long Island or Brooklyn (these are civilian yards), a ship from Norfolk or Jacksonville was sent 500 to fifteen hundred miles away from home base. There was no place in the formula that add-on extra expenses could be costed out. You can cost out to a certain extent the additional costs incurred by sending a ship twelve hundred miles from its home base, such costs as family separation pay. At that time we had a small family separation pay, it was good and it helped morale. We had to bring the men back to the Fleet Base for schools as they were located in Norfolk, and in the case of carriers they were in Jacksonville. We had also the cost of bringing the men back to homeport for medical care as there would be no hospital or dispensary in these civilian yards. I tried to get such costs into the contract competition. Some work was awarded for political reasons by Washington officials, over the protest of the Commander in Chief. To send a Norfolk based ship to Philadelphia for overhaul was a crime. But it was done.

Q: How much control did you have over budgetary monies that were allocated?

Adm. D.: In a sense I had complete control after monies were allocated. If I ran out of money for overhauls, I didn't overhaul "X" number of ships, and this occurred to both Fleets. The Fleets would run out of overhaul funds and the "X" ships would go on a list of what they called "deferred maintenance." This is almost a constant condition in the Navy. The Fleets ask for a certain amount of money for maintenance and it is usually cut all along the line. Money requested is based on a specific number of overhauls with estimated costs. Several things happen--it is cut at several echelons, Defense, OMB, and in the Congress. Perhaps inflation has set in and they would not let the Fleet or the Navy include inflation costs with the budget request. By the time you get your money, the ships needing the least slip into the next fiscal year. I had control to the extent that I could spend X dollars and my staff said that X dollars should be spent on the carrier. The staff advised what could be done, what could not be done and how the money should be spent. We did, of course, run out of dollars. What I did not have was the power to say that the money will only be spent to send my ship into a naval shipyard, or to a civilian shipyard in the home port--I was for that. I wanted to build Navy and civilian yards up in Jacksonville and in Norfolk because of my strong belief in of having repair facilities--civilian or Navy--in the home port. We had quite a capacity in the Norfolk area.

To compound my problem, and this is almost of current interest, was the fact that the largest and most capable private yard in the Norfolk area adjacent to our biggest fleet concentration in the United States, was the Newport News Shipbuilding Company. They refused to bid on our overhauls for our Amphibious Force ships and our Service Force ships. I talked to their President, a Mr. Diesel (this was a Tenneco firm and still is). Tenneco put Diesel in as President, a man who had run a production line in Ohio but who had never built a ship. He was basically capable but he had no sense or feeling for the Fleet, and these aspects I have been talking about were foreign to him. His point to me was that they couldn't be bothered with that type of work, they made more money on new construction and also they made more money on what was called a "set-piece" repair of merchant ships. The big merchant lines had comparatively simple ships in relation to the complicated Navy ships. The merchant ships would have a regularly scheduled overhaul to perform maintenance. They knew exactly what had to be done. They took the merchant ships as a package, they could trim the cost and the overhead and so the yard made money on it. I thought Newport News Shipbuilding was most uncooperative. I perhaps made the mistake in not taking the point up with Washington. In retrospect I think I should have stood up on my hind legs and insisted to Washington that they tell the Newport News Shipbuilding they must take some of my ships.

Q: In recent years Newport News has had some difficulty in getting paid for some of their government contracts, was this true in '70 and '71?

Adm. D.: There was not that trouble then. It is true that Admiral Rickover (as he has been with others) was tough with Newport News Shipbuilding. I was going to mention another incident with this same President Diesel in charge and only shortly after I retired. Because of the fact that Newport News wasn't satisfied on their claims (I do not know if the claims were just or unjust), the Newport News Shipbuilding Company said they would build no more nuclear powered carriers for the U.S. Navy. This was widely considered (by me and most of the Navy and also by a fair part of the public) as blackmail.

The United States Navy needed nuclear carriers for national security and Newport News Shipbuilding had learned the technique on U.S. Navy money. Of extreme importance, Newport News was the only supplier in the entire world. In effect they Newport News Shipbuilding was saying, "we will control the defense of the United States, we will not build another nuclear carrier." If you remember, there was some talk in Washington that the shipyard should be nationalized. I would not be too surprised if Admiral Rickover started this talk. For the first time in my life I felt some sympathy with nationalization, though I oppose it generally - I believe the government should be kept out of business as much as possible. I am strongly opposed to socialization or to nationalization, which goes with it, but in that case I did not believe that a private commercial company should tell the United States that it will not build one of the essential units that the United States needs for its security. I did not think that was tolerable. Apparently Tenneco felt the same way and disposed of President Diesel by kicking him upstairs and putting my successor as CinCLant Fleet in as President--Admiral Cousins. It was quite obvious that this talk of nationalization was not quite idle, the United States simply could not have the biggest, most capable yard in the country tell them no, we will not build something vital for defense. There are other ways to solve that. I mention the above incident because the same shipyard forced my ships to go up to Bayonne, to Long Island and different places.

To compound my difficulties, there was a U.S. Navy decision to close bases, in which I basically concurred. It had to be, with the budget cuts we were suffering. Concerning shipyards only by request I gave my priority list for closing them. My recommendation was that we close the Philadelphia Navy Yard. The Atlantic Fleet was the prime user there. And I recommended that we keep the Boston yard open. The Boston yard was a high-cost yard, it was union controlled and didn't have the political clout in the Nixon administration that Philadelphia did. The point to be made is that the Fleet C in C, responsible for all the overhauls and for every ship in the Atlantic, was forced by Washington to keep the Philadelphia yard open. It was up a river--a day's steaming--a little dangerous, and could have been blocked so easily. It was not a home port for any Fleet ship. So, I was forced to send ships for overhaul up to Philadelphia, not near any schools, not near any Fleet centers. I could see no excuse. Boston, on the other hand, was our only U.S. Navy controlled shipbuilding and repair capacity up in the northeast area. It was on the great circle route to Europe. We had ships based in Newport. CNO did not support me on this nor did he explain why he did not. I can only assume that political pressures were brought to bear from powerful figures in Pennsylvania, on the President and on the Department of Defense. I don't think the CNO would have turned me down because I was responsible and he had confidence in me or I would not have been there. I think I should have gone to Washington personally to see the Secretary of Navy and CNO.

Q: Your recommendations were based on fact rather than on any consideration of political background?

Adm. D.: Yes, and there is a political consideration one must admit. Not only the fact that a Congressman wants a facility for his district, and sometimes they should not have it, but the fact that there should be some geographical spread of Navy resources. To make an extreme case, we would not want the whole navy in Norfolk Virginia. It would be ridiculous from every standpoint. It would be dangerous. It would be unhealthy for the country. Industry and jobs should be spread. It seemed to me we had reached a point where the Navy had modernized and operated in a certain way so that Philadelphia had become obsolete compared with the location of Boston, which you can get in easily. I did not get support. I understand that there are other questions that govern the distribution of jobs and that political pressures are brought on. I will say for the Congressmen, although I am sometimes very unsympathetic with them, they represent a constituency and unless there is an awfully good case made that a Social Security computer can be put in one specific place, if I were a congressman I would try to get it in my district. It doesn't matter where a Social Security computer is. It does happen to matter where certain U.S. Navy facilities are. I thought that somewhere along the line the Secretary of the Navy and the CNO really should have stood up for the U.S. Navy in this particular case. Secretary Chafee had been as much, if not more conscious of personnel matters than any Secretary I have known. He was more conscious of people and what could and should be done for them. I do not remember whether Secretary Chafee was still in office at that point. I have a feeling he had left office to run for Senator in Rhode Island, incidentally he was unsuccessful. John Warner succeeded him.

Q: He first ran in '72, did he not?

Adm. D.: Your memory is better than mine on this; I wish I knew because it would better explain to me why he did not stick up for Boston. After all, he is a New Englander. In my own mind I was turning over the fact that perhaps he had gone.

Through a great deal of work in the Fleet, and because my staff knew that I was very serious on this subject of overhauling at home port, that first year we actually got all but two ships in their home ports. We used every stratagem known to man. I had a superb Fleet materiel officer named Russ Bryan. He is still on active duty and he is now a Vice Admiral which not many EDO's get to be. He is the head of the Ships Systems Command. Due to Russ's effort and his knowledge we ended up with almost all of the Fleet overhauling in or very near the home port. There was a civilian Baltimore yard that wasn't too bad. We arranged some special buses for the crew.

This period, October 1970 to 1972, were the final days of Vietnam, and it did affect the Atlantic Fleet in a great many ways. We still provided units to the Pacific for long tours to Vietnam. We provided carriers, destroyers, amphibious ships and Service Force ships. As usual the carriers stayed the longest, nine or ten months, the other ships got back a little earlier, perhaps seven months. As was well recognized in Washington, we really wore the U.S. Navy out in Vietnam and we continued to wear them out in 1970 and '72. Perhaps someone will write about this some time. It would have been better to end operations there abruptly and leave, and thus preserve our men and equipment. Then the U.S. Navy could have gotten back in shape much quicker. You know now what has happened. The decision was made, and this started in Tom Moorer's time, that we simply had to shift what money we could get our hands on to build some new ships because we were going to inherit a Navy that was just old and worn out. Now it has come to the extreme point where we are getting a new navy but the total number of ships in the Fleets has fallen from about nine fifty to about four fifty. Then Washington cut the new shipbuilding program. We were stretching the ships as far as we could and remember we are still stretching them.

Q: How much notice did you have on the request for ship units from the Atlantic to serve in Vietnam?

Adm. D.: We had a pretty good schedule barring sudden emergency. Washington would compute the number of carriers or the number of amphibious ships needed on station in Vietnam and allocate the Atlantic Fleet a certain number, allowing for transit time, which was just plain awful in the case of slower ships. We knew it was necessary but that did not make it more palatable to the crews or to their families. Our problem in the Atlantic was that we had to maintain combat readiness there regardless of Vietnam. I have spoken at length on this in discussing CinCLant. If the Atlantic line of communication were severed in a war with the Soviet Union, there could not be a conventional war in Europe, except a short one of perhaps thirty days.

Q: The resources are already there....

Adm. D.: They are already there. We would be faced with a--defeat, or b--all-out nuclear war; both of which I believe are unacceptable options.

Q: You did make it clear last time in your interview on the Unified Command, that the top thinking in Washington wasn't necessarily concentrated on the Atlantic or the threat of Soviet units in the Atlantic. You recalled the briefing given by the two intelligence man who mentioned only one Soviet ship in the Atlantic....

Adm. D.: I am glad you reminded me that I mentioned this. It is true that throughout my tour and in the three hats I was certainly not supported by the CNO and I later give some of my beliefs as to why I was not supported. I do believe that students of warfare who were not emotionally or mentally involved in Vietnam would come up with the same conclusion I have arrived at--if you do not hold the Atlantic, you can forget the Mediterranean, it is gone; you can forget any land war in Europe. A war would come to a very quick, and very tragic, halt if the communications lines in the Atlantic were not maintained.

I felt we were in a crunch, we were required, and wanted, to send combat units to Vietnam because the burden had to be shared. I felt it absolutely imperative and my responsibility to maintain the combat readiness of the Atlantic Fleet for a different kind of action, for a war of survival with the Soviet Union. It wasn't that it was threatened this day or that day, it was a threat that was there, had been there for many years, and it is there today.

One of the reasons I felt we were in a crunch was that the families and the crews would expect to have a long period of rest after coming back from Vietnam. They had been in action, men were killed, aviators shot down, there were prisoners of war, the surface ships had been engaged in shore bombardment, the amphibious ships and craft were heavily involved. To have the units come back and have the Atlantic Fleet Commander say "you are not in good shape for a war in the Atlantic and you need a lot of training"-this had to be done with some finesse. The unit we received back from Vietnam was not trained to fight a war in the Atlantic with the Soviets. Take the destroyer, we received the ships back and they had never in 8 to 10 months had one hour's practice in anti-submarine work. They had not practiced on a live submarine, that is a live friendly one, and they didn't have any live unfriendly ones. I have spoken before of the danger in working in a sanctuary--all of our Fleet sat in a sanctuary off Vietnam. It is not training for war with a great power--to sit out at sea and be able to launch planes with no regard as to whether you would be sunk with a torpedo or with a cruise missile. Their consciousness of risk was not there. The units returned with no consciousness of the anti-submarine threat and with no practice. The carrier aircraft, the attack aircraft--reconnaissance aircraft--came back superbly trained in the very latest electronic devices, some of which we didn't even have in the Atlantic. They had been in combat which is the final test so the attack, the reconnaissance, and some of the fighter aircraft were really in superb condition. However, the anti-submarine aircraft were used to go up and down the coast looking for merchant ships. They had no training with actual submarines, yet in the Atlantic that would be their main job. I received back a Fleet that was not trained for the Atlantic. Therefore, I was forced to schedule, to the best of my ability and as appropriate, training exercises to bring this fleet up to combat readiness for combat missions.

Q: In the meantime the personnel was war weary?

Adm. D.: They were tired, their families were not only tired but disgusted with the long deployments of seven, eight, nine months. To have a ship brought back and then say "You have a lot of training to do" wasn't a popular thing. When the ships were brought back the crews were given a month alongside the dock and they were then given work-ups gradually.

The carriers, having always been pressed, had to face getting ready to go to the Sixth Fleet for six months deployment. In addition to that the C in C Atlantic Fleet had to put them into exercises to ready them for cruise missile attacks at sea, to be ready for the various missiles that the Soviet aircraft had at that time, and to be ready to repel the standard attack aircraft. I also had the mission of training them to work with foreign navies, which, in itself, requires some doing to make them effective. We did this to the best of our ability. I hope and I think we reached a reasonable balance of sharing training, upkeep time, maintenance, and at home time. We did not do this sitting in isolation in our headquarters. I called in the Type Commanders, the Carrier Division Commanders, I went on ships and talked to people. We also tried our best to explain why the schedule was necessary and that is not always an easy thing to do, to get them to understand we weren't doing this by rote to check off some training missions, we were doing it for real.

Another factor in this crunch which I have described, was that we were in the period of cutting manpower. These cuts continued in the 70's because everyone said the Vietnam war was going to be over so you cut money, men, ships, and you let ships rest. There was a tremendous turbulence of people being moved. Men left the Navy, ships went out commission, units were phased in or out, there was a great personnel turbulence which accompanies these periods of reduction. It isn't orderly.

Q: Wasn't it fortunate that you were there in the Atlantic as a man who throughout your career showed a sensitivity to the needs of personnel?

Adm. D.: Perhaps it was fortunate that I had a realization of what was going on and what was causing it, because many people just railed against the turbulence--said "let's stop it". I knew enough of the facts to know that it was a thing we had to live with and do the best we could. I did have difficulty convincing Washington of the fact that I had to keep the combat readiness in my Fleet up to do a different sort of job. It is so obvious to say "we have just been in the fighting, with men who have been killed, what are you doing training your Fleet?" That is a superficial type of thinking. Nevertheless, I did not get much support in Washington because there was what I would call a Vietnam bias, and a lack of awareness.

Most of the high officers in power in Washington at that time, had been brought in from the Pacific by Zumwalt. This is not an unnatural thing--one surrounds oneself with trusted people--he had seen many of these men in action, he had seen them do a great job in Vietnam, he was loyal to them, there was a preponderance of people close to the CNO who had a Pacific bias and not much sea experience. That does not mean the weren't smart. One gets emotionally wrapped up in emergency operations. One gets to feel that this is the only goal of the Navy, it is the most important thing. "Forget all this other stuff, including forget education, forget everything, we have a war going on." The fact of people being killed and seeing those casualty statistics on the board every morning is a very traumatic thing. Then to have a C in C come along and talk about what he needs in the mid-Atlantic didn't go down too well with some of these people. I mentioned earlier the low priority that education and training such as having more Army officers at the War College than Naval officers. Slipping back somewhat to CNP days, I have a memorandum that may be of some interest and you wish to attach. It was a reaction to the feeling that permeated the Pentagon--"well, Vietnam is about over and we can just discontinue all this education stuff." Navy had about depleted the Post Graduate School in Monterey, we were not sending the top officers to the War College certainly. We were not by any means filling the educational billets. The Army being larger, and as I have said having a wisdom that "the world goes on" kept on educating their people. It doesn't matter what is happening the Army has always kept sending their people to schools; we did not. I heard a lot as Chief of Naval Personnel and I heard more as Commander in Chief to the effect, Let's cut out all these training schools, the war is over". I wrote the memorandum before I left Washington to all the Secretaries, pointing out that the Navy needed more training, that we were getting new equipment and that training was not going to get less expensive, but that it would be much more expensive than it had been in the past. Recruit training had to be lengthened, not shortened. This is a recurrent thing the Service goes through with in every emergency. When an emergency comes we have to have the men on the ships, we pump them through recruit training as fast as we could. Against our better judgment we reduce the period of recruit training. I believe in WWII it was seven weeks. Eleven weeks we used to consider optimum, obviously it is not absolute, as there are no absolutes in this. When Vietnam came along recruit training got down to nine weeks--it may have been eight-- I don't recall exactly. I told them this must increase, that we must give the Fleet a better trained man. It is so typical of what occurs in the military and in Washington at the end of a war. There is always a feeling that the trouble is over, we can forget all these things and just go back to spending a lot less money and training people less because the crisis is gone. I attempted in my memorandum as CNP to put them straight on this, that there should be more officers in graduate school, more officers in War College, more enlisted men in longer courses in some new weapons we were bringing along. I don't know how it was received but it was quite a fight trying to get the money and men for these things.

I was saying that the majority of the officers brought in by Admiral Zumwalt, had little or no flag experience in the Atlantic. Many of the young close advisers had little broad experience. Among flag officers there had been very little experience. The Chief of Naval Operations himself had had one flag tour in the Pacific as a Commander of a Cruiser-Destroyer Flotilla, at a time when the Pacific Fleet had not gotten around to giving the surface commander any real tactical responsibility. Zumwalt's tour was foreshortened, as happens so often with the brilliant, coming officers--somebody wants them.

The same thing happened to Worth Bagley, who later was Admiral Zumwalt's Vice Chief of Naval Operations. Bagley went from an eight-month tour as Flotilla Commander (about, and I am not sure whether he deployed or not) with only this brief junior flag officer experience in the Pacific. He went from that brief experience in the Pacific, to the Vice Chief of Naval Operations, through the very key assignment of Op 090 (that is the Plans and Programs) without ever having other Fleet job and never having an Atlantic job of any responsibility. Whatever the brilliance and competence of these men, undeniably there was a lack of awareness of the Atlantic in some of these officers.

Zumwalt's close advisors had become a rather senior group, some were promoted very fast. Their reactions in the European and Atlantic theatre were devoted primarily to the Mediterranean. I would guess that was because of some Congressmen and some in the State Department who focussed on the Mediterranean as the most important part of the European-Atlantic theatre. It had a lot of merit, especially in the political field. Anyone--you have talked with Admiral Rivero--who knows that southern flank of NATO will tell you the Italians, the Greeks, the Turks, time and again will say they want to look down there and see those U.S. Navy ships. There were people in the State Department who went so far as to say that if the U.S. pulled the carriers from the Eastern Mediterranean the Greeks and Turks would pull out of NATO. I don't believe that, but I think they were sincere. In a time of surprise all-out war the first thing to do was to be to get them out of there. That does not mean the U.S. and Nato navies could not operate in combat in the Mediterranean, the point is the 6th Fleet should not be there when surprise war occurs. They can be sent in later as appropriate.

The thread of the story I was trying to carry was, that the people around Zumwalt, insofar as they looked at Europe at all, looked at the Mediterranean. They tried to get me voluntarily to increase the Mediterranean fleet, when even the NATO adherents well knew that the Mediterranean Fleet was primarily important in peace time and for political reasons. This was the opinion of the planners on my staff and of the students of naval warfare whom I knew. When I was forced, under this crunch I have been describing, to try to build up the Mediterranean Fleet, thus having longer deployments, I naturally reacted as strongly as I could.

Q: Were the deployments longer than six months?

Adm. D.: No, but a lot of them had recently been to Vietnam. If I had to put more destroyers, more amphibians, more carriers days in the Mediterranean it would lengthen the total time of the Atlantic Fleet out of its home port not to mention decreasing the time available for training.

I have said earlier that, in my opinion, Admiral Zumwalt had at that time very little understanding of Europe, of NATO, or of the Atlantic. He didn't have time to devote to it. He was running the Vietnam war. This obviously had nothing to do with his brain power which was great. If he had had the time to put on it or if his experience had given it to him automatically, he would have been superb. As I saw it as Commander in Chief, he just did not look toward the Atlantic or Europe and when he did it was on a political basis. It made it hard for us in the Atlantic to make our point. I think you will find most military students will agree with my assessment that in the early days of a surprise conventional all-out war with the Soviets that the Sixth Fleet couldn't stay in the Mediterranean initially. It was my opinion that we should have abandoned our twenty-five year rut of maintaining a set number of ships there for a set time. I advocated having an irregular force in the Mediterranean, sometimes perhaps no carriers for a month, then perhaps four carriers. I thought that this would confuse the Soviets more than having them checking out each carrier as it came in--they knew the schedules as well as we did. The carriers relieved each other always in the Mediterranean and usually they wanted us to have the relief in the Eastern Mediterranean, which was another two or three days to get over there. We had a feeling that the Sixth Fleet should probably be brought out before or in the initial days of war. We felt it was the wrong place initially for one of the primary forces of the Atlantic Fleet. Mind you, I don't mean that we should have ever discontinued the Sixth Fleet as an entity, nor should we ever have left the Mediterranean completely bare of ships. We could have changed the numbers of units, changed the schedules and areas of operations and I believe that really would have helped us with the Soviets. Part of the word that came from Washington, and I believe this was political, was that ships in the Mediterranean were "forward deployed"--that is the phrase they used and they use that phrase sometimes now. The military student who thinks about it, or a civilian student of naval warfare, knows that in the modern day conventional war with the nuclear powered submarines, the war can start off Norfolk, Mexico, Guantanamo, the Panama Canal--anywhere. In a sense I believe there is no such thing as "forward deployed" for big units. Nuclear war could start anywhere in the world. In thinking of "forward deployment" in the Mediterranean--the ships were not near the Soviet nuclear submarine bases which were all in the Barents Sea. The Soviets based no submarines in the Mediterranean and they all came through the Atlantic to get to the Mediterranean. They had none in the Baltic.

Q: Relatively inaccessible to the rest of us?

Adm. D.: Home base was inaccessible. Of course our job was to see they didn't get from the Barents Sea to Norfolk or to the Mediterranean, although in peace time they went where they wished. This term "forward deployed" still concerns me. It is misleading. I see it in the papers and I believe we should be more mature than that and realize that with the nuclear powered submarine things have changed. The Soviet nuclear submarine has a cruise missile, I don't know why the United States is letting the press indicate that we are introducing a new weapons. It happens to be a better one than the Soviets--but they had cruise missiles with nuclear warheads back in the early '70's. They could be at sea and fire at Norfolk. They could fire at carriers anywhere, including the Mediterranean. The Soviet subs did go down to the Mediterranean, but made their transit through Atlantic waters. It was our job to try to keep track of them as they went and we did to a certain extent.

We had to use almost schoolboy arguments as to Atlantic strategy part of the time with the CNO. I had many exchanges on this--CNO wanted us to put more nuclear powered submarines in the Mediterranean especially. I mentioned the location of the Soviet bases and used such simple analogies as the fact that the Atlantic area was X times the size of the Mediterranean area, the numbers of Soviet nuclear submarines in the Atlantic was X times that in the Mediterranean, and therefore there was in my opinion, no excuse to build up in the Mediterranean because the Soviet Atlantic threat was six to ten times greater than to the Mediterranea. That seems rather a schoolboy analogy but I got down to that point because I was afraid some of his staff hadn't thought about that. I even got someone to compute the square miles of the Atlantic vs the square miles of the Mediterranean and tried to use that.

Q: What happens to the value of all these courses in global strategy and so forth?

Adm. D.: Well, I can only guess that Navy had neglected to send people to War College. Also there were the emotional ties to Vietnam where the men were dying. That just becomes overwhelming and these other considerations are aside. Maybe they did not think very deeply about them. Perhaps some congressman said we ought to have more nuclear submarines in the Mediterranean, maybe some Greek lobbyist had gotten after him, or maybe an Italian lobbyist. Or maybe there was more press coverage in bolstering the Mediterranean.

Q: Not a Turkish lobbyist certainly?

Adm. D.: Not a Turkish lobbyist, they didn't have enough unfortunately. I felt that the greatest threat in the Atlantic was the nuclear powered submarine of the Soviets. I believe it today; it may change in the future, but the nuclear submarine both the ballistic missile submarine and the attack submarine were the greatest conventional war threat and a real substantial nuclear war threat.

Q: You have promised to discuss this later, but I think it is essential to round out the picture, that you comment on this very real, almost inordinate, fear that the Russians were going to jump into the situation in the Far East, and what this did to the thinking at that time in '70-'72. How did this influence the fact that they overlooked the Atlantic completely because they were afraid they were going to confront the Russians in the Far East?

Adm. D.: It is difficult for me to assess how much this affected them. Analysts in the office of the Secretary of Defense would come up with scenarios of war geographically by sections. I have mentioned this previously. They assume the Soviets go to war, they enter the fray in Vietnam, what do we need then; the Chinese march into Korea, what do we do then, how many ships do we need to fight the Soviet Union in the Pacific? Any naval person would almost refuse to discuss fighting an enemy navy in one portion of the globe, because that is not the way navies work. How credible did they believe the threat of the Chinese and the Russians to assist in Vietnam? They both did do so. How credible was the belief that they would actually enter the fray, that maybe the Soviet submarines would start sinking our ships, that maybe the Chinese would use that road they built up in North Vietnam into China and pour into there. I cannot say. I was detached and the people I knew felt that the Soviets would never go in where we were actually fighting in any strength that might provoke an all-out war, in that sort of area. That is not the way the Soviets would start, at least that was our belief, because that is not the way they would win it. Frankly, outside of aggrandizement and taking some more rather vital territory, it didn't mean that much to them. There was also the play which we read about in the paper and in intelligence dispatches, and on which I am not an authority, the play between the Chinese and the Soviets, as to which Communist faction would rule. So it is difficult to answer your question. I was never confronted by the CNO or by a message from Washington Navy saying, forget this stuff in the Atlantic, the Soviets or the Chinese Communists are going to start something in the Pacific. I wasn't confronted with that sort of thing. I am sure it was in their minds, there was a lot in the papers but I am not able to assess the degree to which that influenced them focussing on the possible Soviet actions in Asia vs the possible Soviet actions in Europe.

Q: I thought it was important simply to add that to your previous remarks on the fact that they overlooked the Atlantic because it's a part of that picture. I don't think we can underestimate the importance of these ideas embraced by the analysts because they were terribly important.

Adm. D.: And I think it is possible to accuse me of a biased view, or any other who happens to believe as I do, that the most important section of the world for the Soviets to win, if they really want to win over the United States without a nuclear war, is Europe--for obvious reasons--the biggest industrial base, the biggest population center; it is obviously the place they would like to own vs. Vietnam. What does Vietnam mean to them? Nice real estate, but compared with Europe, nothing. One could say I was biased the other way. They did not use this on me, I guess is a good way to put it, I was aware that people speculated on it in messages.

I was talking to you about the fact that I didn't feel the senior officers under Admiral Zumwalt appreciated the Atlantic or the areas the Soviets thought was important. It was where they put their ships--where they knew they could use them. I mentioned this in telling of a Unified Commanders conference held by Tom Moorer when I heard General Bennett talk. General Bennett, as I told you, mentioned only one Soviet warship in the Atlantic.

Q: You didn't identify him in that previous talk.

Adm. D.: He was head of DIA. I wrote General Bennett. He replied very nicely and I will be glad to leave those two letters with you. They may be of some significance. I can only guess that Bennett was fed his naval information, as high officers must be, by a naval section and the naval section was responsive to the general naval thought in OpNav and CNO's views. I think this letter would astound most warfare and strategy students. Another example I want to mention, and in a way more difficult for me. I went also to Fleet Commanders in Chief Conferences held by Zumwalt. These were pure Navy C in C conferences. Admiral Clarey, C in C Pacific Fleet, Admiral Bringle, C in C Naval Forces Europe, and I attended. We all went to what was supposed to be the normal briefing in the briefing room which CNO went to every morning. That was the first thing in Pentagon routine--you went through briefings on intelligence, world events, everything. I had attended the briefings almost every morning 1968-1970 when I was Chief of Naval Personnel. I also did as C in C Atlantic Fleet 1970-1972. When I had gone up to visit Bud on some matter I slipped in to the briefing to find out what they were talking about. I found there was no mention of the Atlantic. So I wrote Admiral Rectanus, head of Navy intelligence, a letter which I am going to leave for you if you wish it. I told him that in a briefing the only reference to Soviet naval activity in the Atlantic naval command area was passing mention of a single noncombatant. To an Atlantic commander this was absolutely amazing. I gave him some examples of where the Soviet forces were deployed and what they were doing. I had known him slightly and considered him then and do now an able officer. It was his briefing team who had absorbed what I will call this Washington atmosphere. They didn't care what went on in the Atlantic. I sat through two briefings and I heard about one Soviet merchant ship, nothing of nuclear submarines that were off New York and off Bermuda at that time, which we knew about. I had to classify this letter. So that you may attach it--it was written back in 1972 and I think in 1978 I can de-classify it as I was the originator of the letter. I do not want to disparage Rectanus for whom I had considerable respect. I believe you can see that I had many frustrations in this period. Some natural ones due to the world situation, and specifically those related to the CNO, but actually in most cases it was with the very close and very tight circle of his advisers. I will discuss this aspect of my relations with CNO after I have set a proper background.

To continue with my attempts to illustrate the flexibility of naval forces, which we were discussing earlier, and the strategy of the Soviet naval war in the Atlantic and the folly of our set operational patterns, I did make some moves that were partly successful. I attempted from time to time to get the strength of the Sixth Fleet varied, those attempts were not very successful. After much effort, I did get them to send one carrier out into the Atlantic for one week, to join in an exercise the Atlantic Fleet was having, with some other nations--one of our tri-laterals or bi-laterals. The exercise was held around the entrance to the Mediterranean. My idea was that they would send their Sixth Fleet out, exercise with the Atlantic Fleet, go back in and thus confuse the Russians a bit. I only succeeded in getting our carrier out for one week.

Q: Was that the Strong Express?

Adm. D.: No, they wouldn't come up to Norway for that one, that was too far. The other thing I did, because I had the authority to do this, was to schedule Atlantic Fleet carriers that were going to relieve for a normal tour in the Med., along with their accompanying Service Force ships and destroyers, up via United Kingdom or the Bay or Biscay, to take part in an exercise, sometimes on a bi-lateral and sometimes a NATO basis, simulating delivery of ammunition on targets in Europe from different launch points. I reversed this process also by taking operational control of a carrier just relieved when it came out of the Mediterranean. I would schedule it perhaps for six days operations up into the Bay of Biscay toward the English Channel, to give them experience in different launch points, working with different air restrictions, which are very different from Northern Europe. I believed I owed this to the carrier pilots--they had to be ready to launch from various points and they had to be ready to accept new targets. This I did on my own and I had to compensate for this, because what I was doing was extending the very deployment which I deplored. I felt it was worth it and I arranged to give them extra time in port to compensate, when they came back. So that was a minor victory.

Q: Did that settle the dust as far as the personnel was concerned?

Adm. D.: I had no flare back or poor reactions from the people. The pilots liked it, various skippers liked it. One thing one has to watch of course is that the skipper may like something but it is hard on the crew. The skipper is only there a short time and he wants to do everything. However, I did my best and I continued to go around to the ships and talk to people. I can't say I got absolutely exact feelings but I gave them the opportunity to say things they wanted to, I even asked them leading questions.

Q: Did you also convey to them some idea of the situation?

Adm. D.: I tried to do that through the command chain rather than directly to the men, because if I didn't succeed through the command chain I didn't succeed at all. I mainly gave the crews the opportunity to talk, and while I am not expert at it as a psychologist would have been, I was not totally inexperienced. I had found before that with leading questions such as "Isn't that terrible bread they are having in the general mess?" You get quite a bit. I did not get adverse reactions after I extended the time in port. As I have said, I did have trouble convincing Washington that I needed to continue with my training. I would have thought that the activities of the Soviets would have convinced Washington and I would not have had to do the arguing because the Soviets were being very expansive, very flexible. It was the first time we started to talk about the real world-wide ocean going navy of the Soviets. They made long excursions into the South Atlantic, stayed at sea for months with a submarine alongside a tender. They were quite visible, they sent a cruiser over off New Orleans at the mouth of the Mississippi River, they went to Cienfuegos in Cuba, they were quite obvious. They went to certain ports in Africa.

Q: This was a deliberate policy on their part?

Adm. D.: This was a deliberate expansive policy and the sort of thing a Navy should be doing--learn to stay at sea, learn the seas of the world--they are becoming global. I had thought this would attract Washington's attention. They did pay some attention when the Cuban seizure of a ship took place, which I earlier described. They noticed the extensive use of Cuban ports by the Soviets. So I thought I wouldn't have to argue, but I did.

Another thing I thought would help my case was the tremendous success of their intelligence gathering ships--normal naval terminology is AGI. They were first disguised as fishing trawlers and later they abandoned that disguise and put out these small ships. They weren't fooling anyone, they were superbly equipped with electronic devices. You may remember the press talked about "spy operations" concerning one of our U.S. ships. We had Soviet AGI's stationed off the East Coast, especially they were stationed off any submarine base--

Charleston, New London, Holy Loch, Rota--checking off every exit. The Soviets accompanied our exercises, they read every communication that we had, they recorded all of our radar frequencies and there are techniques for analyzing radars so you can tell the frequency, they were always on our missile firing range down in the Culebra in the Carribean. The Soviets were there for every Poseidon launch. How they got the word on this I don't know, but they were there. There are certain electronic emissions that can be picked up that are of value. They were doing a terrific, sophisticated, superb job. I don't know why the press was never alarmed about his. Seems if the U.S. does something, we are "spying", if they do something, there isn't much made of it.

Q: It isn't the same kind of crime?

Adm. D.: One of the points about these trawlers which I thought I might get the press on. I was assigned to make a speech at the launch of a container ship for the merchant marine, probably in Boston. I thought I would give the press a little something to write about, in addition to the importance of the merchant marine, which they had heard many times. I told them there were intelligence ships off our coast which were being supported by the Canadians and to a certain extent by the United States, and I had pictures to prove it. What happened was that the Canadians especially, and we the U.S. to a much lesser extent in Boston, would allow the Soviet AGI mother ship-- the fishing fleet mother ship and these were authentic--

to come in and fuel and supply in Halifax, Nova Scotia. The U.S. even allowed refuelling in Boston (I don't know about other supplies). I had pictures of these same ships, having been checked out of port, refuelling and intelligence gathering in the sea triangle between Boston and Halifax. I told the press this and of course they wanted the name of the ship, the name of the port. There were certain classified restrictions I couldn't go beyond, although there was nothing very secret about the way we took the pictures, the Canadian Navy and the U.S. Navy merely flew its ASW aircraft over while the Soviets were refuelling and took pictures. We did this a lot, there is no secret about it, nor is there any international law to prevent it. They wanted me to give real details. Then they asked the State Department and typically they sort of pooh-pooh'd it. I don't know what the State Department's motivation was, perhaps they wanted to encourage a little trade with us by the Soviets, but I thought it was a pretty glaring example of supporting an enemy fleet right off your own shore. However, I didn't really get any great press out of that. It made my speech a little more interesting than it would have been otherwise.

There is one item I would like to go into at this time which did give me considerable concern, one where I was not able to convince the CNO and staff. Perhaps for the first time the evidence surfaced that I was absolutely ineffective with CNO's close immediate staff. I am not talking about the whole staff of OpNav with whom we worked very well, but this close "court clique" that formed around Bud. I was ineffective at convincing them and I realized it. By the way of background, ever since WWII the Navy has been over-extended. This is pretty well known. The U.S. Navy has insisted rightly or wrongly, on keeping high deployed numbers of units in the Seventh Fleet and in the Sixth Fleet. The units had to be exercised and have maintenance when back in home waters. The U.S. Navy has been over extended. Some people said the U.S. Navy has never been able to relax after WWII. It is true that we kept up a pretty high pace. I had done some arguing, earlier in various positions in the Pacific and in the Atlantic, for diminishing the over-seas deployments for a lot of reasons. Other people did not agree with me for various reasons, but their reasons all came together so that it was business as usual and we kept those deployments. I discussed with you earlier of my concern and actions when I was operations officer of the Pacific Fleet. You may remember that our staff arrived at the conclusion, after extensive study, that with the number of units and transit times being fixed quantities, the only way we could get more ship days in the Western Pacific was to home-port unsophisticated units such as amphibious ships (LSTs) in Japan or Subic. This procedure eliminated long wasteful transits. We felt homeporting in Japan and Subic would be attractive to a considerable number of Navy people. We put some amphibious ships, some oilers and other simple Service Force ships, and some older destroyers in WestPac, overhauling in Japan mostly. We got more work out of Yokosuka for the same money than we did out of a U.S. shipyard. We had repair ships to work on the more classified repairs.

Q: Was it still less expensive in those days?

Adm. D.: Much less expensive by one-sixth--some political overtones here but much less expensive. I really originated and did the first post WWII overseas home-porting. When I became Commander in Chief, Admiral Zumwalt really got onto overseas home-porting as a cure for all ills. He also may have had other thoughts about it of which I was not aware, perhaps using homeporting as a show of power could have been one of his reasons. He started negotiations. To praise his exceptional ability at persuasion, he sold it to the State Department and to the Congress, which is not easy. He practically negotiated single handed with the Greek Government, about building a dock, getting airfields. He really went after it in his usual effective manner. I got extremely concerned when I found he wanted to home port a carrier and its aircraft in Greece, and one in the United Kingdom along with some other new ships. It was the carrier I was worried about. Remember that at that time, it has been improved now, there weren't even missile firing ranges that we could use that were really good, they had no telemetry. There were no sophisticated ship yard facilities that could yet repair much of our equipment, there were no sophisticated repair facilities for the aircraft ashore, where they could be retro-fitted with new devices. Having studied such a project in the Pacific, having the responsibility, knowing how much more sophisticated ship and aircraft were now some twelve years later than when I had studied it, I opposed it. I sent a dispatch to the Chief of Naval Operations noting some difficulties and recommending caution. I asked for the CNO' reaction and the CNO staff replied that they hadn't bothered to show it to the CNO because it was "negative". That was one of my first inklings that I was running into trouble with the CNO's personal staff. I got an appointment with the CNO by telephone. I had a direct link with him as I did with the JCS chairman. This wasn't the first appointment I asked for, nor the last. He was always ready to give me an appointment, he was completely open, assigned me the time, was always courteous and he listened. I made two trips up to Washington concerning homeporting carriers in Europe and I simply got nowhere. I don't know why, I got no answers, he listened politely, and that was the end of it. He continued with tremendous thrust to make his project go.

Q: There was a great PR campaign too.

Adm. D.: Well, I wondered. It was a flamboyant move, it was a PR move, it was big world stretegic stuff, and I wondered if that had something to do with it. As a Fleet C in C, and I believe pragmatic, I was opposed to it, and I was the one concerned and responsible, but I got absolutely nowhere. That particular item was solved by several events. The Greek situation got worse and worse and finally the Greeks wouldn't let the carriers in, they even kicked the destroyer squadron out. I had not opposed the destroyer homeporting.

Q: The wives had something to say about that?

Adm. D.: I didn't hear about that. We had thought, on the Pacific Japanese homeporting, that there were a certain number of Navy men and families who would like overseas home-porting, it would be glamourous. I thought there would be enough people and we would allow swaps between ships going and not going. I thought we would easily man a destroyer squadron with volunteers, I think there are that many people who want to go overseas. What I was against was the risk, the danger to this modern aircraft carrier--we had only so many carriers and to put one permanently in Greece gave me the shivers. I didn't think the carrier or its aircraft were going to be kept up to date in training or maintenance. The United Kingdom regretfully reported they could not accommodate the carrier group--I think it was a matter of docks and accompanying airfield. It had to be a place where the carrier could offload its aircraft. I lost on the CNO's decision. But I didn't lose in the long run because the CNO was never successful and it has never been brought up again as far as I know. Strategically it was all wrong. Transit time to the Med. could be five days. In the Pacific, not so. They have a carrier in Japan--it used to be the _Midway_, I don't know who it is now.

Q: _Midway_ is there now.

Adm. D.: I have no direct knowledge but have heard no great repercussions. It happens to be quite a different situation. The Seventh Fleet belongs to the Pacific Fleet, the Sixth Fleet does not belong to the Atlantic Fleet, just to cite one aspect. So this overseas home-porting caused me great concern and when he wanted to put one in the United Kingdom, it would have caused me even more concern because while in port the carrier group would have been under CinCUSNavEur. Admiral Zumwalt was keen to have a carrier in northern European waters such as the United Kingdom, but he envisioned it would come under the CinCNav Forces Europe.

As we discussed in the CinCLant section CinCUSNavEur does not have control of operations of units at sea in Atlantic waters. When the carrier would go to sea it would only exercise under CinCLant Fleet. It appeared to me this split was not good. I doubt that this facet had ever come to Zumwalt's attention. I was also concerned about the overhaul of the aircraft and the ships. I will say that in the cases of home-porting which had existed, namely the Sixth Fleet flagship cruiser and I believe one repair ship and a couple of Service Force ships in Italy, they were home-ported only for three years and then brought back for overhaul, and the same could have been done in the United Kingdom. These were simpler ships with no aircraft. They returned having been very poorly trained. I have mentioned this before. I believe this is one of the several instances where Admiral Zumwalt was wrong and did not listen to those people with experience, instead listening to his close circle of advisers who considered only a very flambuoyant and dramatic move, which it was. Reflecting on it with the advantage of time it seems to me that the CNO's drive for European homeporting stemmed from a desire to do something dramatic and newsworthy. He is a dramatic man. It was not militarily sound.

Q: We enter a new phase now.

Adm. D.: I want to discuss a new aspect of operations. One of my concerns as Commander in Chief, and one of my responsibilities, was about what I considered to be the inability of my Task Force and the numbered Fleet Commanders, effectively to engage a sophisticated modern enemy in combat in a multi-threat environment, with our own sophisticated multiple defenses, all complicated by the new technology and by extremely complex real-time electronic intelligence and electronic warfare. I mentioned this facet as Com2nd Fleet. I now had a broader responsibility. This is not a criticism of the officers concerned, or of their basic qualifications or abilities. I thought I had a superb group of young flag officers. It was just that I questioned whether our current system of rotation and some emphasis on shore duty over sea duty could produce a really skilled Task Force Commander and staff. The swiftness and the complexities of events were such as to overwhelm the human mind in trying to control a battle. There were developed many automated aids to help the Commanders by presenting to them in visual form, selected threats and selected pertinent, pressing, intelligence. As C in C I went to sea several times for short periods on as many exercises as I could. I was not encouraged by what I saw. Our equipment capabilities were ahead of our officers' ability to employ them to full effectiveness. I made an off-the-cuff estimate that in simulated combat we were getting only about sixty percent effectiveness of our total combat capabilities. Now, that sixty percent is purely a finger in the breeze estimate--it has no validity. I had no analytic measure taken of how well they were doing--it was my estimate.

Q: Being totally cognizant of the situation, you could make a fairly good estimate?

Adm. D.: I knew we were way short of a hundred percent. I took some initial steps to improve the situation using the electronic war-game player in Newport. This was not new to me, I did emphasize it though. I used the very excellent electronic training devices out at Dam Neck, Virginia. We sent staffs to play their problems out before they went to sea, and we tried to expose these young Flag officers to complicated situations just as if they were at sea. Then when they went to sea we did try to impose on them as complicated situations as my staff could conjure up. Frankly, I should have done more and I count it as my failure that I did not adamantly insist on a longer tour afloat for young Flag officers in combat units. I think I also should have tried to bring up Flag officers who were more specialized in commanding complicated modern sea operations, just as the Navy has swung to breeding a group of officers who are management experts. I think that perhaps in our rush to each new fad or fashion as it comes along, and as it is sometimes imposed upon us for example by the McNamara regime, that we tend to belittle the very specialized matter of command at sea and using all these complicated and wonderful things that the scientists have given us. We take command at sea as a matter of course, "any naval officer can do that". Well, any naval officer can not do that.

Q: We recognize that in terms of the enlisted man, don't we?

Adm. D.: We certainly have. At the task group level, the Flag officer must have possession of a tremendous number of facts right at his finger tips that high executives usually are not supposed to have to have--they are supposed to call in the experts. Things are happening so fast this officer must himself know the capabilities of torpedoes or missiles, and know facts such as the interference patterns of frequencies and certain characteristics of electronic waves between our weapons, and so on, ad infinitum. These sorts of facts cannot be learned once you are in action nor is there enough time for the staff to say "Admiral look at this" and "Admiral look at that". The scientists have given us some wonderful aids. They are going to have to go further, in my opinion. Electronic warfare is so fast--all that goes with it, it is on every new weapon that is introduced, there is an interface on interference-- and the officer has to know what weapon to use and what this effect means. He has to know details of our own and enemy weapons and sensors. It really overwhelms the mind that one has to handle all this instantaneously.

Q: In order to achieve this kind of development to which you aspire, will it call for a reorganization of the whole personnel system?

Adm. D.: I had thought some about it. In helping to rework the operations course at the War College--I saw there that even some of the people writing the course did not understand this facet as well as I did. I wrote up a little paper and left it for them hoping some student might take it up. In this I proposed something like what you suggest. What I said was that at the junior flag officer level we should select specialists in going to sea, and fighting the ships at sea. It will be interesting to see if this comes about. I left the paper with the President of the War College, saying that perhaps some student would like to take that as a paper to write on, pro or con. I became convinced some change was needed through actually watching Flag officers operate at sea and also through what I saw was being taught at the War College, which wasn't bad but it didn't get on to this particular problem.

I understand, third hand, that the present CinCLant, Admiral Kidd, has jumped on this weakness, which he too perceived and that he has made considerable progress by various methods of using our training devices and subjecting these Flag officers to instant decision making under simulated conditions. I wish that I had done more. This may be another argument for something I mentioned earlier, having a four-star officer devote full time to the Fleet rather than to the three jobs, because this is very important to the United States, and to the Navy.

I also tried, operationally, to encourage a very active anti-submarine warfare effort in the Atlantic, both real and in exercises. I think the Atlantic Fleet did very well. My principle concern in the Atlantic was the Soviet submarine threat. All the rest depended on handling that. I put a lot of effort into this field. I cannot relate to you all the fascinating events due to their classification but we were in an era of electronic marvels, both in the United States and Russia. I was given certain classification clearances as a four-star officer for the first time in my life, even though I had had command of the Second Fleet as a three-star officer. I was given clearances for compartmented intelligence and told things that were going on that startled me. I suggested that these compartmented intelligence clearance be broadened and given to my major operational commanders. Perhaps it has been done now. I found out some things when I became Commander in Chief that I should have known when I was Commander of the Second Fleet.

The Atlantic Fleet, in anti-submarine work did some superb work and especially intelligence did some superb work. Operationally the nuclear submarines did some superb work. I am not a submarine officer but I became tremendously impressed. I was briefed every time one of these young captains came back from one of his long missions, and I cannot praise them too highly. The attack nuclear submarines gave astounding performances. They had brilliant, capable, aggressive young skippers, young crews and young officers. The anti-submarine aircraft also came along fast, we were getting materiel improvement aboard them--electronic improvements and some weapon improvements--and they did good work.

Q: In that connection, should the carriers based in the Atlantic have anti-submarine aircraft in substantial numbers or just attack planes?

Adm. D.: It was during the period I was there that we did what was called "experiments"--of putting detachments, and it ended up a squadron, of anti-submarine aircraft on a carrier. Some traditional attack aircraft aviators did not want them around. They complicated the launching schedule, they took up room that other aircraft could have used, they took up maintenance space (they themselves had most complicated electronic equipment). If money is no object I would like to see the anti-submarine effort off into the smaller carriers. You remember we had the old ASW carriers. What brought this experimentation to a head was the obvious phasing out of the old carriers, the writing was on the wall, and has been for some years. The U.S. Navy was not going to be able to afford to carry this large number of carriers. Right or wrong, we were not going to get the budgeted funds to do it. So if the carrier-based anti-submarine plane was going to go to sea it was going to have to be on the big carrier. And the ASW aircraft had to go to sea on carriers. We experimented (I didn't call it experimentation, I knew they could do it). There had to be some "give" all around. We put one squadron on a carrier out of Jacksonville and sent them to the Mediterranean for a full deployment. This was the first time that had been done. We had put them in shorter exercises before and we had put detachments of them aboard, three and six. At this particular time we saw that we had to combine these carrier missions. So we put on an entire ASW squadron. The Division commander was Bob Baldwin who is now the Commander of the Seventh Fleet. He took the first full ASW squadron over to the Mediterranean. I kidded him when he came back because one of his briefers, who was supposed to brief us as to how this went, spent all of his time talking about the number of hours "up" that the A6--the attack aircraft--had. All he was thinking about was the impingement on his attack squadron. Bob did a fine job on this particular project and made a very good report.

Q: I suppose, as a footnote to this, in case of a conflict in the Atlantic with the Russians, would they employ their attack submarines to attack our ships, or would they use them to screen their ballistic submarines?

Adm. D.: Of course I don't know the answer to that. In my opinion they would attack our ships, especially in the period of the early '70;s. Things change all the time. The ballistic missile submarines have been pretty invulnerable. This may change. In my time in the Fleet, I don't think they needed all that protection and I don't think ours did. I don't think anybody could sink our ballistic missile submarines before they got their shots off. On the other hand, the nuclear attack submarine could and did trail our carriers, close aboard and could fire in an instant. We could not chase them off, we couldn't out-speed them, we couldn't drop depth charges on them, we could do absolutely nothing to these submarines in peacetime. In war we could do plenty.

Q: Goodbye Nimitz?

Adm. D.: That is what we were afraid was going to happen in the Mediterranean. I'm not telling secrets because the Russians know it, we know it, anybody who wants to bother to find out knows that in peacetime a submarine cannot be interfered with in international waters by dropping a net, dropping a depth charge, acting like you didn't know he was there and practicing depth charging or that type of thing. It would risk confrontation. It was my opinion that our large ships and our important, high value ships, were targeted. I don't mean there was a nuclear submarine on every one of our ships by any means. I do say they were nearby certain operating units. They made no secret of it. In my opinion, they would at their comparative leisure have eliminated much of our merchant fleet. I don't say every one because we have powerful counters. We have our own superb attack submarines which can attack enemy nuclear submarines. Today perhaps there is some sort of a stand-off between the two--Soviet and the US submarines. The Soviets were technically superior at that time in their cruise missiles. They could stay further away, further than we could detect them and could shoot a cruise missile at our big ships. That has changed, we now have a cruise missile coming on also.

I think a lot of the Fleet was targeted, it was one of my biggest worries and one of the reasons I put so much emphasis on anti-submarine warfare. I haven't discussed the other air ASW protection we had which was coming along fast, that was the land-based anti-submarine aircraft. We were getting better equipment, better crews, they were getting more enthused about their ability, and they were being better recognized in the Navy. Twenty years ago large carrier aviators paid little attention to the people who were doing land-based anti-submarine work.

Q: What was their range?

Adm. D.: I think at that time in the late sixties they ranged only about eight hundred miles. Now it is greater. Today as we fly from Bermuda to Iceland to Azores to Rota with Norway, U.K., Portugal, and Madeira, there is in a sense no limit. They go out on very long patrols, we have improved aircraft. We cover the whole oceans, but the catch is to have numbers of aircraft to be many places at once. We made giant strides in the past fifteen years in these aircraft. As to your question as to whether the carriers are all targeted and are they going to be sunk. They certainly would be an enemy aim. Against them we have our own SSN, we have surface ships with good although not quite as revolutionary advanced equipment, and we have the landbased aircraft. I happen to think still that it takes all three of these plus carrier based ASW aircraft. In other words give them the multi-threat from under the sea, on the sea and from the air which would make it very difficult for them to defend themselves. We are by no means helpless. Because of my background and my feeling of responsibility for the Atlantic, I figured that my principal responsibility was to counter the Soviet submarine threat. Then I knew our ships would get across. I had to substantially do away with the Soviet submarines. I was not as worried about the Soviet aircraft, except where we would be fighting up North. At that time as far as getting merchant ships across the ocean the aircraft were not as much a concern--short of nuclear war. I did take my responsibilities seriously in anti-submarine warfare and I must say it scares me when I see people trying to sweep the threat under the rug.

Turning to other operational aspects, I spoke earlier of my concern about a tropical navy and of my success as SACLant in holding a large NATO exercise in north Norway to get into some cold weather.

Q: That was the Strong Express?

Adm. D.: Right. On the Fleet side I continued my emphasis. I was determined to exercise the Atlantic Fleet by itself. in the coldest weather, including the Marines. I believe one attempt is worthy of note and it indicates some of the many facets of American society in "post Vietnam". It has its amusing aspects I think. I had a meteorologist make a study and advise me where the coldest weather could be found in the United States in January. He advised me it was in the Gulf of Maine. The Gulf Stream veers out to sea there, favors Nova Scotia and keeps it ice free, so the Gulf of Maine is colder than Nova Scotia. So we planned an exercise in January of 1972 which culminated in a Marine amphibious assault on coastal Maine at a public park called Reid State Park. I had wanted to go on up between Greenland and Canada to the Canadian Labrador which is colder, for a more rigorous exercise. I made a couple of feints toward this goal but there were too many diplomatic complications. We weren't post-Vietnam, we were in Vietnam. Holding operations on Canadian soil just wasn't popular so I was told to lay off, so I went ahead with my plan for an assault at Reid State Park. We received immediate violent reactions from alleged environmentalists. Actually, in my opinion, these people were "anti-Vietnam war" activists who were simply out to get the military. One of the groups filed for an injunction to stop that exercise which was denied, I was glad to hear.

Q: Were these people Maine residents or some who assembled from along the Eastern seaboard?

Adm. D.: They were mostly a New York based clique, some from Maine, but mostly New York financed.

The New York Times, for which I have respect, not for its opinions but for its reporting, wrote an editorial in 1972 in very strong terms, condemning the "stupidity" of the military and condemning the Atlantic Fleet for wasting the taxpayers' money to land on the beautiful coast of Maine and desecrating it. This seemed to me to be almost unbelievable. I thought and my staff thought we were carrying out the duties with which we were charged, which was to be ready for combat action in any part of the Atlantic at any time. In years past The New York Times would not have given such a relatively small exercise five lines on page twenty. The New York Times published a special editorial on the subject.

Q: I suppose the environmentalists had a pipe line to the editorial page.

Adm. D.: They must have had. Fortunately I had the support of Governor Curtis of Maine, which helped a great deal. I also had the enthusiastic support of Mrs. Louise Reid Butler, whose father had contributed the park to the state. She wrote me a very nice letter after the exercise which I probably left in the files at CinCLant headquarters, saying how nice the park looked--that it looked better than it did after an average weekend of civilian use. I also had a letter from a Maine resident, a retired major in the Washington area who owned extensive coastal property there, offering his coastal land for the exercise. I will say we were determined to leave that park spotless. We weren't going to have reporters going up to take pictures of a desecrated park. The Maine authorities, as well as Mrs. Louise Reid Butler, notified me the park was very clean indeed and they had had no clean-up to do after us.

This was in January 1972.

At the landing we had pickets all around. They apparently intended to come out and prevent the Marines coming ashore in the landing craft. Mostly hippie types. I had hopes of having the landing craft crashing through scattered broken ice in order to hit the beach. The pickets were going to stop it but the Maine police would not let them in the park. There was something about picketing in a public park being against the law. They were allowed to picket on the road outside and we didn't mind that at all. I didn't want the Marines in contact with the hippies.

In the winter of 1972 we saw what I would consider to be unreasoning anti-military feeling in this country, typified by an editorial in this country's most influential newspaper. I would ascribe the objections not to an aroused or aware environmentalist concern, but to the era of Vietnam emotionalism and its effect on our country. A very disappointing anticlimax--not important to them of course--was that after my determination to have the Marines land in snow up to their ears, they landed in very scattered snow and it was forty degrees that afternoon! So my meteorlogist did not make an accurate prediction for that date.

Q: Through your exercises and in other ways, did you make some evaluation of surface ships in modern warfare in the North Atlantic?

Adm. D.: Well we did not test a condition that I mentioned earlier, where we got severe icing conditions on ships through any reason to dodge it. I did not get to send one out to east of Greenland, which is a nice location for getting iced up, just to see if they could handle it. I tried to schedule my exercises such as Strong Express in Norway-- so that the whole Fleet would experience severe cold. I did not locate a place where it was very cold and rough and then send the ships up there, there wasn't that kind of flexibility in the Fleet. I had to schedule so far in advance anything that I did that I was then at the mercy of the weather-- bad or good.

Q: Did you make an evaluation of the usefulness of amphibious ships in those northern waters?

Adm. D.: We knew that if the amphibious ships ran into rigorous weather conditions they would have had trouble, trouble launching their boats, the rigging would have frozen up. We thought they could navigate through light ice at the beach and that is about all we would expect anywhere we would operate. On the coast of Norway, due to the ocean action, and on the Gulf of Maine, normally you don't get heavy icing close in. You have to go a lot further north beyond Greenland to get that sort of heavy icing--that would have stopped them. Our desire was to operate in what you might call light beach icing. We thought our landing craft would make it all right. We thought their gear would work. We thought our amphibious force was capable of handling the sort of scenario that we envisaged that we would land in. We never really got to test the Marines as the Marine General and I would have liked to. Each time we ran into better than usual weather. We ran into some nasty conditions up in Norway, cold, windy, rainy, but we did not run into deep snow or severe below zero weather. I did make the Marines aware. They did send observers to other countries and they did renew sending their teams to Norway to get ski training. They sent certain cadres--instructors.

Q: Is there any danger of the potential enemy coming at us through the Davis Strait?

Adm. D.: I think there is a danger of submarines, I do not think there is a danger of their amphibious craft. Very definitely danger from the submarines. One of the reasons I wanted to practice in Maine was that I felt the Marines would be used if there were an all-out war in Europe. Under one possible scenario we would want to use them to get into Norway before the Soviets could take it--that would have to be done awfully fast. I felt we certainly had an awakening interest in cold weather operations but we really didn't get the practice that we needed. We couldn't be absolutely sure that they were good at working in rigorous weather conditions with deep snow. That was in 1972. We weren't afraid of the enemy bringing surface ships, certainly not to the United States or Canada. We were concerned with a round the North Cape quick amphibious move by the Soviets. That is a possibility today. We were aiming not so much as combatting that move as getting into Norway against opposition or on our own to establish ourselves. Norway is so thin between the ocean and the Soviet border, and the ocean and the Swedish border. The Norwegians do not have the people to hold for long.

Q: I have often wondered if there wasn't the possibility of the Russians, without any outward military effort, suddenly appearing in Norway in ordinary commercial ships.

Adm. D.: I think that would be well within their capabilities. It was not one about which we speculated a lot. Their merchant ships were pretty well tagged--it was not hard to follow them around North Cape. It would have been pretty hard to effect a surprise because at North Cape, as in every country, you had radars out on points and the Norwegians knew every ship that went around. We were more concerned with an air envelopment of places like Iceland and Spitsbergen. We thought they could be either taken or an attempt made to take them within a short time after a war declaration.

Q: Would this also encompass the Orkneys and places like that?

Adm. D.: If they thought that important enough. We didn't particularly concentrate on that because the Soviets would have then been taking less important places very near NATO's opposition, such as United Kingdom fighters. Iceland is a little isolated and the United Kingdom would have been thinking about the United Kingdom. The United States is a long way away and that is of course, why we used to stress that we have to have the force in Iceland to protect Iceland.

Q: In that area the Norwegians have certain coastal warships, do they not? Of what value are they, and are they in sufficient strength to withstand a sudden Russian attack?

Adm. D.: They had two kinds of coastal ships--one a fast patrol boat, light guns and torpedoes, and they could run in and out of the fjords.

Q: Was that the NASTY boat?

Adm. D.: Yes, but they had a later one and I believe it was a little larger. I went out to sea in the squadron. They were capable of inflicting serious damage on any Soviet amphibious move. One other ships the Norwegians have, and they have developed it quite nicely and I think fits their particular circumstances, is the small seventeen man submarine. It didn't have great range, they weren't out to patrol the ocean lanes, they were to protect the oceans near Norway, not only from attack but also from any transiting Soviet craft.

Q: What kind of torpedoes do they carry?

Adm. D.: They had small torpedoes. The submarines were conventionally powered. They were awfully hard to detect. I may not have told you we had a little fun putting our own anti-submarine units on them and sort of foiling our units in a way, because these little submarines would lie very quietly and escape detection unless you were really very good. They were of no value for high seas work. They couldn't catch a nuclear sub but if they were in the path of a nuclear submarine they then might well do great damage to it.

This is an important area of the world and I was determined it wasn't going to be forgotten in a drift to a tropical Navy.

We were speaking of environmentalists. I might mention that my years '70, '71 and '72, were at the culmination perhaps, of various of their attacks on the Navy. These people didn't really care about the environment at all, they were simply after the military, it was just a Vietnam reaction. In a low-key way, not overt way, they were even in the U.S. government. Starting about that time we had to prepare the most detailed environmental impact statements for every exercise we held in the Atlantic Fleet. I had a man who did nothing but prepare environmental impact reports. Even for an exercise out at sea--we reported the fish we might kill. We reported firing in bird sanctuaries and everything of that sort. It extended to areas that might surprise you. We had many Marine landings at Marine-owned land down at Cherry Point, North Carolina, which is the big Marine Base on the east coast (aviation and land site also). This land was purchased for the purpose of holding Marine infantry exercises. It never occurred, but we heard talk the environmentalists were going to try to get it discontinued because the exercises disturbed the wild life.

Q: Aquatic birds?

Adm. D.: Any kind of birds. They didn't want the Marines to disturb them. That action never took place but we still had to file the extensive environmental reports.

Q: Does this go on today?

Adm. D.: We still have to file the environmental impact reports, how aggressive the environmentalists are at this time in the anti-military area, I am unable to tell you. They were very aggressive at that time. The environmental impact report is now a way of life, you can't do anything on either coast or on any marsh land without an environmental impact report. You can't build a power plant, or factory. I am sure you know of the current California story of Dow Chemical trying to for two years and giving up. San Diego Gas and Electric has been trying for three years to build a nuclear power plant at Sun Desert--I hope they don't give up but I wouldn't be surprised. They have to file these reports for all alternate methods of getting energy.

Q: You yourself tried to get a breaker off your property and ran into this problem, is that not so?

Adm. D.: Exactly, and it was studied by two different agencies for its environmental impact for a year.

In this period we were just talking about, was the culmination of the environmentalist drive to require the Navy to stop using Culebra Island as a live gunfire target. That subject has pros and cons and the Navy might have decided to stop using Culebra anyway, nevertheless this particular attempt was successful and the Secretary of Defense did stop live gun firing and live air drops, after a set period.

Q: Am I right in thinking there were no people on Culebra?

Adm. D.: No, there were people on Culebra but not in our area. The Navy had command posts and tightly controlled gunfire. We never killed anybody there. Nor did we ever fire into a town or put an air drop into a town. The weather there is so beautiful and you have complete control. We had observers out there watching and spotting every shot and we had communication between ship and shore. Under pressure to abandon Culebra there were studies made of possible alternate sites, including the cost of building an island in the ocean, starting from scratch. In one of my messages I pointed out it would be just a matter of time until wild birds settled on the island and we would then be unable to use that island. I think there are undeniable arguments that by the Navy firing live ammunition and dropping live bombs on Culebra, we did deprive people of the beach. But I think there is an undeniable argument that we also saved American lives by practicing gunfire and air bombing and we had no other such place. The Navy had been using Culebra at least since the thirties to my personal knowledge. I don't know when the Navy acquired it. We also had Vieques Island, an invaluable asset, although we did not use it as well and we did not have it instrumented as well. However Vieques could be used for Marine landings and tank maneuvers. I would guess that the navy has now shifted to Vieques and I would further guess that it will come under equally strong attack from the anti-military professional protesters, under the guise of environmentalist concerns.

Q: Are there people on Vieques?

Adm. D.: There are even more people on Vieques, as it is a bigger island. Navy bought only sections of it, which is unfortunate. Especially on Culebra Navy should have bought it all and they would then have been glad to sell. The Navy, or I should say the Government, being penny wise and pound foolish only bought the sections they wanted to use and let the people stay on the other sections. That was way back when the Caribbean was very poor and anybody was glad to get a little money. Culebra is only a small island but the Navy wouldn't buy the whole island. Then before WWII the Navy also bought parts of Vieques. The anchorage between Culebra and Vieques was to be used for the British fleet and the American fleet. In Vieques the Navy does kill cows occasionally because the ranchers let them wander over the firing range. I am sure they collect money for every animal killed.

Q: Who gets the meat?

Adm. D.: I think no one because it is over in the dead ammunition area and people don't particularly like to venture over there. I would suspect Navy would have been most welcome to buy all of that island because the people were poor and needed the money. I do not think now though that we will ever get Vieques entirely. I do hope we retain on each coast a place for live firing. I don't see how the Navy can really be ready if they don't practice live firing on a rough terrain.

Q: I think there is another island mentioned--Mona Island?

Adm. D.: In Mona Passage. I think it is Navassa Island which is just a great big rock, but it is a bird sanctuary. I don't know what ever happened on Navassa Island. It is a rather sheer island. We like areas that have terrain contours so that if there is a miss we go over and spot the exact location of fall of shot. It isn't as if you are firing toward a flat surface, when you fire at a rapidly rising hill you get a very small change of location of falling shot for a big change of information. If you miss a hill the shot goes three miles beyond. We need rolling terrain for both air drops and live firing.

Just to show you further how far the protesters went in their campaign---they came out and camped on our firing range so we coudln't fire when they were there. At the time when Navy was abandoning the firing, we decided to clear up the beach area so that people could safely use it. There was unexploded ammunition in shallow water. We sent our underwater demolition teams down with divers. They would dive, find a bomb or shell not exploded, fix an explosive to it and explode it--this in order to make the beach safe for people to swim. This operation was at the risk of our sailors' lives. The anti-military demonstrators came down from New York in canoes and every time they saw our underwater demolition group go out they went out and stayed right by them so that an explosion would blow them up. This defeated us clearing the beach. The protesters said our explosions would kill fish. And they won, we had to call it off. It would appear they were more concerned about fish than possible loss of human life.

Q: So they had constitutional rights, even down there?

Adm. D.: They really didn't. Three miles offshore is in international waters, though we were a little closer. The tenor of the time put Navy on the defensive. I would say that probably forty years ago Navy would have physically removed the protesters. But of course, we couldn't do anything in the atmosphere prevailing in the U.S. Navy was trying to save human lives.

Q: Do we have any rights in any other area of the Caribbean? Didn't we once use Trinidad?

Adm. D.: We used Trinidad as a base. We got that as a part of the "destroyers-base" deal with England in 1939-1940 and we used it during and shortly after WWII. There are still buildings down there which we built. It was a convoy assembly anchorage. We used the base right up until Trinidad became independent and asked us please to leave and we did. You know the importance of Trinidad because it was an assembly place for oil convoys. It was not used for live firing.

Q: Is there any use for the naval base at Bermuda?

Adm. D.: Yes, our naval base there is now in a rather quiescent state. We have ammunition there though I am speaking as of three or four years ago. There was no pressure to get out of Bermuda. In the early 1970s we had some docks left and some buildings and we kept it in caretaker status. We used the airfield. We controlled our facilities through the same old "Base" agreement of 1939-1940. After WWII Navy took over the former U.S. Air Force airfield down near Georgetown on the other end of the island. We used that for two purposes-- as a staging point and base for our anti-submarine warfare aircraft and for the Military Air Transport Command as a fueling station. As CinCLantFlt I landed there when I flew back from the Azores. My old propeller plane wouldn't make it all the way back to the mainland and usually had to land in Bermuda and fuel in order to get home. It was also used by commercial flights. That was part of a later agreement with the U.K. or the Bermuda government. PanAm could use that airfield. As far as I know that airfield is still under US control, although these things change rapidly and I could be out of date. Bermuda is important, just as every island in the Atlantic is important. Every island you could mention is important for anti-submarine work. Bermuda is not vitally important any more. Navy had it in WWII as an escort base where we did some ship and air training. Navy prepared the escorts to pick up a convoy. It might still be used as a convoy assembly point as it has a large area protected by a barrier reef. We would use it more to base anti-submarine aircraft and its future there extends as far as I can see. There is also the negative aspect of preventing its use by an enemy.

Q: There are repair facilities, aren't there?

Adm. D.: They are British.

Q: How important is Guantanamo to the fleet? We hear from time to time reports that maybe we should give it up.

Adm. D.: I think one must say that no place is vital in an absolute sense. There is no place without which we cannot operate. There is no one place on earth that I would say is absolutely vital to the security of the United States. I think Guantanamo is extremely important, it is the best harbor in the Caribbean, it will take the whole Fleet. We invested millions and millions of dollars in Guantanamo. Of course, we have thrown millions of dollars away all over the world, so there is not a reason to stay there just for that investment. We have some good repair facilities there, we have a self-contained place that can do all sorts of things. It supports a population which trains the Fleet. We still have a big underway training group down there. The ships are one minute out of the harbor and they can shoot--air, surface, or sub-surface--your exercise area is so deep you steam out of the harbor with no difficulty. The weather is always good, it is a great training place. We have two airfields there. To work a ship up, there is no superior place in the world. Ships and aircraft can go down there and shoot every weapon. They do their day's work of shooting and flying and then return to Guantanamo and get ready for the next day's work. It is a wonderful fleet base. There is no comparable substitute for the U.S. Can it be done without? Yes. However, I would say the crux of the reasons for not leaving Guantanamo is this--the day we move out the Soviets move in. I put it, and we are into current things now, in an entirely different catagory than the Panama Canal. I happen to think we need a treaty in Panama. In Guantanamo I wouldn't give an inch. A. We have a treaty now and we could not negotiate another one.

B. It does not impinge on Cuba.
Their vessels have a right of access through the bay, they have always had, up to their cities of Camianera and Guantanamo City. We have never interfered with that, we do not interfere with it today. Soviet ships go through the bay escorted by our tugs. If we left I would say it would be a Russian base very quickly. Our use does not substantially affect Cuba, it does not bisect their country as the Panama Canal does Panama. Some people try to make this analogy, but I say, not so. Guantanamo is important to us to keep. We have a much more valid treaty than with Panama. The real crux of the situation is that Cuba is a country that has threatened us. They have had nuclear intercontinental missiles set up in their country, aimed at our

country. I don't see how people use this as an analogy with Panama which has never threatened the United States in any way. In Cuba we have an enemy country, maybe the term is a little strong, but it was an enemy country. I would like to see us get better relations with Cuba. I have enough faith in democracy that I think maybe our way of life still might prevail. Give up Guantanamo, no, I would not do it.

Q: Why then is the Navy seemingly reticent to make this fact known to the American people?

Adm. D.: Well, I think there is a group terming themselves liberals (I don't like to give that name to them) who say that we should, that this is another evidence of colonialism. I do not see it in that light inasmuch as we have a treaty, we rent the place. The rest is, of course, ludicrous--it was made in 1898-1900--$3,000.00 a year. I think any time the Cubans want to renegotiate, we should increase that. I can't give you a figure but certainly a million a year or more-- whatever a reasonable figure might be, we should pay them that rent. The treaty reads that this arrangement will continue until both countries don't want it any more. We do want it. The treaty was made with the Cuban government when we fought to obtain their independence. If you want to talk about colonialism, not many countries would have done this. We did occupy Cuba at that time. We could have had it as a colony, but they chose to be independent, and we gave them their independence which was right. I do see in a better day renewing the treaty and giving the Cubans a decent rent. It is a wonderful harbor and a controlling harbor in the Carribean.

Now, rather summing up Atlantic Fleet operations, I have been more fortunate than most men to be associated with the people of the Fleet. I had the chance to go on any ship I wanted to and to visit any aviation squadron. I went on every type unit we had, I talked to the crews from every type. I had an association with the junior officers and with Commanding Officers which to me was invaluable, both as a personal experienc and as a professional experience. I quite honestly felt I was as close to what made them all tick as was the CNO or anyone in the Navy. I felt that my continuing experience with this sort of thing had given me a considerable sense of what goes on in a unit, and an ability to talk with everybody from seamen to officers. When I say "talk", I do not mean "Address". I mean I sat down to talk with individual men, such as the fireroom crews. I have assembled petty officers and talked with small groups. I count that as one of my invaluable culminating experiences and I continued that on a very broad scale. I also visited every Fleet base in the Atlantic with the exception of Antarctic--I just couldn't carve the time out for that, and Diego Garcia which was building. The Atlantic Fleet had started building the Diego Garcia base, we had dispatch the ships and the Seabees but I did not feel it was important enough for me to go way over into the Indian Ocean at that time.

I do not recall if I mentioned an exercise feature of Fleet operations of both political and military significance. That is our mutually agreed exercises once a year (at that time) with South American countries. CinCLant designated certain units, with emphasis on anti-submarine warfare--surface, air and subsurface, to circumnavigate South America. At each country there would be an exercise with that country's Navy and Air Force units. In many instances there would be a more complex exercise with 3 or 4 countries involved. We could work with countries which would not work with each other. It helped solidify the U.S. and our friends to the South, politically, personally, and militarily. It gave them the advantage of working with advanced equipment (such as nuclear submarines). If a war came, we could work together more effectively. We may have done more in a "social" sense than efforts by "agencies" who were usually condescending. The project was called "Unitas"

I would like to shift now and devote considerable time to discussing the relations between CinCLant Fleet and the Chief of Naval Operations who was Admiral Zumwalt. I think the relations are important because all of the ships in the entire Navy were assigned either to the Atlantic Fleet or to the Pacific Fleet. No other Fleets had permanently assigned ships. The two Fleets had the combat strength of the United States Navy. I want to talk about it, not just because it was rather an interesting thing--my relation with a very unusual man--but the fact that Admiral Zumwalt will be probably the most thoroughly discussed CNO since King and Nimitz. This is because he did controversial things. He created change and he had a natural flair for dramatizing himself. These were the characteristics, of course, that brought out very strong feelings, either for or against, within the Navy, especially in the retired community, and in the Congress. You will hear everything from the extreme opinions that he was the greatest officer the Navy has ever seen, to the opinion that he wrecked the whole US Navy. You can get almost any opinion you would like to hear about Admiral Zumwalt. Before going into our relations as Fleet commander in Chief and CNO, I should give you some perspective by telling you the background of my past relationship. I do this because there are hundreds of people who know Bud Zumwalt better than I do, but there are not hundreds of people who at that time had this Fleet Commander in Chief relationship--there are only two--Clarey and I. Therefore I want to tell you of my past relationship with Zumwalt. It wasn't a fellow that I just recently got to know. This narrative is now reverting from the period 1970-72 to the periods of 1954 and following.

I have known Bud Zumwalt for a long time since he was a Lieutenant Commander in the Bureau of Personnel back in 1953-1955. I was at that time Executive Assistant to the Chief of Naval Personnel, who was Admiral Holloway, Senior. Bud Zumwalt was Lieutenant Commander in an organization I later headed, called Pers A (that is Plans and Programs and Policy). I had thought of Pers A as the executive branch of the Bureau of

Personnel--policy and executive branch.

I believe I mentioned that Zumwalt first came to my attention when I went to a presentation given to Admiral Holloway on the really dire situation in the Navy concerning the lack of doctors. This may sound familiar to you, it is now with us again. We had more regular Captain doctors in '53-'55 as we wound down the Korean War than we had Lieutenants in whole doctor corps, reserve and regular. We had more reserves than we had regulars anyway.

Q: A dying service?

Adm. D.: Well, that was projected. If medical officers continued to leave in droves and the regular medical officers retired, the Medical Corps would die. This BuPers group, Pers A, got up proposals for the Chief, which was customary. As was customary and very nice of Admiral Holloway he always took me along to all decision briefings. Bud Zumwalt happened to be the presenter that day of his proposed solution to get on with it and try to solve the medical officer situation. I would say, typically of him, he faced the situation very squarely. He said "We will forsake the search for the Holy Grail and get on with the problem". His solution was to give doctors additional pay to try to keep them in the Service. This took courage at that time, for a Lieutenant Commander or anybody else, to suggest to a group of line officers (as was everyone else in the room except a couple of doctors) that a staff corps officer get more money than the combat line officers got. It took a lot of courage and it was not received with great glee by everybody present. Really, it was sort of revolutionary.

Q: How did Holloway react to this?

Adm. D.: Well, I immediately saw it was the only available solution. We had to forget this business that we could do nothing of the sort because the line officer runs the navy. We could not get doctors and we could get line officers. It wasn't whether the Fleet Commander in Chief was more important than the Surgeon General--that was not the point--the point was we had good line officers and we had hardly any doctors. So it appeared to me Bud had indeed hit on the correct solution of having a differential pay.

You asked what Admiral Holloway thought of it. When I walked back with him, he didn't commit himself (and he usually did not) at that point. We talked about it and I said I thought it was correct though not a palatable solution, and that we would have to do a lot of preparatory work and would probably have to increase the bonus in steps as we went along, to make it acceptable to line officers. I said he had just seen a Lieutenant Commander who was going to be a Flag Officer and who was going a long way. At that time, we had two other outstanding Commanders in Pers A. I liked them and I believe Admiral Holloway liked them very much. After my comment on Zumwalt Admiral Holloway replied "Yes, but he won't go as far as (and he named the two captains), the Anglo Saxton fruit ripens slowly". That was one of Admiral Holloway's favorit expressions, he liked to quote from authors. What he was inferring there was that the name Zumwalt meant he wasn't an Anglo Saxon and the others were. Zumwalt was an early bloomer and was striking and would step out early while these other two fellows would show up better in fifteen years or so. For what it is worth, one of them became Vice Admiral and one never made flag rank. Admiral Holloway, too, recognized that Zumwalt was an outstanding young officer. It should not be inferred that Admiral Holloway was prejudiced at all, he was merely stating what he thought was an historical fact. Through that first encounter Bud Zumwalt and I became fairly close friends, in a business way. I would occasionally cut him in on something that was coming up that was in his field, and he would come up and discuss something with me. I did not meet him socially during that period at all. I never, during this time, met his wife. Frankly, we were all working so hard, as usual in the Bureau at least in the key offices, that there really wasn't much social life. Admiral Holloway's wife had cancer so he had had practically no social life. I didn't know Bud socially at all. The next time we had any contact was when I was operations officer of the Pacific Fleet. I thought back on the BuPers days and I saw a spot where I thought Zumwalt would do well--he was then a Commander. I requested the Bureau to send him to Pacific Fleet Staff operations. The Bureau sent back word that he had been asked for somewhere else and I did not get him. I told him about that when I encountered him in a Pentagon corridor a month or so after I had asked for him.

He laughed and said he wished he had gotten out there. I don't even remember what job they had for him.

The next time I saw him he was a Captain, in 1963, that was when I was a Rear Admiral and the head of Pers A in BuPers. Bud had just graduated from the National War College and was ready to be assigned. I guess from the way he talked, maybe it was a month or less before detachment. His detailer had insisted that he was to go to the JCS staff. I think the detailer was very wise, he was trying to jack up the JCS staff and give them a good man, I have no quarrel with the detailer. However, Bud had been offered a position on the staff of the Secretary of Defense in the International Security Affairs office, headed then by Paul Nitze. I have already said that I felt the Navy had never given proper credit or proper emphasis to manning the positions in the office of the Secretary of Defense. That is the true name for it though it is generally referred to as DOD or OSD. Bud came to me and told me he was going to be assigned to the JCS and that the detailer insisted on it, but that he believed he could be of more assistance in ISA because there were hardly any military people there at all and that the JCS staff was not as important in his opinion. From what I have already told you, you can imagine my reaction because I wanted exactly what Bud was asking, I wanted bright, aggressive Navy people who could compete with the bright, aggressive civilians in the OSD staff. I went down to the detailer and convinced him that Bud could do a better job for the Navy in OSD and that is the story of how he got into ISA.

I do not say I put him there, if he hadn't come to me he would unquestionably have gone to some other person, because he clearly saw how effective he could be. Whether he had ever known Paul Nitze before I cannot tell you, I do not think so. I believe that both Bud and Jim Calvert wrote outstanding papers down at the National War College that year and I think Nitze had his eye on such graduates. Of course, I thought it was a very good idea. I wanted the Navy section of the JCS staff to be strong, but the OSD moved so fast that about all the JCS staff could do was to react to the OSD initiatives. It was quite disappointing to tell you the truth.

So, Bud went to International Security Affairs under Paul Nitze. The next slight involvement was in the same position. In 1964 we heard that Rear Admiral C. C. Kirkpatrick who was superintendent of the Naval Academy, was going to be the Chief of Personnel, succeeding Smedberg. Kirk was an old friend of mine and he called me on the phone and asked me a lot of questions and asked me to do some things for him, which I gladly volunteered to do. He said he would like me to get up a small team to make a round-the-world tour before he relieved, touching every Navy concentration or base, to get a feel for the Navy before he came in to his position. Rather typical of him incidentally, it was preparation for his coming job. He said he would like me to get hold of Bud Zumwalt and an officer named Jake Finneran (later Vice Admiral) and have the Bureau transfer them to the Bureau of Personnel right away and for me to form the team and get the itinerary and get the clearances, etc. I actually sent the request for clearances out all over the world and asked them for detailed schedules. As I have earlier told you, Kirkpatrick had a heart attack the night before he was relieved as Superintendent of the Academy and never became Chief of Personnel. However, this incident indicates the wide reputation and recognition that Bud had at that early period. I was informed shortly after my request for Zumwalt that Kirkpatrick could not have him, that Paul Nitze wanted him. So that showed that he left his mark fairly quickly in ISA.

Subsequently, as almost everyone knows, Paul Nitze became Secretary of the Navy, as I recall relieving Fred Korth. What is more natural than for him to bring Bud Zumwalt along as his senior aide? I saw Bud Zumwalt fairly often in this period. Though I was only on the Assistant Chief of Naval Personnel level under Smedberg, I had a special relationship with the Secretaries due to some personality conflicts. I was over there at the Secretary's office quite a bit and Bud and I helped each other a lot by telling each other what was coming down the line, what to expect next, and perhaps to try to prepare the way for a paper that was coming over to the Secretary's office. So we got to know each other a little bit then.

You can see how Nitze would be attracted to Bud Zumwalt because Bud had a brilliant mind, he was quick, perceptive, forward thinking, ready to step out on anything, and he did know people. A year later, in early '65 I believe, just before I left ComCruDesLant, I was on my first Rear Admiral

Selection Board. It was my first Selection Board assignment.
It was the line Rear Admiral Board. I believe that Corky Ward--
Admiral Ward of the class of '32--was the president of that
board, that is my best recollection. Bud Zumwalt was in the
eligibility list but not in the zone, he was far below the
zone. He was selected for Rear Admiral by the Board. At the
time he was selected, I believe his age was forty-four and he
was the youngest flag officer selected under the modern
selection system (I am not going back to the days of Farragut
when one was a Captain at twenty-one). He was the youngest
flag officer selected and five to six years later he became
the Chief of Naval Operations. As usual, it was rumored that
Paul Nitze had influenced the Selection Board to select Zumwalt
because he was his senior aide. Bud was disturbed about this,
I remember at that time. I was not stationed in Washington, I
was in Newport, and he called me on the phone and asked about
this rumor and I told him there was nothing in it. The next
time I saw him in the Pentagon he asked me directly if there
was any pressure brought to bear and I assured him that no
statement of any sort had been made by the Secretary or by
our Board President to the Board as a whole, and that no one in
or out of the Navy had said anything to me personally urging
his selection. Now what the Secretary said to Admiral Ward I
don't know, if anything indeed was said. Ward said absolutely
nothing to the Board as a whole about selecting the Secretary's
aide. In the first place Ward would not, in the second place
Boards are notoriously reluctant to accept that kind of pressure.

Duncan #19 -1840-

I know it possibly has happened but it would be unusual for this to happen. I have already recited to you certain cases I knew about, such as the Rickover case and cases of officers being taken off the list but as far as saying select Bill or Joe because he is my aide, I don't know of any such cases. I assured Bud that he was not suggested to the Board for selection. Of course, all of us on the Board were aware that Bud was the Secretary's aide, it was on his record. I was not one of those assigned to review his records. Not revealing any secrets, each Board member is assigned a whole stack of records to review in detail in order to brief the whole Board. The Board aspired to look at every record and they do, but they cannot go into all details, time doesn't permit. I did not review Bud's record in detail and I don't know who did. We all knew he was Aide to the Secretary but that, in my opinion, was not the determining factor; it was his over all terrific record. Actually, people might have urged his selection to me because there was a feeling that the Boards divided up into little cliques, aviator clique, submariner clique, surface navy destroyer clique, and other surface cliques--it was not so on our Board. I do think that possibly the aviators came in with a prepared list, because members indicated to me that they had a list of senior officers' preferences. I don't think there is anything greatly wrong with this. They were not slavish to it nor did they say that "this is the way it's going to be". I was aware that they had a list of who the senior aviators thought ought to be selected. No group except the

Secretary could order selections. As a matter of fact it was against the oath of office to receive any orders. I do think the submariners knew the submariners, the aviators knew the aviators. I didn't know who the senior surface people wanted and I selected from the record plus consideration of Service reputation. There was no unofficial communication with me at all. The only reason I mention this is because I was ComCruDesLant and one might think that people would approach me, but no one did. It was true, and the Secretary spoke to us on this subject that he was pressing for younger flag officers. As I have said, this is characteristic of Secretaries.

I saw Bud several times later after this event, after his very short sea tour as a Cruiser-Destroyer Flotilla Commander on the west coast. After he was brought back to Washington as a Rear Admiral and made head of the Analysis Section under Op 090. I was made Chief of Personnel. I thought Bud's assignment was quite a wise assignment as he had an analytic mind. Incidentally, he superintended the OEG and the Center for Naval Analyses, the Navy's think tank.

Q: Rivero had that job I think?

Adm. D.: Rivero set up the office of Op 090 in the early '60's. That was the overall boss of the division Bud had. The Center for Naval Analyses was technically under the Franklin Institute. They ran it for us, however it was really run by Op 090 and specifically by Bud Zumwalt who was head of the Analytic Section. When he first was there I was at sea in the Atlantic.

I talked with him in Washington a little about whether I should take the job as Chief of Personnel--I had not been offered the job but I had had a couple of telephone calls indicating that the offer was going to be made. At that time I was Commander of the Amphibious Force. I honestly didn't want to be CNP particularly, I felt I could do it but I was not seeking it. I really liked being in the Fleet--that was a little selfish--and I talked to Bud about it. He said he thought that maybe I should come to Washington and asked what other things was I interested in. I said I was interested in Plans and Operations and Personnel. This is the sort of friendship we had, though I think at that point I had not yet met his family. This may all seem rather inconsequential The reason I am relating these details is that I am going to say some critical things about Bud. Things that can be taken as critical--not about him personally, but about the way he ran things or allowed things to be run. I hope I am objective--maybe I am not--but I think it is a picture of a CNO who is fascinating and it needs to be drawn, and I just want him to know it is being drawn by somebody who wanted him to be the best CNO ever. Bud was a very attractive and magnetic person. It was a pleasure to work personally with Bud. I admired him a great deal for his keen mind, his fearlessness in expressing his convictions, and his consistent superb performance of which I was aware, not only in general, but through my Selection Board work. Bud Zumwalt was one of the most capable officers I had ever known.

Duncan #19 -1843-

By the time I came to Washington as Chief of Naval Personnel, Bud was still in this Analytic Section and we exchanged views fairly frequently. The Secretary of the Navy at that time was Paul Ignatius, an able man. After I became Chief of Naval Personnel it became evident that we were going to make a change in the Commander of Naval Forces Vietnam. The gentlemen who was out there was a good man, he was a two-star officer and in my opinion he needed three stars to hold his own with his peers in the Army and the Air Force. We felt that to hold the Navy side up we should have a three-star officer. The powers that be, although I suppose I was one of the powers, did not feel that the officer there should have three stars. It was about time for him to leave, so how to get an aggressive three-star guy out there? I did not initiate sending Bud to Vietnam. It may or may not have crossed my mind, I don't remember, I would guess it came down from Ignatius, to Moorer to me. I don't remember where I first heard that Bud Zumwalt would make a good guy to take that position. My only comment was that he would be a good choice, that he would do a whale of a job wherever he was sent. I was for it. Usually the Chief of Naval Personnel initiates what they call flag officer nominations but when you get to the three and four-star level--it comes from many sources. In any event Bud did get the position and he was very junior at that time. Remember he had been selected in the spring or summer of '65 and had probably not made his number until the summer of '66. He had probably been a Rear Admiral in fact for no more than two years or so at that time. At that point he was moving along fast. I think the nomination met with favor everywhere, I don't know of any objection. Paul Nitze had moved up to be Deputy SecDef. Incidentally, there was some word that Nitze had been promised SecDef and he was disappointed, nevertheless I can't say about that. I think there was some Congressional opposition to him. He was a good Deputy SecDef in my opinion. There is always a group to object if any man gets ahead, saying "how did he get it" and "it should have been me". There was the usual talk that Nitze told SecNav to send Bud to Vietnam. All I know is that the suggestion came in at my level, I thought well of it, and he was sent out to Vietnam. Bud and I kept very close personal touch because with "in-country" Vietnam, it was personnel all around in the Navy. We had the river boats, the SEAL teams, a little river boat tender and base personnel. It was ninety percent personnel action. In Vietnam it was a young navy and this impressed Bud. He loved those young officers out there and felt they were doing a great job. I felt the same and we sent young officers out there with really no experience but they were good men. By no means, as was bruited about, did we send cast-offs. The Navy might have wanted to send cast offs for two reasons. In general Navy people considered the riverine type operation as an aside, it not being the main game in the Navy. If officers had been asked, "would you like to go and run a little river boat" they would have said no. If they had been asked, "Would you like to get in the action in combat?", they would have said yes. These were good men. One very good reason for the situation was that Mel Laird said Vietnam had number one priority. He told Bud Zumwalt and he told the other Services. Armed with that, I got a dispatch from Bud almost every other day wanting more people, more people and more people. I told him to get rid of some of them, he was trying to pile them up on me. We had quite a correspondence and exchange of dispatches and I got to know him somewhat better. He had his son out there. Through our official relationship as Chief of Naval Personnel and Commander of Naval Forces Vietnam, we had hundreds of exchanges of messages and I did my best to help him. Mel Laird told me to and I thought it was my duty, we were fighting. I will say I did not accede to everything Bud asked me. I would not have acceded to anyone where I felt it was not right. Normally, if people or activities pressed too hard, I would take it up with my superiors saying I am not going to do it. The CNO and VCNO could fire off the message if they wanted to. In the case of Bud, if he became convinced that I was sure it was not the way to go, he accepted it, so we had a good relationship. I certainly did my best for Vietnam in the way of sending good people, keeping them as near allowance as possible, but not letting them stockpile people, or build up pools of men awaiting orders. There are lots of ways to get the system. We had a good amicable relationship I think.

Many officers who you are going to talk to or perhaps you have already talked to, know personal details on Bud's selection for CNO. Possibly you have talked to Bud or you are going to.

In any event he has written a book. I don't expect I have as accurate knowledge on certain aspects as perhaps others do.

Q: Moorer had a very intimate knowledge of it and he told me.

Adm. D.: I think perhaps mine will complement Admiral Moorer's recollections rather well because I was Chief of Naval Personnel under Tom Moorer and knew his thinking pretty well. I saw what was coming, I think. Others may have details I don't know about, many know Bud Zumwalt better. I doubt there are many who were closer to the exact sequence of that action than I was. I do have a quite complete knowledge of the sequence of events and some of the happenings as the new Chief of Naval Operations was chosen that spring and summer of 1970, which we all knew was coming up. We were all pretty sure, I believe it had been announced, that Admiral Moorer was going to be Chairman of the JCS.

I am out of my Commander in Chief Atlantic Fleet role temporarily and going back to when I was Chief of Personnel in order to build this personal background before I discuss some of the differences of opinion between the CNO and CinCLantFlt I realize there may be some repetition- As Chief of Naval Personnel in the period 1968 to 1970, I was a close personal friend of John Chafee the Secretary of the Navy who took office in January 1969. I liked him, I think I know his strengths and weaknesses just as he knows mine. I knew his family. I knew pretty well how he reacted and what his enthusiasms were. He helped me a great deal in personnel matters. He also consulted me a great deal. Many civilians who come into the Secretariat and into the OSD are a little suspicious of the military. Civilian friends have come up to them and said, "Don't let the Admirals take you over, don't trust them, don't believe what they tell you, go check on it". So John came in with a little bit of a wary feeling. Because of my previous experience in Washington and watching these new people, watching them get briefed and watching the questions, I decided that if I ever landed up there with a new administration I was going to try to help them understand the Navy. I would tell them we needed their help and that these Admirals were the guys who should be best friends and should give the best advice. In turn the civilians should support the Admirals if they saw it their way. I invited John to the house to have dinner just with me and my wife, no one else. He had not yet moved to Washington, his wife was still up in Rhode Island. I only mention this to show the relationship that I established, not with the idea of getting my things through but trying to make a Secretary feel at home in the Navy Department. I told him then, I remember the night very clearly, that he must get to know the Admirals, to trust them, ask them questions, to rely on them and help them. I was trying to solidify what I saw as the four years coming up and make it a good working team. How much good this did is something I can't say. He called on me many times asking me my opinion and consulting with me. He helped me many times when I wanted something for Navy people. He would go down and argue his best with the Defense people, he didn't always win but he always did his best and he was sincerely interested. It bothered John Chafee that we didn't have younger flag officers, that really bothered him. He frequently showed me a bar graph chart that he had had made up in his office showing the number of Vice Admirals from each year group. Of course at that time the longer bar graph went out from about year groups '33, '34 and '35. He said, "Why do we have all the Vice Admirals from the classes of '33, '34 and '35? We don't have any out here in '40?" I explained that, at least with the system as it was without arguing whether it was good or bad, an officer simply could not become competitive until he had done this, and this, and this, so that he could compete with his peers to become a Vice Admiral. Well John hoisted that aboard but he didn't really concur. In effect he said I am forty-four years old and I am the Secretary of the Navy, why does an Admiral have to be fifty-five years old to be a Vice Admiral. And he pointed out other examples of which we all know--thirty-six year old heads of corporations and other examples. I explained, or tried to explain, the nature of the Navy. That Naval officers' peers expect them to have been through the actual experiences. Also that you don't try them for two months and then fire them. You pick the man you think can do the job, or you would really have a lot of reverberations in the Navy.

John's thought was, get younger CNO's, younger Admirals. He pushed me real hard and he pushed Tom Moorer to try to get the law changed about the number of officers who could be selected below the zone. There was a limitation. I think we did change the law. I specifically told John Chafee at the time that if we got flexibility into the law that we had to be careful because politicians are stronger than Secretaries and could come in and pressure to select everybody below the zone. The Navy might have thirty year old Admirals. After all, we had thirty year old Congressmen and we could have thirty year old admirals. I didn't think that would work. He said we would consult and he would hold it down and he quoted some figure, I believe fifteen percent, on how many below the zone. The basic Navy idea was to try to advance or accelerate officers at each promotion point, not wait until a person came to the rank of Admiral and then skip all the jobs that really make a man an Admiral--that really give him experience. At each point the best could be accelerated, if an officer is a real star he will last and if not he may flame out at some point along the way. John felt that we did not have at the helm--at the top--necessarily those best suited and the most dynamic, but merely those who had successfully checked off each rung of the ladder. I think we all tried to write into the precept for the Selection Board instructions not to concentrate too much on past record or performance, look at the potential of what the man can do for the future. The key factor isn't that an officer shot down thirty planes in WWII thirty years ago, it is what he can do in the future in the modern Navy. I think we all accepted that, and John was especially strong on it.

I have already told you that all Secretaries of the Navy feel this way, that we should move on. And I think the Navy move on plenty. We might get some younger Rear Admirals, but I don't really think examples like Bagley retiring with four stars at age fifty sets such a good example.

Q: I personally think it is an awful waste.

Adm. D.: It's a terrible waste and if a man is that good we shouldn't turn him out to pasture.

We have changed a great deal over the years. In fact we used to have five Admirals who were in their sixties, and by 1970 had at least two who were about 50, Bud Zumwalt and Ike Kidd. Admiral Moorer as CNO believed in gradual change, not radical change. I don't know how Admiral Moorer would put it but there is no question that Moorer and John Chafee did not see eye to eye on a great many things. They didn't get along all the time, there were times when I was almost a go-between in personnel matters. It was difficult for the CNO, it was probably difficult to the Secretary. I tried to bridge the gap in my area of responsibility. They were both good men, they both were strong men, and there is no question but that they bumped heads some. There is no question but that John Chafee infringed on the CNO's prerogatives, in my opinion. Secretaries had done that many times, including firing Admirals. This is nothing awfully new but he did try to infringe especially in the area of flag officer assignments. He did not succeed there but in promotional policies he did succeed. I am not at all familiar with how they got along in the material or budget areas.

At the time of picking the new CNO--we are back now in July of 1970, right back at the time of choosing the new CNO. I must revert to my CNP experiences temporarily to build my experiences. John Chafee was absolutely determined, and I am sure he had the backing of SecDef and maybe even the President. He was determined to get as young a CNO as he possibly could. I don't think there were any limits that he set to get a young CNO. The President can appoint a Captain as CNO if he wants to, and I think if Chafee had known one that he thought would have measured up, he would have recommended him. Tom Moorer very strongly recommended Chick Clarey, who was a fine man and who was Vice Chief of Naval Operations. He knew the Pentagon routine and the Washington routine. He was in the year group of '34 and I think there was no question but that he would have made a fine CNO. Clarey was typical of several officers who were caught by age. Maybe had he been ten years younger he would have been CNO. He knew that Tom Moorer was trying to nominate him and in the ensuing events he took it very well and acted as a good vice chief to Bud as far as I know, after Bud was selected. Chafee went through a procedure, maybe this has been recited, I think it was sincere but almost partly for effect--he wrote all four-star officers and he asked them for their recommendations on officers to be CNO. He then proceeded to interview numerous officers who were eligible--people who had been recommended for

CNO, people who had been suggested from the outside, people whom he knew--he by no means stuck to the list. I had not seen the list, nor do I even know it was formally compiled. I suppose it was, as I know of some people who were on it. But he went through the motions of interviewing people, including even me, and I knew he was not considering me for CNO at all, but he wanted to give the appearance of having really gone into this thing and talked to these people.

Q: What was the rationale behind this? Why did he consider this to be so terribly important?

Adm. D.: I think that he was truly determined to have an extremely young CNO. I am speculating--he wanted to justify in his own eyes and in the eyes of the Navy and everyone else, that he had considered everybody who might conceivably be a good CNO. Therefore, he went through the motions of interviewing-- I guess he interviewed every four-star officer in the navy and a lot of three stars. I don't know how many, the interviews were set up by his aide.

Q: What was the virtue of youth, as such?

Adm. D.: He never explained it to me too much, except that occasionally he would say "I'm only forty-four years old and am head of the Navy" and he would point out the youth of some well-known figures in industry. I think it was the feeling that we were making people go a set route, rather than saying "Who is the best, most talented, brainy, dynamic guy we can get?", and making him the CNO, regardless of age, rank, or anything else. I think it is very important that, in spite of endowments, a man should have wide experience in the various ranks. Secretary Chafee was not convinced of this, Paul Nitze was never convinced.

Q: He didn't rely on experience at all. He discounted it.

Adm. D.: No, he never did. John Chafee having gone up fast in politics--elected four times governor of Rhode Island, started in his thirties--was determined the Navy was going to have the best, rather than the best ready at the time. I am speculating now. He had me order Bud Zumwalt in to Washington (Bud had been in a couple of times before) to brief the Navy on how things were going in Vietnam. I am not that dumb, I knew he wasn't ordering Bud Zumwalt in to lecture the Navy. He installed Bud in the visiting flag officer's office across from the CNO. After a couple of days Bud called me and said "I don't find people very interested in Vietnam around here." I said, "Well, they are interested in Vietnam. You have done some good in these briefings, but in my opinion you are back here to be interviewed for CNO." I assume Bud knew this and I suspect other people had told him. I went over to see him in his little office, the little cubicle across there from the CNO's office, and we discussed the thing at some length. I told him quite frankly what was up--that the Secretary was determined to have a young man (I don't think Chafee knew Bud Zumwalt other than this trip back). I told him there were other contenders who were well thought of in the Navy. I remember he said something about feeling a little guilty to be jumping over other officers and I said (and I believe it) I didn't think it was his choice, that people do not make themselves CNO, they are made and therefore there is no use wasting time feeling guilty about that. I remember the schedules of the interviews, and I remember the day Bud was to go down. Right after the morning conference which Bud always attended, I went up to his office and we chatted and I walked down to Chafee's office with him. I told him what I thought Chafee was looking for, which was a man with innovative ideas, with concern about young people, and willing to step out regardless of the consequences, and Bud went on in for his interview. Neither of them ever told me about that interview, but I learned very shortly afterward that Bud had been chosen.

Before Bud went back to Vietnam, he had been informed that he was going to be nominated--it apparently had been cleared orally with the powers that be. Chafee called Chick Clarey and myself into his office, along with Bud. Chafee wanted, and Bud apparently wanted, Bud to come back as head of the Flag Officers Selection Board for that year, which we had set up for June, before Bud was to become CNO. Bud was a Vice Admiral. Tradition required a four star Admiral as President of the Board. Chafee's proposal was that Zumwalt be brought back while he was still Commander in Vietnam, and be made head of the Flag Officers Selection Board. This was quite obviously an effort to select young people who were in tune with the coming times. It surprised me that Chafee would suggest this; I was extremely surprised that Clarey did not object to it at all. I don't remember whether he encouraged it but he did not object to the Sec Nav proposal. I said that I thought it would be the worst thing for a young CNO who would be under scrutiny in any event, to be brought in to select the coming Flag Officers before he had ever occupied the position of responsibility. It was not done. I mention this only as a footnote to history.

Bud was brought back to be CNO in July (on the first I believe). I was Chief of Personnel for a couple of months-- July and most of August. Bud immediately started to work on a million things. He directed me to make up charts of promising young flag officers, so that when he left (he was fifty then and said he would be fifty-four when he left) there would be available three or four officers under fifty-four years of age who have had at least a year or two experience at four stars. So he had me make up proposed schedules on four or five flag officers to show how they could be brought up and given experience in a four star billet of at least a year before he was ready to be relieved. He said he was going to retire after his tour as CNO and he wanted the Secretary to be able to choose from at least three contenders who had had experience. I believe this shows an inkling that he knew he should have had some of this experience. I was fifty eight years old at that time and I never put my name on any chart at any time. I had never put my name on any chart, nor did he discuss the matter with me at all. I put my own remarks in, and I pushed another four-star officer who was doing well.

I had known him a long time and I pushed him as the next CinCLant Fleet. I did not mention myself in any way.

Then in early August, I was informed that Secretary Chafee and Zumwalt were going to nominate me to relieve Admiral Eph Holmes as Commander in Chief of the Atlantic Fleet. I was not interviewed or consulted by either one. I am positive that John Chafee had a big hand in it. I owe a debt to Zumwalt and I owe a debt to John Chafee. Bud told me later I was the oldest officer that he nominated for promotion after he became CNO.

Q: That is obvious, they got rid of most of them didn't they?

Adm. D.: Some people said, jokingly, I hope, that they sent me to CinCLant Fleet to get me out of Washington, because I objected to one or two of his early proposals.

This is the sort of background I feel is of some value and will make my observations of Bud Zumwalt of some significance. He was not an unknown quantity to me.

Bud and I had a general conversation that I would not be eligible to get a renewal of tour, I would be sixty-two before I could complete the tour. The Unified Command is two years, the other tours are open-ended SACLant and the Fleet are open-ende The Unified Command is two years and this is for a political purpose, if they don't like you, the President can say goodbye without embarrassment. Bud did not ask me anything at that time, but there was the general understanding that I would complete the tour. Of course, like any human being I would unquestionably have been flattered and pleased to have served another couple of years but it was no surprise to me to serve the one tour. They would have had to go to the President to get my tour extended into another two years.

I had, by that time, met Bud's wife and his children. I was at his son's wedding, which was shortly after he was made CNO. Another illustration of some closeness--I certainly was never his closest friend, nor was he my closest friend. In Norfolk we had the "Azalea Festival" which Norfolk related to NATO. There was a Princess representing every country, and a Queen from one--that year it was Portugal. That year, Anne Zumwalt, Bud's daughter, was nominated as the U.S. Princess. Frequently it is the daughter of a cabinet officer or someone like that. Bud was on some speaking trip and he asked me to present her to the "court". I presented her at night at the evening ball, and I presented her during the daytime ceremonies. I detail this to show that we were on that kind of terms, good friends. This is a lot of detail but I felt I had to mention it if I am going to criticize a guy that I think had as great a potential as any officer I have ever known to become a great CNO. I think that under other circumstances he could have been one of our greatest. He was brilliant, innovative, courageous, he had a capacity to lead, and he had the initiative to make changes. I think if Bud Zumwalt had had a tour afloat as a Second Fleet, Sixth or Seventh Fleet Commander as a Vice Admiral and a two year tour as Commander in Chief of one of the major Fleets, and especially the Atlantic, he could have become one of the great CNO's. I think he is always going to be controversial, I mean his performance will be controversial.

I was greatly disappointed in the CNO in many ways and I cannot explain what made the changes in him. But I will cite some evidence of changes. One could speculate that it was the frailty in all humans, when they attain the top they assume somewhat imperial stature and many of them surround themselves, almost unknowingly, with a very tight "yes-man" clique. Also, this is only speculation, possibly future ambition for high political office, maybe even visions of becoming Senator or President danced in his head, I don't know. No one in his younger days, or in his first days as CNO could have been a better listener, or had a more receptive mind and attitude than Bud, in my opinion. Within weeks of becoming CNO he had selected groups of young enlisted men and officers ordered in to the Pentagon, perhaps ten in a group. He would order them to Washington for a week, he would give them a week to sort out their gripes and suggestions and talk among themselves and maybe go back to their buddies. Then he would assemble them in the Management Information Center with all of us Vice Admiral Deputies and maybe some of the Rear Admirals and his close staff. We would listen to whatever they wanted to say--these were seamen, third class petty officers Chief Petty Officers, ensigns, JG's, black, white, oriental, men and women. I believe this was the first time in history that this had been done. Its effect worked two ways. It helped morale when it became known in the Fleet that very junior people were encouraged to bring direct to the CNO and his Deputies their frank opinions. Further, it helped senior people, many of whom as flag officers had never given junior people a chance to express themselves. It helped them to know what these juniors felt. They found out that these people felt things the senior officers didn't even know they felt. You could watch them and see they hadn't known. These young people weren't bashful. Young people aren't bashful any more. They spoke right out. I think it is important to note they had been selected by either their Commanding Officers, their peers, or their officers, but whoever did it, and I guess it was done in different ways, they were selected to represent groups and it was a job well done. Bud would sometimes get in groups of skills in which the Navy was in trouble. We were having trouble with engineers, we were working them too hard and were losing people out of the rating and we weren't getting people to volunteer. They were copping out of A school--it had a bad reputation. Bud brought in blacks, he brought in women. We brought in young pilots, we were having some trouble in the pilot program at that time. We got in "nukes". We ordered in different groups of that sort and rank meant absolutely nothing. The young people that I saw and heard were not militants. I think our reaction to militants would have been to leave and say, "The hell with them". I don't think we would have paid any attention to militants. These people were usually pretty well spoken young people and obviously somebody back at the ship had confidence that they could speak up in a reasonably articulate manner. My only criticism of this particular exercise, and it's a rather minor one, is that CNO gave the Deputies no chance to speak up and try to explain certain things to these people which might have helped them when they went back to their community. For example, I heard time and again the common phrase "the Navy doesn't pay enough sea pay" or "the Navy won't pay non-rated men for dependent travel", and in many other cases, "The Navy does this the Navy does that." It would have been so easy had Bud turned to me or another, and said how about that? I would have said "We are with you, we have been trying for years to get this, we have seen the Secretary, we have been before Congress--". Then they would have known it wasn't the Navy. I remember one item that I had personally worked hard on. It was a recommendation that bachelors aboard ship get their BAQ so that they get the same money as others. That would come up in these group meetings as a real gripe. Never did Bud let me speak up to say "We agree with you, we have tried it, we haven't tried enough and we weren't successful". I believe it would have been a little better balanced situation if the group could have gone back to their units and related to their friends that, "They told us some new things and it's true the Navy has tried to get some sea pay." I think it would have put the meeting in a little bit better perspective and I think they would have been more effective when they went home. It would have given us a chance to have given them a little bit of knowledge about the Office of Management and Budget, about the staff of the Secretary of Defense, and the Congress, etc. These were good sessions and I give Zumwalt credit for a very fine innovative action. Concurrently he fired out an absolute flood of sheets and suggestions and options of action to be commented upon. Who all commented I cannot tell you.

Q: Was this before the beginning of the Zgrams?

Adm. D.: It started before. He was formulating the Zgrams, because a lot of them queried us on matters that were later to come out as Zgrams. I could give you a hundred examples, there were quite a few examples where, as Chief of Personnel, I replied or commented in a vein that to the uninitiated would seem negative. He came out with a splendid sheet saying "It is proposed to do away with brown shoes". Tom Moorer and I, and Chick Clarey had tried for three years to simplify the uniform (I did do away with the evening tail coat). Every Service except Navy had one pair of shoes, black. He decided we would do that. I had proposed this very thing a year previously. I was overwhelmed on the Uniform Board when I realized I had run into a very emotional area, particularly with the aviators. We tried to run the Uniform Board in a fairly democratic way. So my reply to this sheet was that I strongly agreed, but we had tried it, the matter got very emotional I was completely outvoted in the Uniform Board. Therefore I recommended against it at this time. I knew that some day the Navy would change.

This is the sort of thing that I believe laid the groundwork for my reputation with his eager staff who came with him from Vietnam. It probably went downhill from there. I am sure they felt "here is this old Chief of Personnel, already he doesn't go along." These sheets were the basis for the Zgrams. Because of my reply on some of these sheets, his staff got mad at me. Bud never told me he was mad at me, I knew he disagreed because he didn't do what I said. I know he understood what I thought. I rather suspect that is why he retained me, but he didn't agree with me.

In these early days started one of the things that I think is a failure of the Zumwalt administration and I will try to describe it just a little. The essence of my criticism is that within a very short period--within a month--the Navy went from one of the most open-minded, ready-to-listen CNO's, Zumwalt, to one where any disagreement with a suggestion or a proposed policy out of the CNO's office was simply heresy. You became the enemy if you didn't completely agree.

Q: This attitude came from him?

Adm. D.: From his staff. He never said this, I don't really know what he thought. I believe he felt I was too set in my ways. I don't mind that. I do not think he was angry, nor do I think he thought I was dumb. His staff thought it because when I would bring up reasons why proposals should not be done, they thought I was an "aginer". So I think one of the failures of his administration was to assemble a very tight clique around him intensely loyal, largely with limited experience. This is not an unusual thing for people in high positions, particularly in the case of dynamic people. Kennedy did the same thing, assembled people loyal to him to the nth degree--if you didn't agree with them, your name was mud, you were dumb. You can't get through that wall.

Dynamic and attractive people do attract such a group. They then take it onto themselves to protect the boss and to see that no other idea can be put forward--everything that the boss says is right. I told you about the home-porting. I did consult him but couldn't convince him. If he had consulted me, or if he had listened to experienced people in the Fleet who knew (and he did not know) he could thereby have avoided a mistake. Similarly, there were a great many personnel items where the mistakes he made could have been avoided, but he would not listen to senior people any more, with the exception of a few among those who surrounded him. One of the injuries he did to the Navy was to weaken the chain of command. It reached the point that a Commanding Officer was really afraid to discipline people, because he knew they could write direct to Washington, run around end to Washington to the CNO. They were especially afraid to even say "Boo" to a black or bring one to mast, even though it was a clear-cut case. The Commanding Officers very definitely lost their authority. The ones who felt it the most were the Chief Petty Officers.

I don't know what the modern chief petty officer thinks, those who have recently made it. I can sure tell you the feeling of the others in 1970 to 1972 because I had the Senior Chief Petty Officers at a Command Conference at CinCLant Fleet. I talked to them as a group and then went out and had coffee with them. I know what they thought--they thought it was horrible the way the chain of command had been weakened and by-passed. I consider this failure was due to the factors I have described. Bud skipped experience serving as an flag officer at sea which would have taught him about keeping friends who would tell him facts, and about relying on experienced people. The other factor was the very tight clique around him.

Q: How large was this clique?

Adm. D.: I can't tell you exactly, and I hesitate to deal in names. Some were, or quickly became, flag officers, some were Commander and Captain types. But he put them in every place: JAG, etc. He placed his man in every strategic spot.

I do not think Bud realized how very tightly he was screened. I wonder what he thinks today if he knows what a tight circle he had, if he knows that a Fleet Commander in Chief was told they did not bother to send him a message on a very important fleet matter, which I had marked "Personal for Admiral Zumwalt". His staff said they didn't bother to show it to Admiral Zumwalt because it was negative. I hardly believe Zumwalt would have put up with that sort of thing, but it was a failure of his that he allowed his people to do it. He listened to those relatively inexperienced people versus listening to a Commander in Chief. I am not the only one who thinks this, a great many people in the Atlantic Fleet thought so. His staff became known as "the cult". There is no question but that they had unswerving loyalty to Zumwalt.

I could give you a few examples to show you how the cult was responsible for him not being the CNO he could have been. One of his action sheets when I was still Chief of Naval Personnel, just before leaving, proposed that all enlisted men be allowed to go to and from the ship in dungarees, just as civilian workmen did. A great many of us with extensive Fleet experience knew and pointed out that men do not go directly home from the ship; they go to a bar, maybe go to play a game, go shopping for groceries, go out on a date, maybe they go to the movies, or go see friends, or they go on a weekend. We knew this and I told him, but this information was very unpopular with certain of his staff. It should be understood that there is nothing intrinsically wrong with dungarees-- it is the same material that Saks-Fifth Avenue sells for ladies now to wear to dances. It is a fairly attractive material, the point is that it was the work uniform where men crawled into boilers, they were required to work on greasy engines, they expected to be soiled and we allowed them to wear them torn for the simple reason of economy. You wouldn't make a man buy new dungarees just because the pocket was ripped off or had a button missing. But, once this permission was given a man could wear these working dungarees anywhere. It was reliably reported to us that Atlantic Fleet men were in Omaha, St. Louis and Chicago in the airports, in dirty filthy clothing. The Fleet was blamed. The Norfolk people came to me and said "What are you doing? The airports are clogged with people in dirty dungarees, and in the supermarkets." Some men would even get thrown out of civilian bars because they were so dirty. I knew all this, I knew how men acted and I told Zumwalt. All that I got from it from his staff was that I was reactionary, I wasn't with it. A lot of things could have been said in his directive, such as "a fresh clean pair of dungarees to and from one's home." There are all sorts of ways to do things. He even came out with a "green sheet" saying he was going to change the regulation so that young people in the Navy could feel the same as their peers in society, they could wear anything they wanted out the base gate and the Marines were to let them. In my dispatch I commented that just the week before I had seen pictures of women naked in the reflecting pool in Washington, and a few naked men. Apparently their peers did do that and they were not arrested. Later they were merely told to clear out. I did not think such an open ended order would work and I didn't think that a Marine at the base gate should have to put up with letting a man or woman wear anything they wanted. I said it is hard to set exact standards but I think we can say such things as, reasonable in appearance. Never a word did I hear back on that.

The Zgram went out on dress and we suffered from it. The Navy's image suffered in Europe. As Commander in Chief Atlantic Fleet I got letters from Europe asking what we were doing. I really think he should have fired me. If the Commander in Chief didn't have any more sense or any better feeling for his men than to be completely wrong, he should have been fired. But I did know what I was talking about and I had people under me who knew what they were talking about. I will say in Bud's defense that I don't believe that, in general, the older generation was "with" the younger generation. I don't know that we should have been all the way. I think it is possible that older people resented things that were merely idiosyncrasies on the part of young people. Perhaps he saw clearly that older senior people were alienating the young people, and he was trying to do his best to show the young that he was sympathetic. He used their language, talked about rap sessions, and so forth.

Q: It was a social revolution that we were in.

Adm. D.: Yes it was. And indeed, how should it have been handled, and would another person have handled it better? I choose to think so. Had Bud had the experience needed, with his wonderful innovative mind, then I think he would have been a really great CNO and would have come up with maybe revolutionary ideas, but things that would have worked. So many of his things just simply did not work. As you probably know he later cancelled the order on the dungaree business but it took several years to learn the unwisdom of it. That particular order set the Navy back in the minds of people (Americans and others) a considerable amount. There might have been a few young people who thought it was great but the public at large thought we had lost our minds and that we were tolerating a very dirty, sloppy Navy.

Another innovation to which I did not object was that he initiated beer in the barracks. If you treat people responsibly you have a good chance of the major portion of them reacting responsibly. I think there is a great deal to be said in this area. However, these innovations coupled with certain other Zgrams that were sent out, encouraged a very permissive attitude. He put out one, I cannot quote the exact content, that noted that men did not have to stay on their ship during working hours for their meals. This I must say, is a little revolutionary. On shore it is all right, they can leave their place of business or work and go over to the club or whatever. But to have a man leave a destroyer or a carrier at noon where there is work going on, for him to go ashore to eat is a marked change for the Navy. What happened was predicted by many but they got nowhere. The energetic club managers went as far as they would let it go. They started serving liquor at eleven-thirty in the morning. My aide and I would sometimes drive around at eleven thirty to the Chiefs' club or petty officers' club (this might sound a little silly and we should have gone in out of uniform) and we would count cars and at two o'clock there would be the same number of cars still there. I don't see why the Commanding Officers didn't stop it except that they were afraid to. The club managers put in topless go-go dancers. What I did in that case was to call in my Commanders and told them this practice would be stopped within one week. I said that there would be no breaking of contracts, there would be nothing in writing for the press to get hold of, that the practice would be stopped orally. It was stopped and there was no more. I didn't stop other entertainment during the noon hour. I wasn't afraid but thought it would be counter-productive. I was trying to work within the system and make it as good as I could and still run the Fleet. In any event I felt this was typical of the sort of practice being instituted that hurt the Navy.

One important issue, and this gets away from the personnel type thing, is Fleet organization. That is the case of sending a dispatch where I did inquire about the CNO's reaction to my views and was told it wasn't shown to the CNO. Fleet organization was an area that I felt was my special responsibility, and also where I had a special experience. I could have gone to Washington and I did on occasions where I thought things were very important and where I might be effective. But I don't know to this day how much Bud saw of what I sent in and how much was screened out. There were stories going around the Fleet which had an unfortunate effect. I don't know that they were true. There were stories of malcontents in the Fleet who, if their Commanding officer told them to do this or that, would get to the CNO. Then the Commanding Officer would be "out on report" and would be made to explain his action. I do know that Commanding Officers were made to explain certain items although I do not know it happened exactly in that way. Maybe it was "Mother" writing, or perhaps a Congressman writing. I do know Commanding Officers were made to explain certain happenings on their ships.

I know this subject has been discussed exhaustively. There are a great many people who feel that this general philosophy of operating from the top directly to individuals far down the echelon, and the general permissiveness that existed, putting the Commanding Officer on trial as it were, resulted in such matters as the near-mutiny on the KITTY HAWK. Now that was an involved matter. It was, as I understand it, a first time in the U.S. Navy of men refusing to work, refusing orders, for centuries. I cannot believe this would have occurred under a different system. I do not believe this can be attributed to race relations in the United States. Bud Zumwalt did make some very good initiatives on race relations. One of the good things he did was setting up human relations and race relations sessions to talk things out. I think this is a well-recognized technique that we had not used in the Service. I have never thought and don't think that the Services' race problems were as keen as the problems in civil life. We can't tolerate that sort of problem when we live close together on a ship. We certainly need to talk things out and I commend the discussion type effort. As in other things, I believe the CNO's execution was lacking in many ways.

Q: Was he responsible for the system of "A voice for the ethnic, a voice for the minorities on ships", etc.---that whole system that was going to reach its way up to the Secretariat?

Adm. D.: Only in a sense. I can tell you something of what started about seven years before, going back now to our days of '63-'64. There was a study on the racial situation in the Navy by a group, headed by a Washington lawyer-Gerhard Gesell-a noted liberal. The report outlined to the Navy certain things that were going on that the Navy really did not know or was not sensitive to. He also had recommendations that we thought were far out, I still think they were. Under the impetus of this report which was quite critical, the Navy started various projects and race relations teams were set up under my organization. We made up several teams primarily of enlisted men. We would hear of racial trouble and send the team to look at the situation. Also we had a survey schedule. I admit that the impetus came from the outside but once into it, we tried to do our best and we did indeed learn. I am reminded of a team sent to Pensacola, Florida, at the Air Training Command. We were told it was not needed, there was no racial trouble, no discrimination, and no dissatisfaction. The team stayed down there a while, they came back and reported the black families were in a state of considerable tension. Black groups had held meetings on various aspects of discrimination as they saw it. Yet when we arrived there the Commander sat down with the team and told them he didn't have a single racial problem on the station or on any station in the Air Training Command, and that all blacks were perfectly happy. Our teams uncovered a lot of unsatisfactory situations. They did not put people "on the report" in the sense that I am saying the alleged Zumwalt "system" did. We wrote letters and sent messages to the Commanders explaining that we had heard of certain situations and suggesting that he look into them, questioning politely whether they really knew what was going on. We were told that everything was perfect at the Air Station in Memphis, but we had heard otherwise. Contrary to later practice, we didn't immediately put the Command "on the report"--we sent a team. They were reasonable, tried and true men and women, black and white. For example they went into the crew's mess hall. This may seem a small incident in the old days, but I think you and I see the significance of it today. In the crew's mess hall on one entire wall was a mural of blacks picking cotton in the cotton field with a white foreman overseeing the work. But the Command said everything was all right in Memphis. Now this was the sort of thing which was turned up. So I would say the line of communication on racial matters was not initially established by Bud. Long before him, we had in BuPers an instant reporting system of racial incidents. It was refined, as these things always are, and it became more sophisticated. We got instant reports on racial incidents, whether or not they were considered racial. If a white and a black fought it didn't matter whether they fought because they were drunk, or whether they were arguing over theft, or whatever, we classified it as an incident to be recorded. I won't say we got them all but we got a lot. We got reports of violence with racial overtones. We would get a report of an incident that occurred on a certain station and a newsman would be on the phone asking "what are you doing about it?-Why is this being allowed?" We had to have reports. At that time certain blacks were getting very aggressive, very militant. We tried to do our own trouble-shooting, we certainly made a strenuous effort not to undermine the Command and we straightened it out to the best of our ability through the chain of command. I give you these instances to say we were very race conscious, we were aware that things were not exactly as Commanders thought they were. We did not send teams secretly. We told the Commanders they were coming, and asked that they be given freedom to talk in bars, to go to people's houses and visit the housewives. We did nothing secretly. The Commander got a copy of the report. Even then it was unpleasant to some Commanders. A Commander likes to think he can take care of every incident in his command. I do believe we opened eyes, it certainly opened mine to the fact that we didn't know. I used to pride myself on my ships that I knew enough seamen, firemen and third class petty officers so that anything that went wrong, from the barber cussing them out to the food being bad, I would learn about. What one didn't learn about then were these very sensitive racial matters.

I would like to add a little on this subject. It is a big subject. The Gesell Report is the one I'm speaking of. Gesell leaned toward setting quotas for blacks to enter the Naval Academy regardless of comparative or competitive standards. We got pressures from various sources to set something like a 13% quota for blacks. People seriously proposed this and this was years ago. Admiral Zumwalt never proposed anything like that. We made some good efforts, we did not go as far as we should have, we went faster than society as a whole. One of things in this field that I did and of which I am very proud, (this is out of chronological context of what we are discussing). I had a meeting in Washington with George Bush the Congressman. We were all concerned about young blacks with potential but who had deprived backgrounds. How were we going to get them to officer status and executive status in the U.S.? There were distinguished people at the lunch such as the head of Phillips-Andover Academy. We got rather tired of hearing that the only reason for lack of success of blacks was due to deprived background. Yet we knew there were blacks with high potential. The idea that all blacks were to go to the top was ridiculous. We knew that the deprived background was part of certain deficiencies that certain groups or families had. We had it illustrated to us. Psychologists had means of testing certain youngsters at the eighth and ninth grade level who, given the right opportunity and instruction, could be stars in college and probably in life. The problem was how to get them ahead, especially for us, how to prepare them for the Naval Academy. One thing we adamantly refused to do was to lower the standards at the Naval Academy or in the NROTC. I would have retired over that, and I think my bosses would have also. One specific thing I initiated was as a result of the meeting George Bush held. Prent Kenyon was in on it. We set up at our training station down in Maryland an operation called "bootstrap". This operation still continues and has been moved to NTC San Diego. It was not restricted to blacks but it mainly consisted of blacks. It was not aimed at remedying everybody's deprived background. It was aimed at taking people with high potential, measured by psychological tests to find out their ability, who we believed would successfully graduate from the Naval Academy if they ever got up to the entry standards. We gave them up to two years of education so they could be competitive. We did not want to enter any one in the NROTC or the Naval Academy who could not enter there fully competitive. We felt that their pride demanded they be fully competitive. I knew fine black officers and they felt strongly about this. Incidentally this was not the total answer to solving the racial balance. We became aware that you had to get these young people early, preferably when they started school, but certainly at eight or nine years old. The Navy could not reach back that far.

Q: It would be terribly expensive.

Adm. D.: Terribly expensive, this was not a cost effective program. You may be aware that Andover had done some very good pioneer work in this field, and perhaps still does. They took people in about seventh grade level who had high potential, gave them a lot of remedial help, and sponsored them all the way through Harvard University. I believe they were the first to do it. By the time they got through they were top stars. George Bush may have gotten his idea to set up a program in the Navy from Andover.

Q: What was his position at that point?

Adm. D.: I had known George Bush semi-socially for some years among Washington groups, meetings, and so forth. He was in Congress, from Texas. I am not a judge and I think history will have to judge about Bud's approach. I felt he went too fast, that he gave the militants a chance and a feeling they could do things that in a military service cannot be done. In society all right, but not in the military. I think he tried to let the militants operate in a military society, and it did not work.

I give him credit for doing some good things. He initiated race-relations seminars. This is a good technique, well known of course, but we had not done it in the Navy. Our white enlisted men did not understand the blacks. Long before Bud was CNO I was surprised at some of the things we were requested to do. I came to understand it through talking to blacks. Such as the request that we put in our ships stores black cosmetics, long combs and allow the men to carry these combs. This sort of thing we would not have thought of doing in the sixties. Everyone is more sensitive now.

I think that in Bud's time, with the Vietnam war--as you said a real revolution of society--we would have had to go faster. Bud did some things the wrong way and he did some the right way.

Q: He opened the box and all sorts of things happened, and then at that point cannot be restrained.

Adm. D.: And, who is to say what the other course might have been. It is true that we found the blacks did not like the Navy Service, for many reasons. He didn't have a Navy role model, he knew a doctor, he knew a lawyer, he probably knew an Army officer but he didn't know any black Admirals. The blacks actually avoided the Navy. We were required by McNamara to send our recruiting teams into black areas in big cities and they were stoned. For reasons that I don't fully comprehend the reputation among the blacks was that the Navy was the worst of the Services. This was rather astounding, as I think Navy was the best. That was the word around the black "ghetto", not from the black first class petty officer in the Navy.

I think some of Zumwalt's poorer results were possibly due to the Commanding Officers being so afraid of what was going to happen to them. They let the blacks run over them, they apparently were afraid to discipline them. Probably the

Commanding Officers over-reacted. We had word of black meetings going on in a ship and the Commanding Officer not breaking them up. That was unheard of in the military. There were meetings of blacks on an amphibious ship. We took care of that successfully in 65-66. Some of Zumwalt's initiatives caused this sort of thing. Zumwalt recognized the rehabilitative capability and also the rehabilitative responsibility of the Navy for alcoholics and for drug users. Here again, due to his insulation behind this little clique of advisers, surrounded by the "row of wagons", he didn't know how it was really working.

Q: Were these people changed from time to time or did they remain with him throughout his entire administration?

Adm. D.: They were added to from time to time, and many remain with him yet.

Q: Did they go out into the field and learn something new?

Adm. D.: None of them ever came to CinCLant Fleet to talk to me during the over two years I was there. He did send a black Ambassador down, he was a fine man and I learned a lot from him. None of the staff clique came. In this handling of rehabilitation of drug users and alcoholics he created a tremendous amount of hard feeling. Everywhere I went as Commander in Chief I tried to talk to groups formally and informally. In formal meetings they were allowed to ask question The modern sailor would come right out with his good questions for the Commander in Chief, which no sailor would have done thirty or forty years ago. The officers wouldn't even ask a question then. These young men would stand up to ask questions, and I never will forget the language of some of them. What had happened was that Zumwalt had set up these alcoholic and drug rehabilitation units in the middle of a Navy base. The base was full of busy men, doing their job and going about their work. The alcohol and drug users being rehabilitated had progressively been allowed the run of the base. They were to be treated normally and trusted. They would go to the movies, go to the bowling allies, eat in the mess hall and did no work. I never will forget down in Charleston at one of my talks, a first class petty officer stood up and could hardly talk he was so livid. He said he just wanted to know what in the world was going on, he had been in the Navy for fifteen years, his friends were hard workers and then, he said, they put these "dingbats" in our midst, they don't work, they have every privilege, and if they are discharged they go out with an honorable discharge. "Admiral, what is going on?" I got the same feeling everywhere I went--that it was a grave mistake to set up a rehabilitative unit where the men could wander around among people who were doing their work. The Navy doesn't work that way. I am speaking in generalities. The Navy man has a violent dislike for the guy who doesn't do his work and gets away with it, and you have seen it in this business of the amnesty. However right that may be socially, for the sailor or soldier who has done his bit and his best and worked like the devil, this sort of thing creates very strong feeling among them. These alcoholic units would have been better had they been put in a civilian setting under an agreement with HEW maybe. Not in the midst of a group of hard-working sailors. I believe Bud was the first to give a real push to the rehabilitative effort.

I don't want to give the impression in talking about Zumwalt that I think the Commanders in Chief should always have their recommendations accepted. Something might be wrong if all of them are not accepted, and there would be something wrong if they were all accepted. They should always be queried and they should always be listened to. It was in the area of not being listened to, where the Commanders in Chief were responsible and in areas where they were cognizant, where they had experience--that was the part that undermined authority.

There is the matter of Fleet organization and flag ships, and I am going to have to be general to keep it reasonably short. I could write a book on it. I agreed with Bud Zumwalt, before I went to Norfolk, that we could streamline the Fleet. I knew it pretty well, I knew that we could reduce some CruDesFlot Commanders and some CarDiv Commanders and I knew we could cut some staffs afloat and some that were shore based. I knew we could cut some air station staffs. I was also very aware from my Washington experience, that the whole Navy was under heavy pressure from Congress to cut staffs and to cut flag officers. This is a favorite whipping-boy, especially of the demagogues in Congress. Not the best ones, they are our saviors, but others make a speech to "cut the Navy Admirals" for the hometown news. This was a never-ending thing. Now actually the Navy had studied this flag officer thing and had been under fire for years. I had been in the midst of it.

The Navy had certain needs and the Navy convinced some of the top officials such as Chairman Mendel Rivers and Chairman Stennis. Even Mr. McNamara.

However, I am advised that Bud Zumwalt and John Warner, and now I am speculating that it was to curry favor, volunteered to cut about fifteen flag officers out of the Navy. Later even more were cut. In any event I was aware that the Navy was under pressure to cut and it always will be.

I had lived with Fleet organization a long time, I had been in the Fleet organization and knew a great deal about it. I had joined the fleet in 1933 when we had none of the organization that we went through WWII with. We had then only one Type Commander--the Commander of the Submarine Force. The rest of the Fleet was divided into Battle Force, Scouting Force, and the Train, it was that simple. Destroyers, aircraft, carriers and battleships were divided into Destroyers Battle Force and Destroyers Scouting Force, etc. That did not work for war and the Navy set up individual "Type" commands. However, there were places to trim, we had too many echelons and we knew it. Some of the following is hearsay. I understood that the most extreme examples of proposals I did not like and that made me fearful came from Worth Bagley and his then Op 090 shop, I think he had become Vice Admiral at that time. A proposal came out that we do away with all flagships afloat. Here was the CNO and OP 090 with never a real Task Force command under them, no numbered Fleet command, never a C in C, saying to Commanders in Chief that no flagships are needed. In the Atlantic, on the other hand, I had been Second Fleet and NATO Striking Fleet Commander. I felt I needed to get out in my flagship and run as many as four Task Groups under me. In NATO there was the NATO Striking Fleet, they went to sea with British carriers, Dutch carriers and U.S. carriers, up to the North Sea. I felt they had to have a flagship, and if the U.S. did not I will assure you the NATO council would have appointed another nation to provide the flag officer. Apparently Zumwalt and Bagley did not believe an Admiral needed to be at sea. They proposed that a Commander on shore could make all the necessary decisions.

Q: I think you communicate better too?

Adm. D.: I was going to come to that. I mentioned earlier that the Commander Second Fleet was also Commander, Joint Task Force 122. CJTF122 had under them Army, Air Force and Navy units. It needed a sophisticated communication and "command and control" ship. The cruisers we had were not the best, not by far, but they were the best we had. The new idea I was told, was that

Admiral Bagley felt that you could command from the shore just as well as you could from the sea. We did have some new techniques, many no longer secret where, from a protected headquarters, if it weren't obliterated or sabotaged or the power didn't go off or if there wasn't a strike, you could tell a great deal about a Task Force maybe a thousand miles away. There will always be a man on the spot in any sea operation, he can be from Lieutenant to Vice Admiral. It should therefore be an experienced man with facilities under his control, at his beck and call, to run the operation. There should be some experienced officer who is going to take command. A destroyer could ram a carrier. A plane could crash land at sea. A decision must be made immediately as to whether to stop the ship and take the risk of being torpedoed while picking up the men. Do we send the helicopter, is it too rough, is it too dark--these are decisions that must be made afloat. They are going to be made afloat and I want the most experienced man in the best flagship to make them. The reports I got from Washington were that Bagley said they could be made either from CinCLant Fleet Headquarters in Norfolk, or even from the Pentagon that we could do away with all operational commands everywhere as everything could be run from the Pentagon. There was a proposal in writing, that we shift all at sea operational command to CinCLant Fleet Headquarters in Norfolk. If I didn't know as much about that headquarters as anybody, I should have been relieved.

Neither of these men had ever commanded a great force at sea. There were some tantalizing new techniques. I assume that this is what got to them. The scientists would tell them they could see when a plane takes off, see when it returns to the carrier, and if wanted, Washington could tell the plane to turn right or left. You don't run complex modern warfare that way. You can see I was truly frustrated when this sort of thing started coming down the line.

We also got proposals of lesser magnitude. I acceded to some because I felt it was better to live to fight another day than to quit. In cases not so important all I could do was to put in my recommendation, based on my experience of having watched the evolution of the Fleet, not only in its organizational sense but in its modern complexity sense. I knew we had a new and revolutionary Fleet, I also knew organizations that broke down under the stress of war, I had lived through them. This did not matter in Washington as experience was discounted. So I accepted some decisions, some did not come in until I had left. They have now combined the three surface Type Commands into a Surface Force. I cannot say this is all bad. It seems to be working fairly well. Eventually I can predict, from my knowledge and experience, that the Amphibious Force will be submerged and that we will lose a considerable degree of knowledge and expertise. Just as the Mine Force was done away with in the Pacific after WWII, we have no Mine Force now. We will lose expertise and we are going to learn the hard way that we should have a Mine Force.

Q: There won't be time?

Adm. D.: These sorts of arguments got nowhere. They said you can have a mine section on your staff. We had a mine section before and as you know in the Korean War we were caught flat on our backs and could not even get into a critical Korean harbor. The same thing in amphibious warfare. I will not say however, that the Surface Force will not work. They retained at least three Type Commandes--the Air, the Subs, and the Surface. With good leaders and a good try they can weld a Surface Force into a good strong community, I hope.

There was even talk of eliminating the Air Type Command and combining it with the Second Fleet, which is ludicrous. The Naval Air Force Atlantic has a tremendous materiel job. I don't think there is any use of me going into this in detail in trying to fight these problems, they are sort of over. I will tell you the details of one.

It was suggested but it never took place on my watch. I don't think I would have retired over it but I sure would have thought awfully hard about it, and made many personal trips to see Zumwalt. As I have described to you, the Second Fleet has three responsibilities, widely varied, very important. Regardless of the three command combination Bud moved the Commands ashore and combined them with the Anti-Submarine Warfare Commander, another Vice Admiral and thereby, on paper, saved a few dollars. In contrast, I wanted to emphasize the Anti-Submarine Warfare Force, I didn't want them combined with anything. Anti-submarine warfare was my major problem, but I did have these other problems of carrier strikes, of joint action and of NATO action. I needed a senior commander afloat, and I needed a much better flagship, not to have the flagship taken away. They have moved the Second Fleet Commander ashore, combined his job with Anti-Submarine Warfare forces. This came out of Washington. Not one of these ideas stemmed from any operating echelon in the Fleet. That particular one was pretty much decided but was not in effect when I left, the decision had not even been formally made but I knew which way it was going. It has been in effect now ever since I retired. I cannot comment on how it works, it can only be tested by war. But I believe if the Second Fleet Commander needs to be off the Norwegian Sea with five carriers of many nations, he cannot at the same time be in Norfolk and run the pole-to-pole anti-submarine warfare of the fleet. I believe I will be proved right on this in time. ASW would be combined with the C in C's staff as a Deputy for ASW, though I don't believe it is the best system.

I do not believe Worth Bagley and Bud Zumwalt knew what they were talking about. That is a hard thing to say about your seniors, both of whose talents I admired. I admired Worth Bagley's mind so much that I tried to get him into BuPers as Asst. Chief of Personnel (Pers A) before Bud was announced as CNO. He was a very bright person. He just simply skipped all the steps through the ranks, as did Bud Zumwalt.

This Fleet reorganization proposal was very hard for me to accept and I was not listened to. I don't recall whether I got any replies to my messages.

I meant to say earlier that I believe in brain-storming. I do not believe in just following routine suggestions. I used to try to practice it on the staff and I believe in a no-holds-barred discussion with really wild ideas. That is the way you get new ideas on doing things. I don't want to leave an impression in this interview that I was a "status quo" man--I definitely was not. But I could not ignore recent factual experience. I wasn't talking about WWII. I was talking about exercise Strong Express which happened in 1972, with the most modern equipment available to any nation. This was not any attempt to maintain the status quo. I don't care a whit for the status quo with one possible exception--be very cautious and deliberate in changing certain aspects of organization that can affect the morale of the men. But that has nothing to do with what we are talking about. We are talking about operational things.

I had told you previously that I made a point of going on all possible Fleet operations, and neither of these senior officers giving me these suggested orders had been on a major Fleet operation with modern equipment. Neither of them had been in the Atlantic as a flag officer, and yet the Fleet C in C was not listened to. Had they instituted certain changes which I felt would markedly have hurt readiness of the Fleet I would have had the moral integrity to quit. I felt that I could best serve the Navy by fighting. I didn't know who was going to succeed me at that time. There were a large number of officers who agreed with me. There were many officers who had served in the Fleet who knew that I knew what I was talking about in my comments to Washington. Many of the messages I worked on personally. Some I let the staff work on and I only collaborated. The staff saw every word I wrote to Zumwalt. They knew they had access to my office and they knew that I was not just trying to maintain the status of the fleet as it was. One thing I wanted to be sure of was not to try to maintain the status quo. The status quo was absolutely nothing like the Navy I had entered, it has changed ever since I came into it. But I could not accept some of these drastic proposals such as "there need be no controlling command except Norfolk", or "there need be no operational command Headquarters, except the Pentagon, etc.", which I think borders on the ridiculous. That, incidentally, was not done and will not be done. We are not the Strategic Air Command, which is quite a different proposition.

You can imagine the consternation of the Fleet, and my own personal frustration, perhaps more than any of my staff's. I tried to encourage my staff to speak freely. I hope they did and as far as I know, they did. I did not want to send out a message from CinCLantFlt in which there were serious disagreements, so I routed them around for comments before sending them out. Admittedly, they did contain a lot of my ideas because I felt very strongly on certain issues because I had had considerable actual experience and I thought I was well qualified. I was open to any one coming up and questioning me on any particular facet.

You can see that there was considerable frustration. To give you an illustration about Bud Zumwalt and how little he knew about NATO: As CNO Bud went on a familiarization trip to Norway, which I know very well, having been on many trips there and I know most high ranking Norwegian officers. My aide in SACLant was a Norwegian. When Zumwalt returned from his trip he made certain appraisals and opinions which were not accurate, there was nothing very wrong, they were just opinions. He didn't say they were accurate only that he thought so and so. He sent out a personal message asking for opinions on his views with the idea of keeping Norway, as he put it, from going the route of Finland and on how the U.S. Navy could get some military infrastructure built in Norway. This is a good illustration. This was a personal message from Zumwalt, after a personal trip by Zumwalt, and he sent the message for comment to officers who were very capable and very experienced and very smart, and none of them had anything to do with military infrastructure in Norway. He sent it to Admiral Rivero in Naples, the Commander in Chief of the Allied Forces South, who reported to Andy Goodpaster as SACEur, and he sent it to Admiral Bringle who was the U.S.-Component Commander of the U.S. CinCEUR, who had something to do with Norway in his U.S. Navy hat but had nothing to do with infrastructure in Norway.

Admiral Zumwalt had a U.S. Commander to call on about Norway, namely Commander in Chief of the Atlantic Fleet, wearing three hats. In the NATO SACLant hat, I had on my desk a list of the approved Norwegian Military NATO infrastructure items. We kept the approved list, SACLant initiated every item. I, and my predecessors, through NATO had built two airfields, an ammunition depot, some classified things and upgraded command posts, because we were the only ones--we SACLant--in a position to do it. I was the only one authorized to submit to the NATO Council a proposal for NATO to spend money on Navy facilities in Norway.

I won't go into great detail on how that is done. Naturally you go to Norway and you convince Norwegians and NATO officials of the need. Admiral Zumwalt knew so little about NATO that he did not know he had a U.S. Navy officer who could initiate any reasonable infrastructure project in Norway, who had permission to operate aircraft out of Norway on anti-submarine warfare missions without permission of anyone, including the CNO or the Joint Chiefs of Staff. SACLant/CinCLantFlt could send U.S. planes to operate out of Norwegian airfields and I could improve Norwegian airfields, and Admiral Zumwalt didn't even know it. He didn't know he had a subordinate U.S. Naval officer who had the power to propose to build a new airfield in Norway. Bud wanted to put some money into Norway and build up the military potential. So he sent the message to two people who had no power to initiate any project in Norway.

I give you this as a rather harsh example. The only reason I knew about it was because one of my SACLant staff officers was buzzing around up in Washington and saw a copy of the message and was horrified. A subordinate OpNav officer then sent it down to me and said that they would like me to comment also. That is the only way we ever found out the news--by one of my staff officers rummaging around.

Q: You say that there were in-staff problems? They should have been cognizant of...

Adm. D.: They had in-staff problems. They had people in OpNav who knew Bud had some awfully good people in OpNav whom I knew were knowledgeable, but were they the people who worked up the dispatch? It did wind up later on their desk and they should have corrected it or done something. But it was the "in group" that travelled with him. He had an executive assistant and several personal staff who did all of these things. He did not use Op 06 (Plans and Policy) in this sense. He did use Op 06 and he used them well on JCS matters. On a personal idea such as this, he had made the trip and he knew more than anyone. He had talked to Norwegians, he personally wrote the message, and sent it out through this small staff (and this is supposition now on my part) who did not know much about the Atlantic or about NATO. They probably had never been to a NATO meeting. As CNO Bud was not eligible to go to a NATO meeting. No head of Service is eligible to go. The Chairman of the JCS goes to all meetings representing the U.S. military. Bud, as CNO, did not ever attend the "Shapex" at SACEur's headquarters during my tour, but he may have gone later. CNO's were invited to that and most European heads of Navies attended. It is the Command Post Exercise run by the Supreme Allied Commander in Europe.

This was the sort of thing that was really quite discouraging. There was no use in my running up to Bud saying, "Look here, why don't you send your messages to the right people?" What I did was to send back and politely say that "naturally you would ask experienced and wise officers their opinions". I said that the NATO Norway intrastructure list was as follows, I wrote it out by number with a completion date and asked him if there were any others he wanted me to submit to the NATO council. I said I frankly did not understand why he didn't ask me in the first place. I never got an answer.

This lack of awareness was pretty hard to live with. He had the right people to advise him and he trusted them and he could have used them.

Another example of what I am talking about--in my fitness reports (and I say with appreciation that Bud gave me very fine U.S. Navy job fitness reports) he never mentioned that I was the Supreme Allied Commander of the Atlantic. Most CNO's would have been proud that the U.S. Navy had the job. I was doing a good job. I had been commended by a couple of countries. I had been commended by the headquarters in Brussels. I had two European decorations. He didn't even deign to notice in the fitness report that I was the Supreme Allied Commander Atlantic. There is nothing in my record that indicates this, except in my original orders that I report for additional duties as SACLant. In the NATO circles they do not make fitness reports on Supreme Commanders--in a sense, there is no superior commander to make it. There is a Committee and there is a Chairman and I suppose he could sign it but he doesn't. I think he is well advised to stay out of national fitness reports. But this is just an evidence of a blank spot--since the CNO was so engrossed in other things-- he didn't have time to fill in the gaps and he didn't trust those who did know. He really didn't realize how much he didn't know.

It was a fair statement, I think, to say he trusted only close advisors. He took some of the group with him when he ran for Senator against Senator Byrd. They were so ingrown and self-centered that they helped Bud convince himself that in rural Virginia a Zumwalt would be preferred over a Virginian Byrd. This political experience is a very good example of a bright man successful in one field one time extrapolating that to a new situation.

Q: They retired to private life too, didn't they?

Adm. D.: Yes. I don't want to go into names but two or three of them went with him on his Virginia effort to be Senator--I know two because I talked with them.

I want to say that I wasn't bitter about the situation. I was sad that I couldn't break through that barrier. I knew that if I got on a plane and went to see Bud, he would say, "Well, gee, I shouldn't have done it, you are right". He would have been courteous and would have invited me to lunch and everything would have been fine. I was sad because it was a recurring thing and I couldn't seem to lick it.

One other important issue, on which I don't think the Atlantic Fleet was given proper weight was on the matter of base closures. As the budget became tighter in '70, '71, and '72 it became obvious that we had to close some shore bases. A very few were not badly needed and we had others that were very good but they would have to go or else we would have to reduce a comparable number of Fleet combat units in order to save the same amount of money. Therefore, each Commander-in-Chief was required to list every shore facility in the Atlantic area in order of priority for closure. Now that is a tough job and maybe I would have done the same thing say to the Commander-in-Chief, "what is your first to go and your last to go". This results in a very revealing document and it was fought all through the staff. I did not say a word to my staff until it reached me, I changed some things but I didn't influence them during the formative stage. I wanted to see what they came up with. It was a tough job.

Now I have already discussed the Philadelphia Shipyard in which I was over-ruled. I wanted to close some shore facilities. Some were no good. In other cases I wanted the base but I didn't want to give up any fleet forces--I wanted to save my forces. I had to give up something so I had to give my bases up. My list was not followed, in fact my recommendation was ignored in certain aspects, and the reasoning--the point is rather interesting considering the CNO's experience in the Atlantic, and mine. I wanted to keep Newport, Rhode Island open for destroyers and for some Service Force types as an operating base for several reasons, which I thought were very sound. From my long experience starting with operating the convoy escorts up in Portland, Maine--we talked earlier about the convoy system. The area around Newport is great for basing some portion of destroyers. In Newport there are destroyers, in New London there are submarines, and in Brunswick, Maine we had the land-based aircraft--in other words, we had in one small area the triad for ASW. They could get together easily and exercise, they could have conferences and then discuss them, they could make a good strong team. I forgot to mention a carrier base (ASW aircraft) was over at Quonset, Rhode Island, which was also closed down. So, of the triad, they took out the destroyers and the carrier base--I must admit that the aircraft carrier base was going to go anyway, but not at that time. One of my first reasons for trying to keep Newport was the anti-submarine warfare triad up on the great circle route. Next, the base complex itself--Newport-- had easy access to the great circle route to Europe where our convoys went. It doesn't matter what war you are fighting, the great circle route stays the same. We thought that maybe we might not send the convoys through the great circle route-- we would send them through southern waters. The great circle route will always be important because it is the shortest distance for the enemy to reach the U.S. by any means, submarine, aircraft, etc. Actually all routes would be necessarily used for shipping. Newport-Boston-Quonset is practically right on the great circle route from the Norfolk area to Europe. As I described earlier, Newport-Boston was one of the first areas we expanded before WWII. We went into Boston and then to Portland, Maine before the war ever started, purely on the basis of strategic location. Newport would be a perfect anti-submarine wartime base. My third reason-- it was the only permanent home port location where ships routinely operated in rigorous weather. You have heard me before on this subject--there is a need to operate not just sporadically, but continuously or routinely in rigorous weather.

Q: You spoke about it earlier--the exercises you directed up in that area in the Gulf of Maine.

Adm. D.: There were two excuses given from OpNav--one official, and one told me orally, when I complained. The first excuse was that it would save money and they listed all the money they would save when all the destroyers and the Service Force ships left the docks at Newport. OpNav (CNO) said that this facility and that facility would close when the ships left as they would not be needed. I thought the figures were suspect. Navy had the War College there, the Chaplains' school Waves' school, Nurses' school, Officer Candidate School, several enlisted schools, the law school-- there was a quite a complex in Newport and it is now called the Naval Education Training Center. I suspect that there are more people on the Newport base today than there were when this action was taken. I doubt anything has been closed. My staff analyzed the proposal and figured there would be no savings. In fact it would be an expense because we had to order out three or four squadrons of ships, with dependents, and transfer dependents and household effects to Norfolk, Charleston and Mayport, where the destroyers were to be scattered. We thought there was an overall expense but our arguments were simply not listened to. Bud Zumwalt later told me that he didn't like Newport because of the way Newport used the Navy. Now I do not know exactly what he means by "Used"--whether he was there at one time and had a bad experience or whether he felt they sort of existed on the Navy. The Navy was certainly an economic factor in Newport, there is no question about that. As I observed as a senior officer there from 1964-65, they treated the destroyers in fine fashion. They ran a YMCA for them. They got people to convert garages for residences, heated them, and helped to house the men because of the housing problem at that time. I thought that destroyers were treated very well.

Q: Didn't he blink at the necessity of training in the northern waters?

Adm. D.: No answer, no reaction on the training in the northern waters. I think the inference was that he could crank up an exercise and send them up there. I thought it was valuable to have two inches of ice on the deck in the morning occasionally. It was a rigorous area and I wasn't trying to punish people--in fact they liked Newport. It was tough operating out of Newport at times, but the ships got out to sea in about two minutes. It was easy to get in and out and it was near the exercise area. But the fact is, except for the mobile Fleet units (the fleet units that were pulled out) I don't think they have reduced the base. I have been up there each year since. I did not of course, analyze the base and so I cannot tell you how many people were there.

Although it was not a major item I also considered that it was nice to have Fleet operating units adjacent to the Naval War College, the Officer Candidate School and the various other schools. The War College was a good contact for the ship officer candidates got to come aboard a ship.

Another far-fetched reason, though I do not believe it, someone suggested it might have been a swipe at former Secretary Chafee who had gone by the time it was executed.

There certainly was politics concerning the Boston yard vs. the Philadelphia yard. A lot of facilities had been pulled out of the northeast. This was administration politics and I won't go into that. But politics was not responsible for moving these mobile Fleet units--that was entirely the CNO-OpNav idea.

Another area where the CNO took a path opposite to the Commander in Chief's recommendation was the importance of shore vs. sea command and which were the really important ones to have. The Navy for some years had rightly been upgrading the importance of Washington duty. I still believe that no senior officer should arrive at high position and responsibility without Washington service. Officers many times avoided Washington. As typified by Admiral Worth Bagley being brought in by Admiral Zumwalt with two stars in the Pacific and advancing to four stars at forty-nine years of age, without ever leaving Washington, Bud perhaps over emphasized the duty in Washington to a considerable extent. Bud seemed to consider sea duty an unnecessary qualification for higher grades.

Concurrently, it was true that large, complex, expensive shore stations, such as airfields, were being poorly managed. I am not picking on airfields, large shore bases in general were being poorly managed and poorly run. By and large they were at that time commanded by officers who could not get a sea command. That doesn't mean they weren't good officers or very suited to their job--they just did not happen to meet the competition for the sea command. They may have in some respect been superior to others for the job--but many times felt their career was over and lacked enthusiasm and drive for their work.

Q: The sea commands were limited?

Adm. D.: They were limited, and now of course, getting more so. Also, the staffs on these shore jobs had a substantial number of people on what they called the twilight tour-- their final tour of duty. They were going to retire and there is no question but that a certain psychological effect sets in there where they are looking to the outside perhaps more than to the inside. In fact, I guess the Navy was saying these shore commands aren't as important as Fleet commands. This just happens to be true.

It is also true that the office of the Secretary of Defense and the General Accounting Office were giving the Navy fits about poor management and budgeting. Now if this situation had to be fixed drastically and quickly, Zumwalt did it as best as could be done and he did it in the right way--changed it drastically. He frequently did move in very drastic and very positive steps. He personally took the major sea command list, which is a selection board process in the Bureau, and assigned the number one aviator captain on the list for command at sea, to command an air station. Bud assigned the captain to Roosevelt Roads as his major command. The officer got no other major command. Naturally that station improved, he was a fine officer. And naturally the officer was selected for flag rank, he was number one on this sea command list, he was a high performer. But, this officer having gone from shore duty to command ashore at Roosevelt Roads, then went back to the Pentagon for two years more shore duty as a flag officer. So the officer eventually appears at sea after maybe four to five years ashore, as a two-year experienced flag officer but really he was not completely up to speed as to what was going on at sea. This particular officer was a smart officer and he learned quickly, but things change in four years. We had new equipment and we had new ways of operating it. This illustrates my contention that, no matter how smart this officer was, he could not initially have fought his task group effectively in combat. What is more serious in the long run, I thought that I detected among the officers in the Navy that indeed, command of shore stations was just as important as command at sea. The move did accomplish Bud's goal of illustrating that an officer can be promoted to Rear Admiral from a shore station.

Just before I left CinCLantFlt I put in my periodic personal letter to all CO's, my own views on the importance of command at sea. I have here a copy if you wish to attach it to this. It is my last memo as Commander in Chief and I felt compelled to do it to remind the upcoming young officers that, in the final analysis, the Navy only exists to fight at sea.

Another aspect of Zumwalt's actions that I found distressing was his treatment of certain superb Navy officers. You may have heard about these, perhaps in more accurate terms. These circumstances are well known in the Navy and they are distressing to most. There is no question but that the CNO took, or allowed to be taken, actions which drove Vice Admiral Jim Calvert to retire. Jim Calvert is, in my opinion, one of the most outstanding naval officers I have ever known--certainly one of the really outstanding ones of our times. He would have made a terrific CNO and I expected him to be one. He was a contemporary of Bud's. However, when he was commander of the First Fleet in the Pacific, about 1971-72, he was harassed by Washington-- I don't mean by Bud Zumwalt personally--I mean by one of CNO's subordinates, calling Jim on the phone and offering him first one job and then another. Offering him a job that might not be too bad--a three star job, and then calling him the next day and saying no, that job is not available. I know this to be a fact. He was not offered command of the Third Fleet. He thought was going to have the Third Fleet and was led to believe he was going to have the Third Fleet, which is a combination of the old First Fleet and the Anti-Submarine Warfare Command, but it was given to another officer whose name escapes me now. Calvert told me he had been orally promised the command and was not given it. He was then offered a sequence of jobs, some good and some bad, and they would call him a day or two later to say they weren't available. He was literally harassed. He submitted his resignation, which I think was intended by the people concerned. I think the CNO allowed this to go on and I don't know the reason for that. It became obvious to Jim Calvert. He told me on the phone he was not in line for four stars and was pretty much told by a senior Washington officer that he was not in line for any future promotion or any future upward movement in the Navy.

Q: What about Johnny Hyland?

Adm. D.: I do not know and have not spoken with Johnny Hyland about this matter. After Jim's resignation had come in, Secretary of the Navy John Warner got in the act. He probably should have been in it earlier. I am reliably advised that Secretary Warner called Jim and intimated to Jim that he could get the four stars. There is some question as to whether John could have delivered. How embarrassing--the resignation was lying there in Washington and everybody knew it.

There are some people who say that Bud didn't want the competition. I don't believe this because he thrived on competition, it stimulated him. He liked the Service competition and he liked the Congressional competition. It is true that when Bud was being relieved, and I know this to be a fact, he was pushing Worth Bagley hard to be his relief as the Chief of Naval Operations. Perhaps as Worth Bagley's brother was Chief of Personnel, you could establish some sort of a plausible scheme of getting rid of competition. I personally do not believe it had anything to do with competition. I don't think it was a scheme--I think it was blundering, inattention, unawareness of people's feelings, and, of course, not as high a regard for Jim Calvert as most have. It is quite obvious that the Chief of Personnel at that time did not have a high regard for Admiral Calvert. Calvert was driven to retire because of the way he was being treated. Ray Peet was another bright and capable officer, who I believe should have been a four star officer.

Peet was working for OSD and Sec.Def. Schlesinger thought highly of him. He was in an important three star billet. He was given the same treatment--seemed to have no future, job running out there, so he put in his retirement papers. Then, after orders for his move were all ready, I am told that Schlesinger said Peet could get four stars. I don't know whether Schlesinger could have delivered either. In each case, the civilian Secretary didn't recognize until too late what he was losing and I believe he was incapable of stopping the show at that particular time. Nevertheless, two of our really outstanding officers felt they had to retire.

The list of items involving the Fleet Commander in Chief and the CNO, Admiral Zumwalt, would be unending. I am sure you don't want me to recite every one and I shall not. The type of action of great concern, in addition to the ones already noted, was illustrated by Zumwalt's determination to put civilian technicians as a permanent part of manning new high-technology vessels, rather than to educate and pay officers to do this work. To put civilians in combat ships' crews will not work!

Q: Is it legal?

Adm. D.: It is either legal or can be made legal. We used technicians on new equipment as trouble shooters. The Fleet called for them and they would fly down from wherever to trouble shoot. Then we would teach our own petty officers. We would send men to the factory to be trained. Bud proposed, since we were having terrible problems in manning ships and air squadrons with technicians, that the solution would be to hire the civilian technician. My solution would be to make the best petty officer technician an officer and pay him. If necessary, make a new title--Technician Specialist-- and pay them twenty or thirty thousand a year; but not put a civilian on a warship who is going to keep exact track of his working hours, who can quit on any trip he so desires. He could strike. I think it is a poor idea and I think he will regret it, if he pursued it. I just don't think it will work, and incidentally it did not work. It never went through while I was still on active duty--I guess he had enough opposition. This example is typical.

Bud put out an order, for example, to institute at once on all ships, a six section watch for the ship's crews. That means standing duty one day out of six onboard when you are in port, that is overnight--after working hours. Nothing we would have liked better. I have a memorandum here that is a little ancient history. We had talked of this proposal for years. As Commander Amphibious Force I put out an order to given it a try and to make a report on how it went. I happen to have one of the Squadron Commander's reports with me. The report made to me back in 1966 was they could not do it unless the Navy would change the personnel situation drastically, over man the ships, and get the proper technical men on board to run them. They simply did not or could not get enough engineers to afford to stand only one day's duty out of six.

Some ships could manage to go to one out of four, One out of three was the best most could do. All these ships tried as this was a big morale factor. It also caused great inequalities because, while certain ratings were full up and could go to the six section watch, others could not. We also tried (this is long before Zumwalt suggested it) cross training--training the storekeeper, of which we had plenty, to stand the engineroom watch. But in nuclear power we could hardly get enough nuclear trained people to put the ships to sea. Even the CNO could not order nuclear powered ships to reduce the required number of qualified people on board.

Q: You were desperate?

Adm. D.: We were desperate for normal demands and the CNO said to put crews on a six section watch in port. The nuclear plant runs in port, it requires qualified reactor operators on board in port. So this sort of order, as if no one at sea knew anything, was a little disturbing. Incidentally it was not done--people tried, we had tried already. Perhaps later when the personnel situation changed, it was done. I told Bud orally because I didn't want to put it in a written message, that he would have to change the basis on which we were manned and to go to the Congress and explain this. We have always thought that one day's duty in three was too much, particularly with our long deployments. This was typical of not listening to experienced advisers, putting out orders and catering to the civilians--it sounded awfully good in the newspapers.

Bud was determined to spend a lot of money, we thought unnecessarily. Here is another example Bud wished to see if in the U.S. Navy we could man a lot of our auxiliary supply ships, such as oilers, with civilian crews. He set up a big program to test this out to see if it would really work. In my message to him, I pointed out that the British had done it for over a century and they could give us very good advice on the pros and cons. We had and could observe them doing it. Many U.S. Navy officers had been in formation with them, as I was sure he had. The British could give us advice on whether they were going to continue the practice. They could give us advice on the savings and how it works, and we could determine the pros and cons from that and spare the whole expense of our testing. That dispatch was never answered. Actually the pros and cons are evident. The decision could go either way-- you do save some money, there is no question. Of course, sometimes the civilian crews get obstreperous and say they won't work after four o'clock or they go on strike entirely and won't go to sea. Almost every one of us of my age has had destroyers fueled and supplied from civilian manned U.S. merchantmen in WWII, usually in port, not so much at sea, although I have done it at sea. It will work and it would work, especially if we had adopted it as a way to go. It didn't work very well as a part time thing because they were so uncooperative. My main point is, he insisted on spending the money although the British could give him a hundred years' experience. Their entire auxiliary fleet, their oilers, supply ships, etc., were

Duncan #19 -1908-

civilian manned. There were some troubles--when the merchant seamen went ashore in a foreign port, they would get out of hand and would not conform to naval discipline. That is a minor point, as I say, there are pros and cons to this. Maybe the ship wouldn't sail at all. On the other hand the Navy could save some money because you don't have a lot of complex equipment aboard and you probably don't have a self-defense ship which is darned expensive. This is an arguable project. What is bad is that CNO refused to recognize what had been going on and insisted on continuing an expensive experiment. The Navy has some civilian manned auxiliaries now, going well as far as I know.

Q: Do you think he ever saw your dispatch?

Adm. D.: It is inconceivable to me that he didn't know the British did it. It is also inconceivable to me, knowing him, that he didn't talk to the British about it. There was something back of this that I never learned--I think it could have been another grandstand play. It got into the press about how much money Navy was going to save. I don't know whether my message ever got to him on that.

I am just reciting some examples that gave me concern. Zumwalt had a real concern for people; really basic. I have given you examples. Then he would take contrary action on such items as keeping the Philadelphia shipyard instead of the Boston yard. He consented to move the Bureau of Personnel (theoretically the BuPers being the most important ingre-

---
The typist inadvertently gave two pages the same number. The following page is also 1908.

dient in the navy--everybody says it) to New Orleans, and that was cancelled only after Bud left office. Another case of him being wrong, doing something against people.

Q: To the great consternation.

Adm. D.: I think I know why he did it. It was because the Chairman of the House Armed Services Committee asked him to do it. But you don't have to do everything Congress asks you to do. It was ridiculous. Personnel is most important and Personnel people didn't like being put down in New Orleans. The Navy did not grow that way. This attempt to move BuPers was nothing new. SecDef's office and Congress would tell us that the Air Force Personnel is in San Antonio. That is quite different, it is almost a home to the Air Force. New Orleans isn't a home to anything in the Navy. We always felt Personnel should be at the seat of government. All of our officers think that way. But here was one of our foremost Personnel men moving the Personnel function far away.

Another example: Admiral Zumwalt sent out some officer's anonymous, intemperate letter for all of us to read at the Commander in Chief level. I believe he went below that level but the Commanders in Chief were the main addressees to do something about the complaints in this officer's letter. As to the complaints--some were good and some were absolutely inane. This officer claimed he had been at sea three years and that there was so much paper work to do he never had time to read Fleet, Type, or numbered Fleet instructions--that he had never opened them, and this was obviously a lie. We didn't get the name of the officer. So, a four star officer had to start a study, and make a reply to CNO based on an officer's letter which hadn't been dignified with his signature. It was humiliating to the Navy to do this. I don't understand the CNO putting this out. I don't know of any other CNO who would have put it out. Maybe this officer was very junior. It looked as though the junior officer's opinion was worth more than any advice he could get from his Commanders in Chief. Maybe some of CNO's younger staff put him up to it.

He also had a propensity to make grandstand plays to the press and Congress at the expense of ship Commanding Officers. Possibly he was thinking of the future; I don't know his motivation. Frequently he intimated to the press that he was going to defend the men against their Commanding Officers. This went over well with the Washington press.

Now this sounds as though I don't have anything to praise and that I have quite a bit to gripe about and to criticize. My critical comments, if they are that, are in the specific field of CNO's relations with his Commander in Chiefs who should have been his closest confidants. If the C in Cs were not, he should have fired all and gotten people whom he trusted to carry out his desires. Then he could just have called us on the phone about this officer's letter and said, "Do it." and it would have been all right. He was speaking to Commanders in Chief who had had considerably more experience at sea than he, but he did not listen to them-- at least not to me. I don't know whether he listened to Chick

Clarey or not. When you interview him you might ask.

In summarizing, I feel that Zumwalt represented the greatest waste of talent that I have seen in the Navy. As I have already mentioned, with extensive experience afloat and in charge of sea operations, he could probably have been the most outstanding Chief of Naval Operations since King. He had the brains and the perception. He was always courteous, even solicitous, directly to me. I bear him absolutely no hard feelings. That would be ridiculous because I would never have had the chance to be CinCLant Fleet had it not been for Bud Zumwalt. Due to the force of circumstances, I consider that the Navy wasted a great talent. Properly brought up, and when I say "brought up" I mean having taken the proper preparatory steps--I don't care at what age, he would have been the greatest CNO. I sincerely believe that and I hope that if he sees this record he knows that my remarks are not a personal thing, it is a Commander in Chief's objective view of what went on. I consider him a friend today. I attribute the greatest importance, as I have already intimated, to the insidious effect of the tight "court clique" which surrounded him. I cannot believe that he knew how it worked because it was the opposite of his nature as I knew him as a younger officer, to isolate himself--but yet his staff succeeded. They kept him from being a much better CNO.

Zumwalt did a lot of good. I haven't recited the good he did because it has been recited elsewhere. One of the greatest goods he did was teaching the Navy that change is possible and that change is necessary. We have to keep abreast of society and we have to know what goes on and acknowledge it, we can't retreat into an isolated Navy which lives entirely separately from society. I think Bud did convince the Navy that there were more ways than one to do things, and he instituted a lot of practices that are going on today that made the Navy better. I hope in the final analysis on Bud that the Navy has learned a lesson that is peculiar to the Navy--it doesn't apply as much to the Army--that the Navy cannot stand many brilliant, energetic CNO's, who haven't had the necessary experience. We must start accelerating stars such as he was, very early. Give these "stars" their chance at all the really important rungs of the ladder, the Washington duty, the Task Force, the ship command, give them all of this while they are younger and then they can be the Commander in Chief at age forty or forty-two years with all the steps covered. These people who are real stars and who show it early must be very tightly career managed.

Q: Is this contrary to BuPers policy?

Adm. D.: As I have mentioned earlier, there has been an evolution in getting younger people at all. We have not yet gotten the forty-two year old who also had the extensive experience at sea with three stars, but we have had a fifty year old who hadn't had those steps. We had Jimmy Holloway who was about fifty-three when he became CNO. Holloway had had the Seventh Fleet, been the Deputy CinCLantFlt, and VCNO before becoming

CNO, so we're getting there. The practice is somewhat resented by some. There might be an inclination to think we are running the Navy to career manage three or four officers who are stars and potential CNOs. The Navy must do more than that--take ten real "star" officers and out of that they might get three. In my opinion that is the way to go--that is what industry does. The other fellows who are darned good officers go along and maybe some get to be four star officers too. Maybe they are late bloomers such as Churchill was.

That completes my section on Admiral Zumwalt. Do you want me to go on with the summary?

Q: Just as you wish.

Adm. D.: I do not believe I have stressed enough the progress made in my later years in the Fleet in the material side. Not a technical man myself, I marvel at the progress made by the scientists and engineers. And it speaks well for the material side of the Navy that these new developments were made successfully operative in the Fleets. The sonar advances, the missiles, the fire control equipment, the electronics, the various sensors, the torpedoes, the highly technical aircraft. There has been a revolution in weaponry and sensors since World War II. It was a pleasure to be a part of the Fleets during these advances.

I would like now to wind up this very wonderful opportunity given me, to put my thoughts down covering a very long period of time. I have taken a long time putting them down. I would like to talk about some disappointing, negative elements about a naval career and then about the rewarding ones. In this summary I want to give my feelings about the Navy as a career. There is no priority in my recollections at all, they are just random thoughts.

One outstanding thing that is of first priority and which I come to last, is my tremendous satisfaction in my naval career. One of the disappointing aspects of naval life was that many of the Congress, much of the public, much of the civilian staff in the office of the Secretary of Defense, assume that the military are, in general, an inefficient bunch; and that neither officers nor men work very hard. I think we suffered from the traditional civilian attitudes toward the land based infantry. In past history, in early unsophisticated days, the infantry officers apparently did not have much to do between wars and engaged in sports and in an European type gentlemanly leisure existence.

Q: And they were very visible...

Adm. D.: They were highly visible. The public knew infantry units. They did not know warships. The infantry troops, when no state of war existed, after reasonable training performed very menial rote tasks and did a lot of "make-work". An infantry division, always excepting in combat, and speaking generally of peace-time, could indeed be assigned any task for a week, or a month, or a quarter. They could be put in a "training mode" for a month or they could all be sent on

leave for a month, or they could all turn to and spruce up
the base for a "visitors' day". Nothing had to be kept
running all the time. I know I have mentioned this previously.
One of my hardest tasks in personnel was to refute the
frequent allusions by OSD staffers, the General Accounting
Office and some in Congress, that the Navy had too many men,
that they did not have meaningful jobs and they did not have
enough work. I could not seem to convince them that the Fleet
was different. At sea in the Fleet, the workday never stops.
The engines ran all night, the bridge was to be manned
all night and the ship conned twenty-fours a day, seven
days a week. And training continued on top of running the
ship. We shot the guns, fired the missiles, flew the aircraft,
held all sorts of emergency drills such as fire and damage
control, battle damage, and so forth. On top of this at
sea or in port, was the incessant maintenance of electronic
and other machinery and equipment, and in some ways we could
never do enough. We were operating, on a seven day a week
basis, some of the most sophisticated, scientific units
ever built by man. We were doing this in the Fleet in a
natural, sometimes hostile, environment of the sea and the air.
Equipment became so technical and so much training was
needed to operate it properly and so much maintenance and
repairs needed to keep it running properly that it became a
de-motivating factor for some of our officers and men. They
were overworked and literally never through. It was a sharp
disappointment to me to see so many compare the Navy to an

infantry division or a civilian firehouse crew who played checkers until an emergency occurred. I know that this affected our men. This attitude was sponsored by the entertainment industry and the news media and it became a part of folk lore. "If it moves, salute it; if it doesn't, paint it", and "Drunk as a sailor". It sponsored condescending attitudes by civilians who still thought of the old days back in the 1700's of manning merchant ships by rounding up men from the waterfront saloons. While, as in any profession or work in life, we had some loafers, some drunks, and some dishonest, it was my experience and a major reward of life to be associated in the Navy with what I thought were the most dedicated, hardworking, conscientious people that I have ever seen. I think the public does not realize it. Speaking for the Navy that I know, the taxpayers are getting the biggest bargain possible for their tax dollars from the people in the Navy. Sometimes I felt that the men were tireless and selfless. There is an interest and involvement in the unit, that is, the ship, the squadron and the aircraft, that was unique. There was a concern for others assigned to the same unit. I have been fortunate in knowing many civilians during my naval career and, of course, knowing and working with many in the five years since I have been retired. While there are always those who are conscientious and overworked themselves, and many who attain brilliant accomplishments, nowhere as a group or profession have I seen the devotion to duty that I saw in the Navy, or the degree of assumption of responsibility for the organization or activities to which they belonged. In fact, I have been astounded now, in my civilian contacts, to see their relative ease of life, short working hours, the attitude among many of being the adversary of one's employer, and the general lack of reliance (comparatively speaking) that one can put on the word of a person that a specific project or assignment will be carried out.

I observed the practices of the civilian world in civic affairs, in the construction industry and in ordinary business, and I find it somewhat lacking in comparison with the Navy. I do believe some of the popular ideas of Navy life stem from the examples I have given you. Also, some navy men still see shore duty as a rest period from sea duty. It was at one time. Now, for the officer in the Pentagon, it is as hard or harder than sea duty. The family dirt farmer is the closest comparison I have ever seen to the Navy people's dedication and work. This has been one of my greatest pleasures--to have worked alongside this consistently devoted and hardworking group.

In thinking back over our discussions it would appear that I have concentrated too much on the problems of the Navy, and what went wrong. I believe the reasons for this somewhat negative or seemingly critical approach are: First, that one does spend an inordinate amount of time and energy on the problem areas. If there were no problems we would not need so many or such good people. Secondly, if this oral history is to have any value, pointing out problem areas would be the major contribution to the future.

I have had simply wonderful experiences when everything went well. The satisfaction of commanding a destroyer in combat in war, with a fine, dedicated, tireless ship's company, was immeasurable. To see these young men, cool under fire, sailing into enemy waters with about one quarter inch of steel between them and death, to watch them perform as enemy aircraft bombed them, was an inspiring experience. To go to sea as ship, division, task group, Task Force, Second Fleet Commander and as Commander in Chief, and see this whole complex mechanism of men and equipment work together was most inspiring. Even though I was relatively sophisticated in what was involved in what we were doing, it never failed to amaze me that all of this sophisticated equipment and this large number of people of a broad base of skills and talent could work together to produce such a symphony of power at sea. I had many inspiring, rewarding times, but to write of the details of these would not be helpful to the future. I have wished so often that naval officers could translate these experiences and feelings to the public. And indeed, very few have ever transmitted to their crews their admiration and appreciation of the tremendous job being done. In thinking back one of my regrets was that I did not express to those in units under me my appreciation and admiration for their performance.

To continue with a negative. I consider one of my major disappointments and one of this country's weaknesses is the fact that with rare exception the Secretary of Defense and the OSD's staff (normally called OSD or DOD) have never considered

themselves as members of the defense team of the United States--
made up of uniformed military and civilian components working
together. Even more rare was the civilian in SecDef or OSD
who considered himself as a leader of the uniformed people,
and I emphasize the word "leader". There was no loyalty,
to the military as such. I am talking now mostly of the staff
of the Secretary of Defense. They considered themselves an
adversary to the military--sent to set the military straight,
to keep them in line, not sent to play their designed role of
being the civilian link between the military and the Congress.
Obviously there were exceptions. Some of the old line civil
servants had the best attitude and the security interests of
the country at heart. Mel Laird, who had been a politician,
as Secretary of Defense, tried hard to play the proper role--
the leader of the whole Defense Department, spokesman to
Congress, etc. By contrast, we had McNamara who disliked
and disdained the military, Enthoven who said that no one
with any brains would ever be in uniform, engine Charley
Wilson's number two man, whose name I have forgotten, who
told the Generals that he was sent there to take the stars
off their shoulders. There was a great arrogance at the OSD
middle and lower levels. On the average they were relatively
young men in their thirties who had achieved little or nothing
except an academic record. Many had continued their education
until they were about thirty in order to avoid service in
Vietnam. They considered that they were hired to bring their
superior intelligence to bear on the military. They generally

spent a substantial effort selling themselves to the senior business men, lawyers and industrialists in the Department of Defense or elsewhere in Government; so that they could leave on their coat tails into a big paying job.

I mentioned earlier the practice of these young neophytes finding a budget item they could eliminate--such as enlisted mens' quarters' furniture--to gain "brownie points" with their civilian superiors. They usually left Defense, going into industry to higher paying jobs as a reward for their hatchet jobs labelled as "objective analysis", which they had performed. This adversary relationship was an unhealthy thing, it wasted manpower, caused lost efficiency and lowered morale. I hope it changes. There is more than enough for all to do, working together toward a common goal.

One of the disappointments to me as I grew up in the Fleet was the realization that many Navy material officers, in varying degrees, did not really have much sensitivity for Navy men. I could give a thousand examples. When I was in the Academy we all respected the EDO's, because usually they stood in the top ten. Similarly we respected those who stayed in the unrestricted line who became technical post graduates such as ordnance specialists and aeronautical engineers. Although there were exceptions, a common thread runs throughout--insensitivity to individuals. Our ships were, despite some criticism you may hear, really amazing in their technical aspects and in their sound construction. Yet the same people who designed and built them, built a destroyer living-compartment in the after part of the ship where it had only four openings--one to the steering engine room, one to the carpenter shop, one to the electronics work shop and one, a steel ladder with clanking steel guide chains--the only access to the after part of the ship. This was their idea of home for eighty sailors on eight month deployment, but it was typical. They air conditioned the electronic equipment spaces first and years later, the personnel spaces. They, the EDO's built the biggest and best overhaul yard on the West Coast, fifteen hundred miles from the Fleet based at San Diego.

Q: Do you mean at Bremerton?

Adm. D.: Yes at Bremerton, Washington--the site of three to twelve month overhauls. My early impression, as a bachelor Ensign, was "how silly it was to send my ship thirteen hundred miles from Long Beach to Bremerton, when all the families were in Long Beach and there were no allowances to move them to Bremerton". I could quote examples by the hundred.

Around the budget table when I was Chief of Personnel in 1969, I had a materiel minded aviation Vice Admiral argue before the Chief of Naval Operations that Navy personnel should be cut in half for two years and the money applied to buy new aircraft, and then hire a new Navy.

Q: Hire a new Navy?

Adm. D.: Yes, hire a new Navy. He was under the impression that the crews could be trained very quickly to re-man the Navy immediately.

There was rather unbelievable naivete about how people worked and what makes people work and what motivates them. This same year I had a most severe battle in the Navy in order to get a new Library for the Naval Academy because it competed for dollars needed for weapons. I have mentioned this earlier. The Naval Academy did not build a new academic building for twenty-five years. At the time I was testifying to get the new Library, it had fewer books than Andover prep school and it had one third the books of a small liberal arts college with one half the enrollment--Trinity College. It had one fortieth the books of a large university such as Yale or Notre Dame. Yet I had a tough argument getting the new Library. This is depressing. This seemingly persistent disregard for the individual by our best technical minds has confirmed in my mind that we must never have the Naval Academy all scientific major, or try to make it an MIT. We must have officers diverse interests, diverse education and diverse backgrounds. We must have officers with technical knowledge but also with knowledge of people and the humanities.

I think that throughout my discourse you will have noted troubles I have had in various jobs getting money for education, getting money for post graduate work, getting money for the associate degree program for enlisted men, etc. Tuition aid ran out in 1969 at the end of the Vietnam war. I wrote a memorandum in 1969 and I am going to leave a copy with you, which was to try to warn the Secretariat what was really coming when the Vietnam war was over--the training was going to get more expensive, not less.

One minor disappointment with the Navy, having noted the near uniform devotion to duty of Navy men, has been the lack of recognition of the expense of naval life. This applies, to some extent, both to enlisted men and civilians, as frequent moves are expensive for all, and long deployments are expensive for all. It was most recently evinced in Senator Proxmire's successful attempt to eliminate enlisted mess management personnel from senior officers' quarters in cases where they had entertainment responsibilities. But it started long before. In the 30's the barge and gig crews and the division officers personally bought the paint for the boats because not enough was issued and it wasn't good enough quality. We used our personal cars for official business year after year. The best uniforms are maintained at the expense of the family; it is always the Navy first and you want it that way. Also, to have the best command, the Commander really should entertain their staff or squadron or ship in their house. I know that this is not accepted by Congress and it is impossible to prove its necessity and some do not do it. It is not absolutely essential but the Navy is better if they do do it. It is certainly more justified than the business man's expense account yacht, apartment, executive jet and three martini lunches as far as validity goes. As Chief of Personnel I tried to have every officer above Lieutenant J.G. in my house for a reception, and all civil service above a certain level--I believe above GS12. This was expensive to me personally but I wanted them to be a team and I think it helped. I mentioned previously that I received zero allowance as Commander of the Naval Base Subic although I had visits from the President, the Cabinet, six foreign Ambassadors, and six foreign Admirals on official visits, and it practically broke us, temporarily. It is not right that officers carry the United States representational responsibility and pay for it out of their own pockets. It is not right that officers spend thirty five or more years in the service of their country and end up as a flag officer with practically no savings, yet I have seen this occur. Of course, the retirement pay given by the government helps tremendously, in fact it is a life saver.

I have given some negatives, not serious ones, just some thoughts. There are overwhelming rewards for a naval career and I have mentioned some of them. One of the things is that there are unlimited horizons if a person wants to work and is interested. There is absolutely an unlimited range of what one can be or do--become a scientist, a teacher, an engineer, a planner, and operator, a financial expert, a weapons specialist, a Presidential adviser, a space man and so forth. To cite my case, all the tremendous experience I have with people, events and position, is an example. I ended up in command of two hundred and thirty-three thousand men--the largest naval Fleet in the world. Commander of the

NATO sea forces, in serious conferences with Ambassadors, foreign Generals, Admirals and Cabinet level officers with private consultations with six heads of State, with responsibilities for the United States from the North Pole to the South Pole and for parts of the Pacific and parts of the Indian Ocean. What more could one ask? Opportunity is there to distinguish one's self in almost any field except that speculative making of a large fortune.

I do not know why we have consistently not been successful in selling the Navy as a career--it offers so much. True, we have high calibre applicants for the Naval Academy, varying from time to time, but it was very hard to interest WWII reserves in the navy life as a career. Partly perhaps the difficulty is the stereotype of the military portrayed by the press--that is, the military mind, boring assignments, and doing everything by rote. We have had the opportunity several times in the past twenty to thirty years of retaining talented OCS graduates. We retained a considerable number. Overall we have had a lot of difficulty in selling them on the tremendous opportunities they would be offered in the Navy. I believe one reason for our difficulty in the enlisted brackets was the fact that the Congress and the OSD have never really recognized the life the US sailor has to lead: uncomfortable, no privacy, no certainty, and long work hours. It isn't just money, the US Navy sailor has never been given recognition by civilians and especially by government officials for what he contributes, and the difficulty of his life compared with his civilian counterpart. There is the great enjoyment by all those I know who have completed long careers, of working with a dedicated group. The opportunity is there in the Navy for the person with a good mind, a disposition to work, and a liking for the Navy. There is no caste system, there are no court favorites. It is amazing to me that more young men do not see the challenge and the opportunity. I would trade my Navy career for no other in the world and I wish that all could know of the over-whelming reward of Navy service in the public service.

Q: I thank you very, very much. Your career has certainly been a great success.

Adm. D.: Well, people will say to me "You were successful, that is why you think it was great!"

Q: You have done honor to the Service and the Service has honored you!

Index to

Series of Taped Interviews

with

Admiral Charles K. Duncan, USN (Ret.)

Volumes III and IV

AIR FORCE, U.S.: Greater percentage of flag officers than
                 navy in the late 1960s, p. 1318; ability
                 to predict candidates for chief of staff
                 several tours in advance, p. 1319; p. 1683;
                 degree of flag experience of officers compared
                 to the Navy, p. 1388-9; policy of retiring
                 3 and 4 star generals at age 55 in the late
                 1960s, p. 1395; needs higher ratio of skilled
                 personnel to total population than other
                 services, p. 1423; availability to commander
                 of the Atlantic Fleet dictated by Joint
                 Chiefs of Staff in the early 1970s, p. 1713;

ALCOHOLISM: ashore and in the fleet in the early 1970s,
             p. 1303-5; p. 1308-10;

ANDERSON, Admiral George W., Jr., USN (USNA, 1927): regarding
                 flag officer promotion lists, p. 1323-4;
                 as chief of naval operations in the early
                 1960s involved with the question of oil
                 or nuclear power for the USS JOHN F. KENNEDY
                 (CV-67), p. 1383-4;

ANDREWS, George W.: Democratic congressman from Alabama's
                 dealings with Duncan as chairman of the
                 Personnel Subcommittee, Defense Appropriations
                 Committee in the late 1960s, p. 1414, p.
                 1451-2; p. 1458;

ANTI-BALLISTIC MISSILE (ABM): battle in Congress over
                 continuation of funding in the late 1960s,
                 p. 1424;

ANTI-MILITARY SENTIMENT: towards U.S. military exercises
                 during the Vietnam War, p. 1813-15; p. 1820-21;
                 p. 1824-25; p. 1705-06; in the Defense
                 Department in the late 1960s, p. 1298;
                 p. 1340-41; p. 1350; p. 1703-04; p. 1918;

APPROPRIATIONS COMMITTEES: process of Navy budget hearings
                 in the late 1960s, p. 1286-7; Senate committee's
                 approval needed for expenditures from "M
                 Account", p. 1445-47; publicizing deficit
                 for Fiscal Year 1969, p. 1450-51; ease with
                 which Navy budgeting could be misunderstood,
                 p. 1452-53;

ARMED SERVICES COMMITTEE: budget hearings for new entitlements
                 in the late 1960s, p. 1414; Duncan's concern
                 for most efficient management of funds
                 appropriated, p. 1452;

ARMY, U.S.: JROTC as a tool for future recruiting, p. 1275-77; a larger proportion of flag officers than Navy in late 1960s, p. 1318; differences between mobilizing Army and manning the Navy, p. 1421-22; needs lower proportion of skilled personnel than other services, p. 1423; fighting to retain anti-ballistic missiles in Congress in the late 1960s, p. 1424; Army flight training not suitable for Navy pilots, p. 1440-41; billeting according to effectiveness in influential positions, p. 1467-68; stronger interest in NATO than Navy, p. 1478; budgeting on a per-exercise basis in the early 1970s, p. 1698; availability to the commander of the Atlantic Fleet dictated by Joint Chiefs of Staff, p. 1713; continues training and educating of personnel in peace time, p. 1781;

ARMY JUNIOR RESERVE OFFICER TRAINING CORPS (JROTC): part of the Army's strategy to have strong presence in civilian life to influence future recruiting, p. 1275;

ASPIN, Les: as Democratic congressman from Wisconsin created press stir and trouble for Duncan concerning Bureau of Personnel budget for Fiscal Year 1969, p. 1451-55; p. 1459;

ATLANTIC FLEET: area responsibility derived from commander of Atlantic fleet, p. 1665-67; rough estimate of size when Duncan took command in the early 1970s, p. 1765; as second fleet as part, p. 1766; homeporting for long overhauls, p. 1766; p. 1774; use of various East Coast shipyards in the early 1970s, p. 1772-74; strain on personnel and equipment during Vietnam War, p. 1775-77; lack of preparedness due to Vietnam duty, p. 1777-78; antisubmarine warfare in the early 1970s, p. 1807-12; environmental impact affects training in the early 1970s, p. 1820-25; base closures in the early 1970s, p. 1894-98;

ATLANTIC OCEAN/ATLANTIC COMMAND AREA: crucial area for the United States and the Soviet Union, p. 1753; p. 1776-77; neglect of area possibilities for Soviets by U.S. in the early 1970s, p. 1756; p. 1787-88; 1791-92; access to by Soviets, p. 1756-57; p. 1786-87; Zumwalt and his advisors' lacking in practical knowledge of command area in the early 1970s, p. 1782-84;

AZORES: NATO/U.S. use of in the early 1970s, p. 1582; importance regarding antisubmarine patrols, p. 1691-92; effect of independence movement to future U.S. military use, p. 1692-94;

BAGLEY, Admiral Worth H., USN (USNA, 1947): selected by Zumwalt as Vice Chief of Naval Operations in the early 1970s despite his lack of experience, p. 1320; while in the plans and programs division in the early 1970s instituted idea of doing away with flagships afloat and the consolidation of some fleet commands in order to free flag officers for Washington duty, p. 1783; p. 1882-87;

BAINBRIDGE, Maryland: use of naval training facilities there by non-military, underprivileged people directed by Department of Defense in late 1960s, p. 1298-1300;

BARENTS SEA: Soviet transit of and bases in during the early 1970s, p. 1756-57; p. 1786-87;

BERMUDA: U.S. Navy use of in the early 1970s, p. 1826-27;

BRYAN, Vice Admiral C. Russell, USN (USNA, 1945): as Duncan's Fleet Materiel Officer, his efforts to use home port for ship overhauls in the early 1970s, p. 1774;

BURKE, Admiral Arleigh A., USN (USNA, 1923): as Chief of Naval Operations in the late 1950s-early 1960s wrote to rear admirals requesting their voluntary retirement in hopes of giving more and younger officers the opportunity to hold flag rank, p. 1387-88;

CALVERT, Vice Admiral James F., USN (USNA, 1943): as Naval Academy superintendent in the late 1960s supported summer program of use of academy facilities by underprivileged youths, p. 1301; conditions surrounding his retirement in 1972, p. 1901-03;

CHAFEE, John H.: as secretary of Navy in the late 1960s was determined to bring about equality for women in the Navy, p. 1310-11; worked to promote selection of younger officers to flag rank in the early 1970s, p. 1375; p. 1848-54; praised by Duncan as "individual-oriented", pp. 1370-71; p. 1773-74; made ruling on

Culebra as site of U.S. training exercise in the early 1970s, p. 1698; Duncan's relationship with, p. 1846-48;

CHAPLAIN CORPS: position in command structure of Navy, p. 3161; p. 1365-66; need to protect from budget cuts, p. 1364; efforts to remove from under control of Chief of Personnel, p. 1365-66; Duncan's futile effort to get a chaplain in charge of the chaplains' training program in the late 1960s, p. 1366; rotation of flag rank chaplain to fleets in the late 1960s, p. 1369;

CHIEF OF NAVAL OPERATIONS (CNO): testifying at congressional committee hearings in the late 1960s, p. 1289; meetings with the CAB, p. 1290-92; p. 1373-74; conflict with the secretary of Navy on selecting flag officers, p. 1315; as military head of the Navy, p. 1316; choosing prospective CNOs in the early 1970s, p. 1320-24; ruling out priority lists in promotions of flag officers, p. 1321-22; age and experience goals for CNO in the late 1960s, p. 1464; not involved with NATO in the early 1970s, p. 1476-77; activates Eastern Atlantic Command upon necessity, p. 1726; use of Joint Chiefs of Staff seat in the 1960s and 1970s, p. 1729; p. 1734; p. 1739; lack of authority under certain emergency conditions, p. 1739-42; demands on time and assets, p. 1766-67; lack of support to Duncan in homeport/shipyard matter in the 1970s, p. 1772; background effecting role of, p. 1776; p. 1780; p. 1782-83; p. 1911; invited to NATO "Shapex" in the early 1970s, p. 1891-92;

CHIEF OF NAVAL OPERATIONS' ADVISORY BOARD (CAB): benefits to CNO and his deputies from meetings, p. 1290-92; used by Zumwalt in the early 1970s as a "hearing board" for junior officers and enlisted personnel, p. 1373-4; importance of representation by Bureau of Personnel in order to insure equal time with materiel proponents in the late 1960s, p. 1408-09:

CHIEF OF NAVAL PERSONNEL (CNP): duties of in the late 1960s, p. 1267; p. 1270-72; p. 1280-81; position concurrent with Deputy Chief of Naval Operations for Manpower and Reserves (OP-01), p. 1268-70; distribution of rank and number of personnel, p. 1281; Military Pay Navy, p. 1281-90; p. 1414; Navy Policy Council member, p. 1291; attendance at secretary of defense meetings, p. 1292; assignment and selection of flag officers, p. 1313-21; chaplain corps under Personnel control in the late 1960s, p. 1361; low manning, p. 1420-22; p. 1781-82; computer used for expenditures in the 1960s, p. 1437-38; Operation and Maintenance budget, p. 1438-41; on uniform board in the early 1970s, p. 1861; p. 1865-68; beer in the barracks in the early 1970s, p. 1868-69;

CLAREY, Admiral Bernard A., USN (USNA, 1934): as Vice Chief of Naval Operations under Admiral Moorer in the late 1960s helped establish rough guidelines for flag officer selection and promotion, p. 1386; asked by Zumwalt in 1970 to make list of possible successors to the position of Chief of Naval Operations in 1974, p. 1320;

USS CLAUDE V. RICKETTS (DDG-5): U.S. destroyer used as trial ship for multinational manning from 1964-1965; implications for security and difficulties that arise with multinational crew, p. 1543-48;

COLBERT, Vice Admiral Richard G., USN (USNA, 1937): as president of the Naval War College in the early 1970s requested a visit by the Standing Naval Force, Atlantic, which had to be denied, p. 1524; p. 1618-19;

COMMANDER, EASTERN ATLANTIC (ComEastLant): Second position held by Commander in Chief, U.S. Naval Forces in Europe, activated only by specific direction; took operational control of a bilateral submarine exercise with Norway in the early 1970s, p. 1726-27;

COMMANDER IN CHIEF, ATLANTIC (CinCLant): Similarity to SACLant position in scope, p. 1475; importance of position to NATO, p. 1475; p. 1499-1500; p. 1557-58; p. 1562; CinCLant fear of losing power one reason some have not backed split from CinCLantFlt, p. 1475-76; unified command chain in the 1970s, p. 1476; p. 1669; p. 1671; invited NATO countries to participate in exercises with U.S. units south of the NATO boundary in the early 1970s, p. 1510-11; peacetime commander of NATO forces in Iceland, p. 1550-51; p. 1556; background and authority of position, p. 1662-68; confusion caused by CinCLant and CinCLantFlt titles, p. 1664-65; p. 1672; p. 1729; Atlantic command area in the early 1970s, p. 1665-66; authority to deal with foreign nations, p. 1666-68; p. 1724-25; effect of Navy being only permanent component, p. 1672-73; staff overlapped with CinCLantFlt in the early 1970s, p. 1676; attempts to obtain airborne command posts in the early 1970s, p. 1686-88; coordinating use and control of assets for unified commander, p. 1689; p. 1721-22; need for innovative exercises and problems in the early 1970s, p. 1697-1702; p. 1705; need for cooperation of higher echelons to make junior personnel of each service truly test mobility in the early 1970s, p. 1699-1702; p. 1707; need for "in service only" criticism of exercises, p. 1704; military and political advantages of joint exercises, p. 1708-10; war planning as major duty, p. 1710-24; exercises with South American countries in the early 1970s, p. 1729; responsibilities in the Indian Ocean in the 1970s, p. 1732; p. 1734; emergency operations off Cuba in 1971, p. 1735-38; p. 1740; protection of the Panama Canal in the 1970s, p. 1745-47; unified commanders conferences, p. 1749-50; p. 1756-57; support from other services, p. 1751; Vietnam as priority during the early 1970s, p. 1752-54; Duncan's reasons for wanting position separated from CinCLantFlt, p. 1761-62; improvement of task force ability with training in the early 1970s, p. 1803-07; antisubmarine warfare as a concern in the early 1970s, p. 1807-12;

COMMANDER IN CHIEF, ATLANTIC FLEET (CinCLantFlt): no set tour length in the early 1970s, p. 1467; responsibilities of position, p. 1469; desirability of separate officer for this billet and CinCLant, p. 1473-75; p. 1761-62; preferable way to allot men, money, and equipment for exercises, p. 1527; working with CinCUSNavEur in the early 1970s, p. 1726; keeping watch on Cuba for CinCLant in the early 1970s, p. 1742-43; desirability of homeport for long overhauls, p. 1767; need for cooperation from Washington in the early 1970s, p. 1769; p. 1779; given no control over use of shipyards in the early 1970s, p. 1769; p. 1772-74; concern over fleet fitness for war in the Atlantic over Vietnam, p. 1777-79; cold weather exercises in the early 1970s, p. 1812-13; p. 1897-98; shore duty versus sea duty for flag officers discusses, p. 1989-1901; Duncan's reaction to use of civilian personnel in the early 1970s, p. 1904-05; p. 1907-08;

COMMANDER IN CHIEF, EUROPE (CinCEur): role in command structure in Europe, p. 1672; p. 1681; p. 1726; working with CinCLant in the early 1970s, p. 1677; airborne command post in the early 1970s, p. 1685; confusion of roles of CinCEur and CinCUSNavEur in the early 1970s, p. 1726-27; had operational control of Middle East Force in 1970-1972, p. 1733;

COMMANDER IN CHIEF, U.S. NAVAL FORCES IN EUROPE (CinCUSNavEur): Confusion by many as to area responsibility and chain of command in the early 1970s, p. 1588-89; p. 1726; p. 1760-61; attempts to make refueling agreement at Diego Suarez in the early 1970s without going through proper channels, p. 1734;

CONGRESS, U.S.: move introduced during the Vietnam War to change the code of conduct for prisoners of war, p. 1287-89; Zumwalt testified before various committees in the early 1970s, p. 1289; Representative Aspin (D-WI) publicizes Navy's Personnel budget deficit in 1970, p. 1451-55; p. 1459; House Appropriations Committee's dealings with the Navy in the late 1960s, p. 1286-87; p. 1445-47; p. 1452-53; Navy's Personnel budget deficit for fiscal year 1969 investigated, p. 1441-55; House Armed Services Committee;s dealings with the Navy in the late 1960s, p. 1414; p. 1452; L. Mendel Rivers (D-SC) as head of the House Armed Services Committee in the late 1960s, p. 1452; p. 1457-58; p. 1462; William Proxmire (D-WI) as senator in the late 1960s felt there were too many flag officers in the services, p. 1317; George Mahon (D-TX) as chairman of the House Appropriations Committee in the late 1960s, p. 1452-55; p. 1459-60; number of naval personnel cut substantially by Congress in the early 1970s in response to the de-escalation of the Vietnam War, p. 1396-1400; p. 1425; p. 1427-29; Edward Hebert (D-LA) as chairman of the House Armed Services Committee in the late 1960s and a supporter of JNROTC, p. 1272; p. 1279-80; legislation passed

to create first fully subsidized medical
school for the military in the late 1960s,
p. 1335-38;

COUSINS, Admiral Ralph W., USN (USNA, 1937): as Duncan's
successor to SACLant/CinCLant/CinCLantFlt
in 1972, their change of command ceremony
was not attended by any number of official
civilians from the Navy Department, p. 1516;
p. 1685; recognized difficulty in keeping
NATO awareness of sea command, p. 1517;
as president of Newport News Shipbuilding
Company, p. 1771;

CUBA: U.S. use of Guantanamo in the 1960s and early 1970s,
p. 1349; p. 1827-30; seizure of vessel commanded
by U.S. civilian in 1971, p. 1735-38; p.
1740; Soviet movement and establishment
of bases in the Cuban area in the early
1970s, p. 1742-45;

CULEBRA: island off the coast of Puerto Rico and under
its control, that came under verbal fire
in the early 1970s as the site for U.S.
military training exercises, p. 1698-99;
p. 1822-26;

DEFENSE, DEPARTMENT OF: declines to expand military billets
at Guantanamo in the late 1960s, p. 1349-50;
budgeting between the services under presidents
Eisenhower and Ford, p. 1402; pressured
for cancellation of NATO exercise Strong
Express in October of 1972, p. 1616; criticized
for blurring SACLant and CinCLant command
structures in the early 1970s, p. 1694-95;
anti-military sentiment within Department
creates problems for planning and exercises
during late 1960s and early 1970s, p. 1298;
p. 1350; p. 1703-06; budget cuts on ship
overhauls in the early 1970s, p. 1768-69;
poor rapport with the military in the early
1970s, p. 1917-19;

DEFENSE INTELLIGENCE AGENCY: Director's speech to the unified
commanders meeting in the early 1970s held
only a brief reference to the Atlantic and
the Soviet threat there, which incensed
Duncan, p. 1756-57; p. 1776; p. 1790-91;

DEPUTY CHIEFS OF NAVAL OPERATIONS: Se OP-01, OP-04, OP-05;

DIESEL, John P.: president of Newport News Shipbuilding Company in the early 1970s who refused to bid on Navy ship overhauls because it was not lucrative enough, and later threatened that the company would build no more nuclear carriers, p. 1769-71;

DUNCAN, Admiral Charles K., USN (USNA, 1933): as Assistant Plans Officer on the Commander in Chief Atlantic/Atlantic Fleet staff from 1948-1951 when unified command concept was being developed p. 1472-74; in Plans and Policy section of the SACLant staff from 1952-1953 became familiarized with NATO operations which proved a great aid when he assumed the SACLant position in the early 1970s, p. 1643-44; p. 1646; p. 1882; as Assistant Chief of Naval Personnel for Plans and Programs from 1962-1964, p. 1268-69; p. 1272-76; as Atlantic Fleet Cruiser-Destroyer Force commander in 1964 and 1965, p. 1546-48; on line rear admiral selection board as commander of the Atlantic Cruiser-Destroyer Force when Zumwalt selected in 1965, p. 1839-41; personal relationship with Zumwalt, p. 1463-66; p. 1832; p. 1842; as commander, Second Fleet from 1967-1968, p. 1803; p. 1882; as Chief of Naval Personnel and Deputy Chief of Naval Operations for Manpower and Reserves in 1968-1970, p. 1267-72; p. 1276-1462; p. 1843-61; p. 1920; initiated first subsidized medical school program for the military as CNP, p. 1334-36; stressed personnel interest in ship design while CNP, p. 1380-85; difficulties with Personnel budget and M Account for fiscal year 1969, p. 1395-1400; p. 1411-21; p. 1428-30; p. 1442-61; as Supreme Allied Commander, Atlantic from 1970 to 1972, p. 1469; p. 1490-92; p. 1495-1661; p. 1678-79; p. 1684; p. 1690-91; p. 1694; p. 1890-92; in charge of largest NATO exercise ever held as SACLant in 1972, p. 1529-32; p. 1536-41; p. 1608-14; p. 1816; as Commander in Chief of the Atlantic between 1970 and 1972, p. 1469; p. 1498-99; p. 1504; p. 1510; p. 1662-63; p. 1668: p. 1678; p. 1682; p. 1684; p. 1686-92; p. 1694-1700; p. 1705-16; p. 1724-43; p. 1745-51; p. 1756-62; as Commander in Chief of the Atlantic Fleet from 1970 to 1972, p. 1469; p. 1498; p. 1510; p. 1589; p. 1678; p. 1682; p. 1684; p. 1743; p. 1765-82; p. 1784-1805; p. 1807-33; p. 1863-70; p. 1873; p. 1878-89; p. 1894-99; p. 1901; p. 1904-12; as CinCLantFlt has marginally successful effort to have ships overhauled in their homeports, p. 1766-74; assessment of his naval career which spanned from 1929 to 1972, p. 1912-19; p. 1923-25;

EISENHOWER, General Dwight D., USA (USMA, 1915): as president in the 1950s set a "planning goal" as the ceiling for his military personnel budgets, p. 1400; p. 1402; as an exceptional choice for first Supreme Allied Commander, Europe in the 1940s became the precedent for people associating that billet with the head of NATO, p. 1478; p. 1483; p. 1514-15;

FRANCE: peripheral involvement with NATO in the early 1970s after pulling out of the alliance, p. 1501-02; p. 1504-05; p. 1514; p. 1648;

GARRETT, Rear Admiral Francis Leonard, CHC, USN: as chief of chaplains in the early 1970s advocated separation of chaplain corps from Bureau of Personnel, p. 1365;

GATES, Thomas S.: former secretary of defense and navy who headed commission in the late 1960s directed to study military pay and other manpower issues, p. 1340; p. 1354;

GATES COMMISSION: formed by the Defense Department in the late 1960s to civilian versus military pay scales and other manpower issues, p. 1340-56;

GERMANY, FEDERAL REPUBLIC OF: Bavarian mountain demonstration of military skills given to Duncan and other NATO officials in the early 1970s, p. 1533-36; Helmut Schmidt, as Defense Minister in the early 1970s, asks that NATO tone down exercises which end in all-out nuclear exchanges with the Soviets, p. 1603-05;

GIBRALTAR: involvement with Standing Naval Force, Atlantic in the early 1970s, p. 1614-18; as a point of contention between England and Spain in the early 1970s, p. 1614;

GOODPASTER, General Andrew J., USA (USMA, 1939): as SACEur during the same 1970-1972 period that Duncan was SACLant, but held the position longer, as Duncan felt Navy should extend his NATO position for future appointees, p. 1468;

because he held position before Duncan assumed comparable duties, was able to offer assistance, p. 1607, p. 1631-32; working with Duncan and heads of state, p. 1490-92; p. 1607; working with Duncan to get German units in the Atlantic, p. 1522-24;

GREECE: Tension among NATO countries as a result of Greek-Cyprus troubles in the early 1970s, p. 1574; p. 1659-60;

GUANTANAMO: use of Jamaican civilians in jobs where military billets not granted in the 1960s and 1970s, p. 1349; use of by Atlantic Fleet in the early 1970s, p. 1827-30;

GUINN, Vice Admiral Dick H., USN (USNA, 1941): as Duncan's successor as Chief of Naval Personnel called for audit of the Personnel budget after finding deficit in fiscal year 1969's allocation for travel allowances, p. 1448-50;

GUNDERSON, General Zeiner: as Norway's Minister of Defense in the early 1970s worked with Duncan in organizing exercise Strong Express in 1972, p. 1610;

HEBERT, F. Edward: Louisiana congressman who chaired Armed Services Committee in the late 1960s when appropriations for a national medical school were granted, p. 1336-37; interest in Junior Naval Reserve Officer Training Corps (JNROTC) in the 1960s, p. 1272; p. 1279-80;

HOLLOWAY, Vice Admiral James L., III, USN (USNA, 1943): As Duncan's deputy in both CinCLant and CinCLantFlt positions in the early 1970s smoothed out difficulties with the staff of CinCEur, p. 1677; knowledgable about NATO as chief of naval operations in the mid-1970s, p. 1476;

HOLMES, Admiral Ephraim P., USN (USNA, 1930): SACLant/CinCLant/CinCLantFlt in the late 1960s relieved by Duncan in 1970, p. 1463; recommended separation of CinCLant and CinCLantFlt billets in the late 1960s, p. 1475; France allows him to visit in the late 1960s only as CinCLant, not as SACLant after they pulled out of NATO, p. 1502; pushed for an airborne command post for CinCLant while in that position, p. 1886;

HOMEPORTING: Homeport versus other yard for overhauls in the early 1970s, p. 1772-74; p. 1920; Zumwalt initiated some overseas homeports in the early 1970s, p. 1798-1803; base closures in the early 1970s, p. 1894-98;

HOMOSEXUALS: Duncan's opinion of their impracticality in the closed service environment, p. 1302-03; naval treatment of in the 1960s, p. 1305;

IBERIAN ATLANTIC COMMANDER (IberLant): as subdivision of SACLant in the early 1970s, p. 1579-80; Duncan works on establishing original boundaries of command in the early 1970s, p. 1643; British/U.S./Portugese tug-of-war concerning the area in the early 1970s, p. 1643-44; NATO quarters for, p. 1645-48; Portugal, as host country, holds great influence in the success of this command, p. 1660;

ICELAND: As an original member of NATO, p. 1548-49; effect of British occupation during World War II, p. 1549-50; peacetime/wartime command of NATO troops, p. 1550-51; political issues including fishing limits and U.S. presence in the 1970s, p. 1551; p. 1553; p. 1560-61; p. 1660; p. 1690-91; controversy regarding black U.S. troops, p. 1553-54; purity of culture, language and entertainment, p. 1548-49; housing difficulties for foreign personnel in the early 1970s, p. 1555-56; importance, militarily, regarding the Soviet Union and NATO, p. 1556-60; p. 1689-90; terms of agreement concerning U.S. presence in the early 1970s, p. 1561-62; p. 1564-65; as politically and militarily naive, p. 1565-66; as a U.S. host country for NATO, p. 1569;

INDIAN OCEAN: command responsibility for the Pacific Fleet in the early 1970s, p. 1732; responsibility assumed by Atlantic Fleet in the early 1970s, p. 1732; p. 1734; Soviet vessels in, in the 1970s, p. 1756-57;

INTEGRATION: racial integration of the military ordered by Truman in the late 1940s, p. 1294; in terms of equal treatment for men and women in the late 1960s, p. 1310; Secretary Chafee as strong backer of fair treatment for all personnel in the late 1960s, p. 1371;

USS JOHN F. KENNEDY (CV-67): when designed and built in the mid to late 1960s, not enough attention given to personnel considerations; the Navy was more concerned that another carrier be added while staying within the budget, p. 1383-84;

JOHNSON, Lyndon B.: as President in the mid-1960s exercised executive privilege in promoting personnel, p. 1326-28;

JOINT CHIEFS OF STAFF: recommend use of U.S. Naval Academy in 1960s for underprivileged civilians, p. 1300-01; General Maxwell Taylor recalled from retirement in early 1960s to chair, p. 1328; close relationship to Duncan as CinCLant in the early 1970s, p. 1667-70; p. 1712-15; allocation of airborne command posts in the early 1970s, p. 1686; p. 1698; ability of the chief of naval operations to use JCS to seat to initiate agreements with foreign powers in the 1970s, p. 1729; emergency authority of chairman, p. 1739-42;

JUNIOR NAVAL RESERVE OFFICERS' TRAINING CORPS (JNROTC): originated under Admiral Smedberg as CNP in the early 1960s, p. 1272; value to schools in the late 1960s, p. 1273; p. 1277; no significant value as a recruitment aid to NROTC or the enlisted ranks in the late 1960s, p. 1274; p. 1276; geographic distribution of units, p. 1277; high cost in terms of personnel and funds for the negligible results, p. 1274-76; popularity with schools, school boards, and parents mixed in the 1960s, p. 1277-78;

KELLY, RADM James W., CHC, USN: as Chief of Chaplains in the late 1960s worked with Duncan in enhancing the chaplains' presence in the fleet, p. 1362-65; p. 1369;

KELLY, Roger: as Assistant Secretary of Defense for Manpower in the late 1960s authorized the use of Navy facilities by underprivileged civilians, p. 1300-01; ease of working with regarding commissions and special studies, p. 1344-45;

KENNEDY, John F.: as president in the early 1960s exercised privilege by appointing retired general Maxwell Taylor to Joint Chiefs of Staff, p. 1328; used authority as president to

-15-

                  put top priority on Polaris submarine program in the early 1960s, p. 1406; p. 1687;

KIDD, Vice Admiral Isaac C., Jr., USN (USNA, 1942): As SACLant in the mid-1970s with problems similar to Duncan's, p. 1517; p. 1685; as CinCLant realized need for more demanding exercises for new officers and more specialized training, p. 1806;

LAIRD, Melvin R.: as Secretary of Defense under President Nixon advises Duncan not to go to Representative Aspin about Personnel budget for fiscal year 1969, p. 1454; helpful and supportive to Duncan in his roles as SACLant/CinCLant/CinCLantFlt between 1970-1972, p. 1455-56; p. 1515-16; p. 1684-85; familiarity with NATO, p. 1516; p. 1639; p. 1683-85; p. 1755; Vietnam as priority in the early 1970s, p. 1752-54; signs National Security Decision Memo in the early 1970s without apparent scrutiny of contents, which advocated reduction of forces in Europe and the Atlantic, p. 1758; p. 1761;

LeBOURGEOIS, Vice Admiral Julien J., USN (USNA, 1945): Duncan's chief of staff as SACLant in the early 1970s; sent to meet with the Norwegian military to iron out troubles preceding NATO exercise Strong Express in 1972, p. 1610;

LUNS, Joseph M.A.H.: as Secretary General of NATO visited Norfolk, Virginia in the early 1970s for the twentieth anniversary of the Allied Command, Atlantic, p. 1515;

M ACCOUNT: account in the U.S. Treasury with cumulative excess funds from budgets of all the services; usually will be used to cover any deficiencies, but was not allowed to be tapped when Duncan's Personnel budget for fiscal year 1969 showed a deficit for personnel transfers, p. 1441-55;

MAHON, George H.: as Democratic representative from Texas in the late 1960s chaired the House Appropriations Committee and was pressured by Representative Les Aspin (D-WI) to take up Bureau of Personnel budget deficiencies with the Justice Department for prosecution, p. 1452-55; p. 1459-60;

MARINE CORPS, U.S.:   stationed in Iceland in early 1970s, p. 1690-91; unified command exercises in the Atlantic in the early 1970s, p. 1697-98; winter exercises and the difficulty in arranging a site, p. 1817; environmentalists complain about the use of U.S. for exercises, p. 1820;

McCORMICK, Admiral Lynde D., USN (USNA, 1915): Did not favor splitting CinCLant-CinCLantFlt position, p. 1475-76; stepped down in flag rank in order to stay in the Navy until age 62 in the late 1950s, p. 1387;

McNAMARA, Robert S.:   as Secretary of Defense in the 1960s promulgated social change through the services, p. 1295; p. 1297; p. 1306; reputed to stress materiel over personnel in making budgets, p. 1405-07; improved budget procedure, p. 1426; requires Navy to designate a Polaris sub for multinational manning, p. 1545; institutes the Nuclear Planning group, p. 1629;

MEDICAL PERSONNEL: study made in the mid-1950s by then-LCDR Zumwalt on problem of retaining in the military, p. 1333; p. 1833-34; Duncan initiates proposal and congressional Armed Forces Committee appropriates funds for a fully subsidized medical school for the military in the late 1960s, p. 1335-38; medical personnel should be seen as maintenance cost for a system's readiness and not necessarily as a personnel cost, argues Duncan in the late 1960s, p. 1343-44;

MEDITERRANEAN: research on by antisubmarine center at La Spezia, Italy conducted by NATO-country scientists in the early 1970s, p. 1650-52; Duncan's views on Sixth Fleet presence in during the early 1970s, p. 1783-88;

MOORER, Admiral Thomas H., USN (USNA, 1933): as chief of naval operations in the late 1960s requests retirement of "peaked" flag officers, p. 1392; felt CinCLant-CinCLantFlt should be separate billets, p. 1474-75; knowledgeable about NATO as chairman of the Joint Chiefs of Staff in the early 1970s, p. 1476; p. 1478; p. 1617-18; p. 1540; p. 1642; initiated Iberian Atlantic Command in the early 1970s, p. 1645;

MULTINATIONAL MANNING: experiment tried aboard the USS
            CLAUDE V. RICKETTS (DDG-5) in the mid-1960s
            with mixed success, p. 1543-48;

NATIONAL SECURITY DECISION MEMORANDUM (NSDM):
            "A Review of Noncombat Missions in Europe,"
            a controversial assessment of necessity
            of troop strength in Europe and the Atlantic,
            signed by Secretary of Defense Laird and
            forwarded to Secretary of State Kissinger
            in the early 1970s, contained some faulty
            research in Duncan's opinion, p. 1758-61;

NAVAL ACADEMY, U.S.: use of facilities for non-military
            personnel in the 1960s, p. 1300-01; Duncan
            helps champion effort for new library for
            in the late 1960s, p. 1921; academic instruction
            regarding NATO, p. 1493;

NAVAL WAR COLLEGE: Duncan feels that command structures
            should be part of the curriculum, especially
            such intricate and important facets as the
            chains of command for NATO and the fleets,
            p. 1727-28; p. 1750-51;

NAVY, U.S.: conflict of unified command versus traditional
            chain of command, p. 1472; p. 1670-73; p.
            1760; budgeting for exercises by oil, hours,
            etc., p. 1698; need to clarify ramifications
            of unified command structure, p. 1732; p.
            1751; refusal of Newport News Shipbuilding
            Company to bid on overhauls in the early
            1970s, p. 1770-71; no priority given to
            maintaining advance education levels in
            the late 1960s, p. 1781-82; p. 1921-22;
            peacetime cut looms in the early 1970s as
            the Vietnam War winds down, p. 1781-82;
            overextension of since the end of World
            War II, p. 1798-1803; fleet organization
            in the early 1970s, p. 1880-88; base closures
            under Zumwalt, p. 1894-98;

NEWPORT NEWS SHIPBUILDING COMPANY:
            refusal to bid on naval vessel overhauls
            in the early 1970s, p. 1769-70; difficulty
            with Navy with payment for contracts in
            the late 1960s-early 1970s, p. 1770; rumors
            of nationalization, p. 1771; threatened
            to stop building nuclear carriers in the
            early 1970s, p. 1770-71;

NORTH ATLANTIC TREATY ORGANIZATION (NATO): General disinterest of U.S. civilian and military as versus European attitude, p. 1471; p. 1479-81; p. 1490-93; p. 1512-13; discussion of boundaries and potential additions in the early 1970s, p. 1482; p. 1506-12; p. 1618; standardization of equipment discussed, p. 1483; p. 1541-44; p. 1591-94; economics of outfitting, training, housing in the 1970s, p. 1488; p. 1542-44; European attitude towards NATO, p. 1484-87; p. 1490-93; effect of Soviet threat on planning in the early 1970s, p. 1487-90; p. 1572-74; France's relationship with NATO in the early 1970s, p. 1501-05; p. 1514; p. 1571; organizational levels, p. 1508-09; European countries' proclivity toward sending army and air representatives rather than navy in the early 1970s, p. 1517-18; permanent U.S. representation p. 1518; need for greater flexibility in use of NATO sea forces in the early 1970s, p. 1518-25; Duncan gets German forces into the Atlantic in the early 1970s, p. 1521-24; Standing Naval Force, Atlantic from 1970-1972, p. 1523-24; p. 1614-22; need for larger and more complicated exercises, p. 1525-26; p. 1528; exercise Strong Express in October, 1972, p. 1528-30; p. 1536-41; in Iceland, p. 1548-66; p. 1690-91; installations and infrastructure, p. 1567-73; U.S. funding of NATO installations in foreign countries, p. 1571; p. 1574; United Kingdom involvement in the early 1970s, p. 1585-86; strong European desire to repel Soviets, if necessary, with conventional and not nuclear weapons in the early 1970s, p. 1601; p. 1605-08; value of Miliary Committee tours to enhancing knowledge and trust between countries, p. 1624-28; p. 1636-43; European tendency to use NATO to air political differences, p. 1656-61; availability of nuclear subs through SACLant/CinCLant combination in the early 1970s, p. 1675; antisubmarine research center staffed with civilians from NATO countries in La Spezia, Italy in the early 1970s, p. 1650-52;

NORWAY: Sensitivity regarding location of NATO exercises because of close proximity to Russia, p. 1487-90; p. 1530; p. 1533-35; p. 1572-73; p. 1576-77; p. 1589-90; Duncan reviews Russian-Norwegian border in the early 1970s, p.1533-35;

NATO infrastructure in the early 1970s,
p. 1569; p. 1581; p. 1585; p. 1588-91;
vulnerability to the Soviets, p. 1818-20;
common market vote and effect on NATO exercise
Strong Express in 1972, p. 1608-14;

NUCLEAR WAR: Allied chain of command for authorization
of use of nuclear weapons in the early 1970s,
p. 1474; "short war" concept versus conventional weapons, p. 1594-1604; p. 1776; reaction
of NATO Nuclear Planning Group in the early 1970s,
p. 1628-35; p. 1642;

OP-01 (DEPUTY CHIEF OF NAVAL OPERATIONS FOR MANPOWER AND RESERVES):
billet held simultaneously by Chief of Naval
Personnel in the late 1960s, p. 1268;
responsibility for personnel transfers,
p. 1268-69; command functions of, p. 1269;
overall sponsorship of personnel, p. 1368;
working with Ships Characteristic Board in the
late 1960s, p. 1384-86;

OP-04 (DEPUTY CHIEF OF NAVAL OPERATIONS FOR LOGISTICS):
as sponsor for the Chaplain Corps when they
have construction needs in the late 1960s,
p. 1368; as budget holder for Operation
and Maintenance and Military Construction
in the late 1960s, p. 1438-39;

OP-05 (DEPUTY CHIEF OF NAVAL OPERATIONS, AIR WARFARE):
after the Bureau of Personnel put in many
recommendations with this department concerning
the design of the upcoming USS JOHN F. KENNEDY
(CV-67) in the late 1960s, few were actually
implemented, p. 1384;

OP-090 (DIRECTOR, NAVY PROGRAM PLANNING):
office set up in the early 1960s by Admiral
Rivero which had control of OP-96 Navy's
"think tank" ably directed by then-Rear
Admiral Zumwalt in the late 1960s, p. 1841-42;

OP-96 (SYSTEMS ANALYSIS DIVISION):
in the late 1960s then-Rear Admiral Zumwalt
directed this division, the Navy's "think
tank", as his latest Washington assignment
before assuming the position of chief of
naval operations, p. 1375; p. 1841-42;

OVERHAULS: use of civilian contractors in the early
1970s, p. 1767; p. 1769-71; strain put on

PERSONNEL TRANSFERS: responsibility of OP-01 in the late
              1960s, p. 1269; activation and discharges,
              p. 1284-85; p. 1305; logistics in filling
              posts when promoting or creating flag officer
              billets, p. 1313-21; travel and re-enlistment
              costs covered by MPN (Military Pay Navy),
              p. 1396; congressional budget actions increase
              number of transfers in 1970, p. 1396-98;

POLARIS PROGRAM: receives financial priority in the early
              1960s, p. 1406; p. 1408; involvement in
              multinational manning program in the early
              1960s, p. 1545; "roving" missile system
              developed in the early 1960s, p. 1546; acceler-
              ation of program during Kennedy's presidency,
              p. 1867;

PORTUGAL: position in NATO infrastructure in the early
              1970s, p. 1577-85; p. 1645-46; p. 1694;
              dealings with Gibraltar in the early 1970s,
              p. 1614-18; IberLant command in the early
              1970s, p. 1644-46; NATO status, p. 1660;
              advantages to U.S. forces and NATO, p. 1693-94;
              cooperation with Duncan in CinCLant/SACLant
              role from 1970-1972, p. 1694-95;

PRISONERS OF WAR: U.S. Navy's unwillingness to change code
              of conduct during Vietnam War while prisoners
              were still being held, p. 1287-89;

PROMOTIONS: initiation of 3 and 4 star assignments in
              late 1960s, p. 1313; recommendation by superior
              officers for promotion to flag rank, p.
              1316; p. 1321; p. 1323; disadvantages to
              promotion by seniority, p. 1322; "promotion
              lists" for flag rank, p. 1322-25; ranks
              not permanent above rear admiral; billet
              justifies the rank, p. 1323; pressure to
              promote individuals from non-Navy sources,
              p. 1326-27; p. 1329; slowed by budget cuts
              in late 1960s, p. 1431; p. 1436-37; greater
              numbers under Zumwalt, but with three year
              reviews, p. 1393-94; lack of promotions
              due to "age gap" during late 1960s, p. 1325;
              p. 1375;

PROXMIRE, William: Democratic senator from Wisconsin who
              harped to the press about "too many generals"
              in the late 1960s, p. 1317;

personnel, p. 1767-68; budget considerations, p. 1767-69; desirability of homeport for, p. 1767-69; p. 1774; complexity of naval vessels versus merchant vessels, p. 1769-70;

PACIFIC FLEET: Command area concerning the Indian Ocean in the early 1970s, p. 1732; use of Atlantic fleet units during the Vietnam War, p. 1775;

PANAMA CANAL: CinCLant conducts study in the 1970s to decide whether responsibility, militarily, for this area should change hands, p. 1745-47; Duncan predicts situation in Panama in the future, p. 1747-49;

PERSONNEL, BUREAU OF: studied civilian commercial personnel practices in the late 1960s to see if they could be applied to the military, p. 1329-33; studies conducted on doctors in the military in the mid-1950s, p. 1333; p. 1833-34; chaplain corps as part of in the late 1960s, p. 1361-70; lack of success influencing Ships Characteristic Board in the late 1960s, p. 1379-86; budget problems with fiscal year 1969, p. 1395-1400; p. 1411-21; p. 1428-30; racial matters and the Gessell Report of the mid-1960s, p. 1871-76;

PERSONNEL, Reduction of: aggravated by congressional cuts in the late 1960s-early 1970s, p. 1396-1400; p. 1425; p. 1427-29; to avoid cutting number of ships or weapons, p. 1415-16; p. 1420-22; arbitrary releases have a negative effect on personnel morale and skill level, p. 1430-33; post-Vietnam reduction, p. 1779-82;

PERSONNEL COSTS: argument of listing as personnel costs those costs needed to re-train personnel on new or updated weapons systems in the late 1960s, p. 1342; medical care as maintenance and repair cost, p. 1344; feasibility of civilian substitution to save money studied in the late 1960s, p. 1346; p. 1904-05; p. 1907-08; lack of flexibility in pay scale for enlisted personnel in the late 1960s, p. 1352; change in retirement system and pay in the late 1960s, p. 1356; release of skilled personnel to reduce costs in the late 1960s, p. 1399-1400; p. 1430-33; p. 1920-21; explanation of entitlements, p. 1396-98; operations and maintenance budget covers everything but air training, p. 1438-41; costs incurred during overhaul of vessels, p. 1768;

RACIAL MATTERS: integration of services under Truman in the late 1940s, p. 1294; equal treatment in the military enforced during the 1960s and 1970s, p. 1310; p. 1371; blacks in Iceland from the post-World War II period to the present, p. 1553-54; Zumwalt on race relations, p. 1870-78;

RADFORD, Admiral Arthur W., USN (USNA, 1916): as chairman of the Joint Chiefs of Staff in the mid-1950s expressed willingness to have destroyers half-manned rather than cut force level of vessels, p. 1416;

RECRUITMENT: JNROTC as possible recruitment base in the late 1960s, p. 1274; p. 1279; incentives for medical personnels in the late 1960s, p. 1335-36; recommendation for direct and demand hiring by commission in the late 1960s, p. 1353; p. 1406-08; fear of overspending personnel budget, p. 1444;

RECTANUS, RADM Earl F., USN: as head of Naval Intelligence in the early 1970s received a letter from Duncan complaining of the cursory mention of Soviet presence in the Atlantic, p. 1791-92;

REHABILITATION: impracticality of Navy being used for this purpose, p. 1295-98; shore duty for alcohol or drug abusers, p. 1303; p. 1308; under Zumwalt, p. 1303-04; 1307-09; p. 1878-80; origin of attitude of services use as rehabilitator in the 1960s, p. 1305-06; resentment from satisfactory personnel toward abusers, p. 1308-09;

RICKETTS, Admiral Claude V., USN (USNA, 1929): as Vice Chief of Naval Operations in the early 1960s tasked with selling the idea of a multinational nuclear force to allied foreign ministers, p. 1545-46;

RICKOVER, Admiral Hymen G., USN (USNA, 1922): contention that there were too many flag rank officers in the services, p. 1318; treatment of the Newport News Shipbuilding Company in the 1960s, p. 1770-71;

RIVERO, Admiral Horacio, Jr., USN (USNA, 1931): worked with Duncan in the early 1970s to coordinate Mediterranean exercises with

Atlantic ones as CinCSouth, p. 1621; briefed top NATO officials during visit to Italy in the early 1970s, p. 1637; as CinCSouth was encouraged to work with the antisubmarine research group at La Spezia in the early 1970s, p. 1652;

RIVERS, L. Mendel: as Democratic representative from South Carolina and head of the House Armed Services Committee supports new legislation for efficient management of appropriated funds in the late 1960s, p. 1452; p. 1457-58; p. 1462;

SCHMIDT, Helmut H.W.: as German Defense Minister in the early 1970s expressed concern over the number of NATO exercises assuming the use of nuclear weapons, p. 1603-05; p. 1639;

SECOND FLEET: Commander, Second Fleet becomes Commander, Task Force 122 in the early 1970s, p. 1714; p. 1882; assignment of ships in the early 1970s, p. 1766;

SHIP CHARACTERISTICS BOARD:
Duncan's dealings with this group in both Bureau of Personnel tours (early 1950s and late 1960s) left him with the impression that because vessels and weaponry are inevitably built under budget pressure, habitability and personnel concerns are often the areas economized, p. 1379-86;

SHIPYARDS: civilian contractors in the early 1970s, p. 1767; p. 1769; improvement of homeport areas, p. 1769; recommendations of closures in the early 1970s, p. 1772-74; overseas, p. 1798-1803; actual base closures in the early 1970s, p. 1894-98;

SIXTH FLEET: pressure from Zumwalt and his advisors to step up presence in the Mediterranean in the early 1970s, p. 1783-88; Duncan's attempt to vary strength and scheduling of in the early 1970s, p. 1792-93;

SMEDBERG, VADM William R., III, USN (USNA, 1926):
as Chief of Naval Personnel in the early 1960s with Duncan as his assistant and advisor, p. 1272-73; p. 1379-80; p. 1836; p. 1838; forbade keeping of so-called "promotion list" for prospective flag officers in the early 1960s, p. 1323-24;

SOLZHENITSYN, Alexander: Soviet defector in a speech aired on the British Broadcasting Company in the mid-1970s exhorted Europeans not to get so complacent in peacetime that they are caught off-guard by Soviet might; a message similar to the one Duncan espoused as SACLant in the early 1970s, p. 1599-1600; p. 1657;

SOVIET UNION: Reconnaissance over Iceland in the early 1970s, p. 1690; use and access to the Atlantic Ocean in the early 1970s, p. 1690; p. 1756-57; p. 1786; observation of U.S. training exercises from 1970-1972, p. 1719-20; bases and movement around Cuba, p. 1742-45; p. 1795; submarines in the early 1970s, p. 1742-45; p. 1756-57; p. 1786-88; p. 1809-12; U.S. attention to diverted by Vietnam, p. 1752-54; p. 1779; p. 1788-89; U.S. naval briefing on in the early 1970s, p. 1791-92; Soviet subs off the U.S. coast in the early 1970s, p. 1795-97;

SPAIN: U.S. base at Rota and sale and transfer of old U.S. vessels helped keep Spanish-U.S. relations friendly and enhanced their willingness to participate in multinational exercises in the early 1970s, p. 1728; their desirability as a potential NATO member in the early 1970s, p. 1728;

STANDING NAVAL FORCE, ATLANTIC: first permanent multinational peacetime group formed in 1968 from various units of NATO members' navies; difficulty getting NATO to agree to have German ships as part of this force in the early 1970s, p. 1523-24; political influences on exercises in the early 1970s, p. 1614-22; possibility of vising non-NATO countries introduced by Duncan in the early 1970s, p. 1621-22;

STEINHOFF, General A.P. Johannes, German Air Force: as Chairman, NATO Military Committee in the United States for various official duties, p. 1515; p. 1684;

STRONG EXPRESS: Largest NATO exercise ever held, in October of 1972 in Norway; Duncan's desire to hold exercise as far north as possible is partially thwarted by Norwegian fears of aggravating the Russians, p. 1530; p. 1532; p. 1816; great interest in the exercise by dignitaries from various countries generated at NATO meeting in mid-1972, p. 1536-38; effects

of press exposure, p. 1538-40; communications
exercises, p. 1540-41; pressure to cancel
exercise from U.S. embassy and other outside
sources due to media coverage of delicate
Common Market vote going on in Norway during
same period, p. 1608-14;

SUPREME ALLIED COMMANDER, ATLANTIC (SACLant):
position held simultaneously with CinCLant
and CinCLantFlt in the early 1970s, but
separate staffs for each job, p. 1460; no
set tour length for billet, p. 1467;
responsibilities as NATO officer, p. 1469-70;
p. 1495-98; effect on NATO naval support
system in the early 1970s, p. 1486-87; Duncan's
meetings with high European officials in
the early 1970s, p. 1490-93; Duncan welcomed
in France after political change in country
in the early 1970s, p. 1502-04; objectives
for Duncan while in this position, 1970-1972,
p. 1506; p. 1512; p. 1518; p. 1525; Duncan
sends message to NATO council regarding
the southern boundary of the alliance, p.
1511; Duncan increases the number of exercises
held in the early 1970s, p. 1513; SACLant
would have command of NATO troops in Iceland
during a war, p. 1550; value of SACLant/CinCLant
dual role for Iceland, p. 1550; p. 1557-58;
p. 1562-63; p. 1690-91; NATO infrastructure
projects initiated by, p. 1577-84; Zumwalt
uninformed about role of in the early 1970s,
p. 1589; p. 1889-93; NATO seats for SACLant
staff rigidly allocated, p. 1626; Duncan
as host for Military Committee tour in the
early 1970s, p. 1640; SACLant staff in the
early 1950s studies Iberian command area,
p. 1643;

SUPREME ALLIED COMMANDER, EUROPE (SACEur):
responsible for first military action if
Soviet troops move into NATO areas, p. 1491-93;
value of U.S. divisions in NATO forces,
p. 1494; SACEur control of German naval
units, p. 1521-24; necessity of working
around reservist schedules in some countries
in the early 1970s, p. 1529; infrastructure
in Norway in the early 1970s, p. 1581; U.S.
bases in England in the early 1970s, p.
1586; involvement in Strong Express in 1972,
p. 1608; seats at certain NATO meetings
not allocated for even senior staff in the
early 1970s, p. 1626-27; vital interaction
with SACLant in the early 1970s, p. 1649;

TAYLOR, General Maxwell D., USA (USMA, 1922):
    Example of presidential power to exert influence on promotions and appointments of flag officers; recalled from retirement by President Kennedy to chair the Joint Chiefs of Staff from 1962 to 1964, p. 1328;

TERRITORIAL WATERS: Misunderstanding by the press and others about the extent of international waters and the high seas in the early 1970s, p. 1730-32;

UNITED KINGDOM: Dealings with NATO in the early 1970s, p. 1585-86; Lord Peter Carrington's comment on "short war" concept in the early 1970s, p. 1598; Iberian command as point of conflict, p. 1643-44;

VIEQUES ISLAND: island off the coast of Puerto Rico used in the early 1970s for naval training exercises; controversy over its use by military endangering the civilian population raised, p. 1697-99; p. 1822-26;

VIETNAM WAR: members of Congress request changes to prisoner of war code of conduct while Americans are still being held, p. 1287-89; refugees from Vietnam housed at Camp Pendleton in California in the 1970s, p. 1306; drug and alcohol rehabilitation during war at Zumwalt's insistence, p. 1308-09; effect of personnel entitlement policies, p. 1436-37; anti-military sentiment effects exercises, p. 1705; priority given to war effort by both fleets, p. 1752-55; p. 1774-80; p. 1799-89; post-war personnel cuts, p. 1779-82;

WENDT, Admiral Waldemar, F., USN (USNA, 1933):
    as Deputy Chief of Naval Operations in 1966-1967 conducted a study on the advisability of making command of the Atlantic Fleet a separate billet, p. 1475; as CinCUSNavEur/ComEastLant planned training exercise with Duncan until his retirement in 1971, p. 1727;

WARNER, John W.: as Secretary of Navy in the early 1970s refused to sign Duncan's Distinguished Service Medal after bad publicity about Personnel Department budget deficiency, p. 1455-56;

WOMEN IN THE MILITARY: Duncan's opinions on equality in the services requiring both burdens and privileges, p. 1310-12;

WRIGHT, Admiral Jerauld, USN (USNA, 1918):
while holding the longest term as SACLant in the 1950s helped establish an antisubmarine research center in La Spezia, Italy manned by NATO civilians, p. 1467; p. 1650;

ZUMWALT, Admiral Elmo R., Jr., USN (USNA, 1943):
champions rehabilitation of Navy personnel in the early 1970s, p. 1303; p. 1307-09; p. 1878; differences of opinion with the Secretary of Navy over flag nominees, p. 1315; makes flag officers take leave between assignments in the early 1970s, p. 1317; starts selection process for his successor as chief of naval operations in 1970, p. 1319-20; accelerates move toward younger flag officers and earlier retirement in early 1970s, p. 1325; p. 1375; p. 1392-94; p. 1464; as LCDR in Bureau of Personnel in the mid-1950s conducts study on problem of retaining medical personnel, p. 1333; p. 1833-34; as CNO makes point to listen to junior officers and enlisted personnel, p. 1371-74; p. 1858-61; clique of officers surround him as CNO and limit accessibility to those who should have his attention, p. 1376-78; p. 1800; p. 1862; p. 1869; requests Duncan not speak to congressional committee investigating Personnel deficit on his own behalf in 1970, p. 1453-54; professional compatibility with Duncan, p. 1465-66; lack of knowledge or interest in NATO as CNO in the early 1970s, p. 1476-77; p. 1784-85; p. 1889-93; Duncan uses as an example of what lack of experience can do to someone in a high position, p. 1588-89; p. 1782-85; notification about Cuban action in 1971, p. 1740-41; effect of his background in Vietnam on tour as CNO, p. 1755; p. 1776; p. 1780; with Secretary of Navy Chafee nominated Duncan for SACLant/CinCLant/CinCLantFlt position in 1970, p. 1765; lack of support for Duncan on using homeport area for ship overhauls in the early 1970s, p. 1772; lack of information about the Atlantic Fleet in his fleet commander conferences, p. 1791-92; establishes overseas homeports in the early

1970s, p. 1799-1803; career before assuming position of chief of naval operations in 1970, p. 1832-55; changes uniform code in the early 1970s, p. 1861; p. 1865-68; race relations, p. 1870-71; p. 1876-78; alcohol rule change, p. 1868-69; fleet organization, p. 1880-88; shore duty versus sea duty for flag officers, p. 1898-1901; role in VADM Calvert's retirement in 1972, p. 1901-03; advocated civilian manning for some positions on Navy ships, p. 1907-08

www.ingramcontent.com/pod-product-compliance
Lightning Source LLC
Chambersburg PA
CBHW080616170426
43209CB00007B/1449